Secret Voyages

Best Wishes

Conrad Thompson

2006

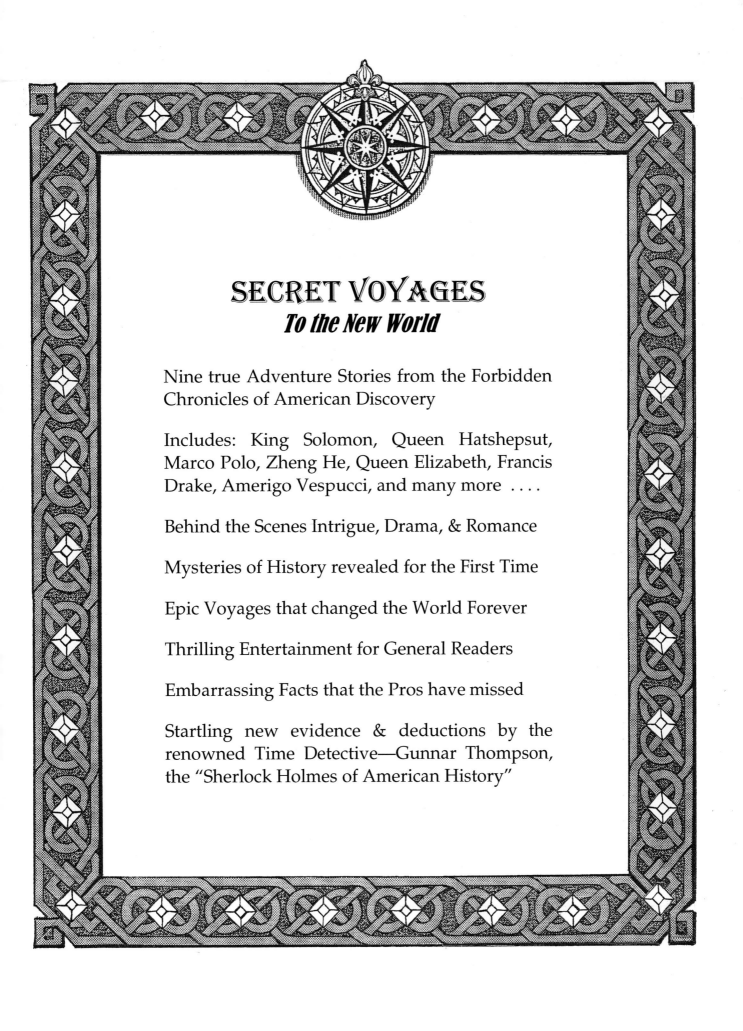

SECRET VOYAGES
To the New World

Nine true Adventure Stories from the Forbidden Chronicles of American Discovery

Includes: King Solomon, Queen Hatshepsut, Marco Polo, Zheng He, Queen Elizabeth, Francis Drake, Amerigo Vespucci, and many more . . . .

Behind the Scenes Intrigue, Drama, & Romance

Mysteries of History revealed for the First Time

Epic Voyages that changed the World Forever

Thrilling Entertainment for General Readers

Embarrassing Facts that the Pros have missed

Startling new evidence & deductions by the renowned Time Detective—Gunnar Thompson, the "Sherlock Holmes of American History"

LEGACY OF THE SECRET VOYAGERS

Ancient mariners changed the course of world
history. They brought back from their
overseas expeditions:

Guns, cannons, & rockets;

Compasses, astrolabes, & telescopes;

Secret hoards of copper & gold;

Manufacturing technology & inventions;

Exotic medicines, spices, & drugs;

Maps of New Lands across the Seas; and. . . .

They told tales about stunning vistas, strange
animals, and bizarre cultures in places that
were far, far away beyond the horizon.

Ultimately, the new ideas that they brought
home helped to inspire a transformation of
positive thinking in Western Civilization.

**MECHANICAL
TIME**

Theatre Sub Rosa Presents—

SECRET VOYAGES
to the New World

Nine True Adventures from the Forbidden Chronicles of American Discovery

By Gunnar Thompson, Ph.D.

MISTY ISLES PRESS
Seattle, Washington—2006

Secret Voyages to the New World
—Nine True Adventures from the Forbidden
   Chronicles of American Discovery

Prime Distributor/Publisher:
New World Discovery Institute (NWDI)
   Imprint: Misty Isles Press
PO Box 491
Port Townsend, WA 98368 USA
http: //www. marcopolovoyages. com

ISBN-13: 978-0-9788916-0-2

ISBN-10: 0-9788916-0-0

Library of Congress Catalog Card Number: *pending*

Cataloguing tree: 1) history—American Discovery, Exploration, Pre-Columbian
Voyages, Indians, Native Americans, horses, Amerigo Vespucci, Old World &
New World cultural contact, diffusion before Columbus; 2) history—China,
Zheng He, Tzu Fu, 1418 Ming Map; 3) history—England, Nicholas of Lynn,
Queen Elizabeth, Francis Drake, John Dee, King Arthur, Edward III, Roger
Bacon; 4) history—Ancient, Bible, King Solomon, Solomon's Mines, Ophir,
Marco Polo, Renaissance; 5) cartography—history of, Mercator, longitude,
clocks in navigation; 6) inventions—history of, telescope, compass, clock, guns,
espionage; 7) Indians—history of, native horse, bow & arrow; 8) human
geography—cultural & plant diffusion, immigration; 9) Mysteries of History.

Printed in the U.S.A. on Recycled Paper

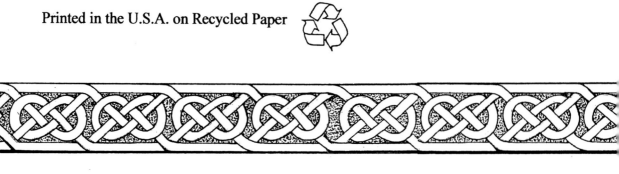

Acknowledgements

This book represents the culmination of nearly thirty years of research in libraries, museums, private collections, and at archeological sites around the world. Several prominent scholars have had a hand in guiding my quest to solve the mysteries of the past. I have had the good fortune to know the Norwegian ethnologist and adventurer Thor Heyerdahl, Native elder and statesman Vine Deloria, Jr., Smithsonian archeologist Betty Meggers, and most recently the distinguished British author and former Royal Navy submarine Commander—Gavin Menzies.

World travelers Bob and Maryann Ness have been a continuous inspiration and resource of vital clues from their trips to Eastern European museums and Mongolia. Bob is famous throughout the Seattle area for his ability to inspire business leaders and nonprofit managers. He introduced the author to the Ethnic Theatre Company of Seattle (also known as "The Group") which served as the inspiration behind the format of this book. Shakespeare made the observation that "all the world's a stage"—and, like the Theatre, some of the most important dramas that influence our lives actually occur "behind the scenes." They are secrets. So it is vital to our understanding of the Puzzles of History to find out just what was going on in the Skullduggery of the Times. It will astonish you.

The author has gained immense assistance from an informal "think tank," of sorts, consisting of a group of eclectic philosophers and problem solvers. Like the "Baker Street Irregulars," who were always ready to help out the British detective Sherlock Holmes (in the tales of Sir Arthur Conan Doyle), they all enjoyed participating in late night marathon discussions that ranged from the enduring Enigmas of History to the social and political problems of the world. Among my brilliant, yet modest associates, are Frederic Jueneman, a retired analytical chemist, and Victor DeMattei, an expert in Balkans history. It was Jueneman and DeMattei who first deduced that Marco Polo had a motive for concealing geographical information relating to what he saw in the New World. When you consider that most historians have completely missed the clues regarding what Marco Polo was actually doing (behind the backs of everybody in the court of Kublai Khan), then you begin to realize that much of our so-called "history" is exactly what Henry Ford called: "A bunch of bunk!" We are typically taught in school—as "Truth"—the lies and misconceptions that were used in Past Ages as a way of indoctrinating people. The so-called "Authorities" wanted people to think in accordance with the dominant cultural entity. During the Middle Ages, that entity was a very backward Medieval Church. The leaders of that organization believed that the world was about to end at any moment. Scientists and philosophers, like myself, were often burned at the stake as a public demonstration of the futility of innovative thinking. We are still burdened with a great deal of "cultural baggage" that has survived from the Middle Ages as Eurocentric supremacy. Of course, the World just keeps on going—so we had better find out what really happened in the Past, or we might get stuck repeating the same mistakes over and over again. The "Irregulars" help keep me going.

Dedication

For Laura Ovette, midwife, and the Rosewind Community.
They have provided the vital intellectual garden for solving
the riddles of the Past and for nurturing a new vision of the
future. They are the *Sin qua non*.

Secret Contents

photo by Lucy Cavender (lucycavender@gmail.com)

Zheng He Map Conference

In March of 2006, Chinese navigational experts, members of the international press, and representatives of the Zheng He Society met in Beijing to discuss the remarkable discovery of a 1418 Ming Map that shows the whole world. Pictured here are British author Gavin Menzies (front), Chinese antiquities scholar and attorney Liu Gang (center), and Gunnar Thompson. The three scholars are shown here outside of Alex Peterson's charming Bookworm Club.

Preface by Gavin Menzies

It is a great pleasure to write this preface to Gunnar's latest book *Secret Voyages to the New World*; and it is an honour to have been invited to do so.

I first met Gunnar in Seattle in April 2004. Gunnar had emailed me about an extraordinary map that he had come across whilst serving as an Associate Professor at the University of Hawaii. That map, published in Venice in 1419 by Albertin di Virga, was the most exciting piece of evidence that has surfaced in the four years since my book *1421—The Year China Discovered the World* has been published. I will explain why later.

To put Gunnar's discovery into perspective: in 1990, I started to write a book entitled simply "1421." It was a book about that year and the extraordinary events which had taken place in Europe—including Joan of Arc's first communion in May of 1421, the union of France and Britain, and the coronation of French Princess Katherine of Valois' as Queen of England in Westminster. Also in May of that year, the world witnessed the defeat of the Holy Roman Emperor by the Hussite army. In December of 1421, the Ottomans crossed the Dardanelles, and they surrounded the Emperor of Byzantium at Constantinople. This effectively severed Europe's only link to China via the Silk Road. The Mamluk Sultan Barsbey thereby provoked Prince Henry the Navigator into setting up a base in Southwestern Portugal in order to find a new route to the Far East. Thus, 1421 was a tumultuous year—if ever there was one.

By the year 2000, my book of over 1500 pages was sold to a publisher—who required many changes. By the early spring of 2001, these changes had been incorporated, and the revised book which was then sent to historians for vetting. One of these historians asked me if I knew of a map showing islands in the Caribbean that had been published by Zuane Pizzigano in Venice in 1424—some 70 years before Columbus reached the Caribbean. I immediately thought that the islands, which were Puerto

Rico and Guadeloupe, must have been discovered by Portuguese secret voyages; so I searched the Portuguese archives in Lisbon.

There I discovered to my astonishment that the Portuguese didn't actually know the location of the islands—because they were still in the process of sending out caravels to look for them! Even more astonishing was the fact that the Portuguese also claimed that the King of Portugal's eldest son, Prince Pedro, had returned to Lisbon from Venice in 1428 with Master Maps of the World. One of these maps showed the entire World from Portugal to China; another showed the Americas as far south as the "Straits of Magellan"—that is, to the very bottom of South America. So here was an astounding claim—that before the European voyages of exploration had started, Europeans already had maps of the *whole* world. If this were true, then the history of world exploration would be stood on its head.

I tried to find these world maps—searching archives in Florence, Genoa, Venice, Lisbon and Coimbra—but to no avail. They had last been seen in the 1520's; but they were all now presumed to have been lost. However the Portuguese claim that these maps once existed was corroborated in Venetian records; and it was obliquely corroborated in the records of the Holy Roman Emperor Sigismund of Luxemburg. It occurred to me that if the maps did exist, then the Portuguese and Spanish kings would have issued copies to their captains before they set sail to the New World. If this had been done, then it was possible that the captains would have referred to them in their logs. On a supremely beautiful day in 2001, while basking in the soft warm sunshine, I found the first gem: in the logbook of his first voyage, Columbus admitted that he had a map showing islands in the Caribbean. Within three weeks, I discovered that Magellan also had a map showing the straits which now bear his name. The same was true for Cabral of Brazil, da Gama of South Africa, and Tasman of Australia. In other words, the whole world had been charted *before* the Europeans ever set forth on their so-called voyages of "discovery." They all knew in advance where they were going!

The problem was that no one would believe me.

Then Gunnar told me of di Virga's map published in 1419. This map had been found in a bookshop in Sbrenica by a collector named Albert Figdor. He took his antique map to the leading cartographer of the time— Dr. Professor Franz von Wieser of Austria. The professor authenticated the map as "genuine." No one has challenged its authenticity since then. The map was stolen in 1932; but fortunately it was photographed before the theft on several occasions. One of these photographs can be seen in the British Library in the collection of Prince Youssuf Kamal.

The 1419 map showed the world from the North Atlantic to Australia. Africa has the right shape; and rivers and coastal islands are in their correct places. Japan is shown a century before Europeans reached this part of the globe; North Australia has the correct shape and size, and it is in the correct position relative to China. All of this had been achieved before European voyages ever started. In 1419, the Portuguese voyages had just gotten under way—with Madeira being the first discovery the next year in 1420. In other words, Di Virga must have copied his map from some other source. From that thrilling moment in 2004, when I received Gunnar's email, I was convinced that one day we would find a Chinese map dated prior to 1419—from which di Virga evidently copied his own map. A Chinese collector, Mr. Liu Gang of Beijing, found the Chinese version published in 1418; and he kindly provided me with a copy in 2005.

Gunnar's discovery of di Virga's map was no accident. These things seldom are accidents; indeed, they are the fruit of a lifetime of assiduous research. Gunnar has forsaken what could have been a successful career as a Professor to pursue his quest for the truth. His guiding passion has been to find out who *really* discovered America.

We first met at SeaTac Airport in Seattle. Gunnar had travelled from his home on the Straits of Juan de Fuca; and I had flown in from Kyoto while on my return flight to London. After a few welcoming beers, Gunnar showed me two of his books: The *Friar's Map* and *Nu Sun*. I was bowled over—as they contained page-after-page of evidence from Chinese voyages to the Americas before Columbus. Indeed, much of that voyaging had taken place even before the era of Zheng He. This collection of evidence seemed to me to be absolutely incontrovertible proof; and I find it astonishing that Gunnar's critics could dispute him. But the historians and anthropologists have managed to keep him out of the academic arena for years and years.

In my opinion, Gunnar is the world's leading authority on voyages to the New World before Columbus.

I therefore unhesitatingly recommend *Secret Voyages*; and I hope that you will enjoy it as much as I have.

Gavin Menzies
London
27th September 2006

Expedition to the Great Wall

The author (center) accompanied Beijing scholar Liu Gang, China tour guide Tony Chen, and Steve Hill (behind the camera) on a trek to one of the Seven Wonders of the Ancient World—Emperor Zhu Di's Great Wall. This trip was part of the author's worldwide search for clues to America's ancient past. Besides enjoying the many wondrous sights near Beijing, the author gained vital clues that will help to identify ancient Ming village sites in the New World.

Prologue

Under the Rose

Codes, secret maps, and intrigues were common in the early days of New World discovery. Throughout the thousands of years that ancient mariners sailed to the American continents before the "official European discovery," secrecy was a common strategy in the survival of nations and in the commercial success of rival businesses. Since these voyagers who traveled upon the oceans left no "footprints" to tell of their passing, historians have often overlooked the adventures and achievements of the ancient sailors. About all that modern writers have been able to tell us is that the old mariners simply "vanished" while sailing towards "unknown lands." Often the historians venture the opinion that the ancient voyagers of China, or Africa, or England were "swallowed up" by the so-called "Sea of Darkness;" or they were presumably "swept away" in a storm. This has been the convenient rationale to dismiss or to cover up any inconvenient evidence that might jeopardize the glory of traditional European heroes.

Until now, the stories of the "lost" mariners **have never been told.**

Sometimes, those who have undertaken the task of examining the ancient archives have come across some vague references about mariners sailing off towards the sunset—never to be seen again. On other occasions, there might be an accounting in the harbormaster's diary of a vessel that showed up carrying a suspicious cargo—such as copper, gold, silk, salt, dyewood, or codfish. The captain of the vessel claimed that they were returning from a simple trading venture to someplace ordinary, like the French port of Calais—but the nature of the cargo suggested the suspicious vessel had sailed far beyond the traditional boundaries of European shipping. Often, the harbormaster took a bribe and looked the other way. But sometimes, he noted down in the daily journal the unusual cargo—just in case a superior wanted to take a closer look in the future. In case there were any questions, he could point to the logbook as proof that he had done the required paperwork.

It was not the harbormaster's job to investigate the origins of suspicious cargoes or to confront devious captains who utilized every imaginable deception in order to avoid paying taxes. Sometimes, just knowing a little too much about what was really going on could jeopardize the harbormaster's life. In modern times, historians who promote the traditional view of history have been equally reluctant to pursue these tantalizing clues to their logical and inevitable revelation that the ancient mariners were sailing to the Americas long before the traditional heroes of discovery appeared upon the scene.

Few subjects have been more controversial or more volatile than the evidence of Old World voyagers who reached the Americas hundreds— even thousands of years before Columbus. Typically, historians have been more comfortable expounding their beliefs about past events than investigating the facts in order to find out what really happened. This controversy over early voyagers to the Americas has pitted armchair academics against visionaries and adventurers like Thor Heyerdahl—a Norwegian ethnologist who proved that it was possible for the ancient Egyptians to reach South America in reed boats. Betty Meggers, a Smithsonian archeologist dared to report her discovery of Japanese potshards in Ecuador dating to the Third Millennium BC. Instead of applauding her brilliant fieldwork, colleagues practically rode her out of the Institution for threatening the Old Paradigm that Columbus was "first."

They say that "truth is stranger than fiction"—and when it comes to what really happened in the hundreds of years leading up to the entrance of the European contenders, it is also much more exciting. The real story of behind-the-scenes intrigues, daring missions, romance, betrayal, and discovery deserve a full accounting in the annals of our multicultural heritage. At stake is a true understanding of how our ancestors attempted to learn about the meaning of existence and our place in the universe.

Finding Paradise

In the beginning, the ancients believed the earth was at the center of the universe. This was a fundamental error that impacted the way that people thought about their past, their present, and their future. It took many centuries of exploring before they learned that the sun is actually at the center of the solar system. That discovery—which is so vital to gaining a true understanding of physics and religion—was reflected in the emergence of rituals, symbols, and monuments (such as the pyramids of Egypt) and the celebration of the supreme Sun God—Ra. Historians haven't quite figured out how the ancient Egyptians reached that remarkable conclusion; but voyages to New Worlds across the seas were certainly behind the advancement to a new level of understanding.

A second fundamental mistake that was prevalent in ancient civilizations was the belief in an Earthly Paradise. Ancient religious leaders sought to understand the meaning of life by finding a suitable analogy in Nature. One popular belief—which was taught as "revealed wisdom" or Truth—was that the souls of deceased humans were reborn in the Land of the Setting Sun in the west. This region was presumed to be an isle of abundant orchards, sweet grasses, good hunting, and plenty of wine, dancing and - merrymaking. Egyptians called this land of earthly delights: *Sekhet-hetepet* or the "Fields of Peace." "the Abode of the Sun." Greeks revered the Promised Land as "the Elysian Fields;" Irish bards praised the Land of *Hy-Bresail* or Yuns yer Affalon—the Isle of Sweet Breezes and Garden of Apples. Christians wrote poems about "Paradise and the Garden of Eden." All of these charming notions about a happy place on earth resulted from the tales of mariners who had sailed across the oceans to the New World. When theologians in Egypt heard tales of the land of abundance across the ocean, this seemed to offer a suitable explanation for what happened to the sun during the night—and where the souls of the dead gained the promise of eternal life.

As long as life remained simple, people were illiterate, and they didn't travel far from home, the idea of an overseas Paradise was of great comfort to those who were dying. It was also a great inspiration for people of the lower classes (surfs, laborers, and slaves) whose daily lives were full of drudgery, whipping, abuse, and futility. Soldiers marching off to war were promised an immediate flight to the Promised Land if they died on the field of battle—thus generals motivated armies with the hope of an "afterlife" as heroes in the Elysian Fields.

When life became more complex, as it was bound to do among the more advanced civilizations of the Sumerians, the Persians, and the Egyptians—then the priesthood recognized an opportunity to make their services more value and indispensable. They envisioned elaborate rituals that supposedly were required for a soul to gain entrance into the Underworld Paradise. This "under" world was literally the land on the opposite side of the globe. We find among the Egyptians elaborate *Books of the Dead* describing the necessary rituals and spiritual "route maps" for reaching the Underworld Paradise. These books not only refer to the Paradise on the opposite side of the globe; they also tell of the "two-ways river" of the ocean. This is a clue to Egyptian knowledge of ocean currents that conveyed mariners westward or eastward across the sea.

When Christian theologians arrived upon the scene (during the early Middle Ages), there were some difficult moments when they tried to fit the real world into the template of Judaic tradition. According to the Old Testament, there were only three continents. So, there was some difficulty reconciling the fact that mariners who undertook voyages to the Western Isles often sailed to new lands across the seas that were not enumerated in Scripture. At some point in the Dark Ages (roughly between 500 and 1400 AD) the decision was made that the Underworld Paradise was the location of the biblical Garden of Eden. Supposedly, this was where Adam and Eve had dwelled before the Deluge—that is, before forty days of rain covered the entire world beneath the ocean. Presumably, this Paradise was reserved for good Christians—with Egyptian pharaohs and assorted warriors of other faiths being relegated to the outlying environs of hell. However, the "chosen" were only allowed to take up residence in Paradise *after* they had been baptized, died, and waited for the Apocalypse (that is, the End of the World). Until that moment, until the trumpet of Doomsday and the "Final Judgment," also the so-called "Last Act of God's Creation Play," Church authorities regarded the overseas isles as "Forbidden Territory." If you were a loyal Christian, you simply didn't go there. Or, if you did, you didn't dare tell anyone because of the sanctions and reprisals that were sure to result. Lips were sealed with respect to the Secret Land.

Of course, the Church's decision to condemn voyages to the New Land didn't stop the merchants who sailed across the seas on trading ventures; nor did it stop the fishermen who realized that the best fishing grounds on the planet were located off the coast of Newfoundland. Sebastian Cabot, an explorer for the English in the 15th century mentioned that there were so many codfish in the region of the Newfoundland Grand Banks that sailing vessels were measurably slowed by the bodies of the fish—like they were thick seaweed.

Fishermen and illicit traders in the New Lands were led to their destinations by following the direction of the north-pointing magnetic compass. The Church prohibition against using such "demonic devices" didn't stop the sea captains from sailing west; it simply meant that they hid the essential navigational tool inside a wooden box called a "binnacle." Meanwhile, the prohibition that Church leaders issued against sailing to the New Lands inspired secrecy, deception, and lying among Christian mariners who didn't want to be burned at the stake. During the Dark Ages, cartographers either didn't mention the overseas continents; or they used cryptic references on maps. Such names as "Icelandic Isles," "Estotilant," "Great Ireland," and "Brazil"—appearing on maps in the 14th and 15th centuries—are clues to the early voyages of secret mariners. These so-called "fantasy isles" have caused modern historians great confusion; but the ancient navigators managed to keep their heads in spite of threats from religious leaders.

During the 13th century, Roger Bacon mentioned that he had experimented with the magnetic compass; he experimented with gunpowder (against a Church prohibition); and he wrote about New Lands across the seas. His superiors in the Franciscan Order confiscated and burned all his books; then they restricted him to house arrest in exile from his homeland. Likewise, Leonardo DaVinci was arrested for suspicion of heresy—but he escaped because all of his incriminating notes about the sun-centered universe were in code. In the middle of the 16th century, Church authorities in Holland arrested the Dutch cartographer Mercator— one of the greatest scientists of the Renaissance. He was guilty of Protestant tendencies; and he committed the unwise "error" of celebrating the honor of another heretic, Amerigo Vespucci. Luckily, Mercator escaped execution—but only because his wife had the good sense to burn all of his personal letters the moment that he was arrested. The Dutch cartographer was subsequently released due to "insufficient evidence."

Nevertheless, he was still required to repay all the costs of his false imprisonment. As late as 1610, Galileo Galilei was censured for using the "demonic" telescope—and for claiming that the earth orbited the sun against the "revealed wisdom" of scripture. After admitting his "theological errors," he added in a whisper: "the earth moves."

Multiply these examples of situations where Church authorities attempted to prevent the advancement of scientific knowledge by a hundred thousand, and you will have some idea of the enormous scope of the problem. The severity of this repression, involving torture and public execution, helps to explain why intellectuals thought it was necessary to conduct their activities in secret.

The phrase "under the rose" came into use during the Dark Ages. Many philosophers and scientists sought to preserve their anonymity and their lives while engaged in the exchange of new ideas. A rose placed above a doorway or held by someone at a meeting had the significance of binding by oath all those present to secrecy. It was thus understood that anyone who broke the oath of silence by revealing the names of those who were present or what was discussed was subject to assassination—because literally everyone at such secret meetings had risked their lives. On occasion, of course, spies managed to infiltrate the secret gatherings. Occasionally, the supposedly secret meetings were followed by mass arrests and executions. In those situations, it was customary for the officials to torture those who were arrested in hopes of revealing the names of additional suspects. Often, their property was also confiscated so that wives and children became destitute. The effort to prevent the development of demonic inventions and to punish innovative thinkers was deemed necessary in order to protect the power of influential leaders in the Church administration or their cronies in government. It was also believed that the best way to keep the peasants and commoners in line was through ignorance and illiteracy.

Those who wrote about scientific inventions, about secrets that threatened the established order, often wrote books that were anonymous. We find many anonymous books in the archives of the Middle Ages. Often, these are books that doctrinaire historians dismiss as having no value with respect to the "official" version of history.

This is a Book of Secrets. The information that is revealed in these pages includes the forbidden lore of new lands as well as the extreme measures that Church and government authorities once employed in an effort to protect their secrets. Everything on these pages was at one time or another "under the rose."

Enjoy reading about the Nine Secret Voyages to the New World— but don't tell anyone where you learned these secrets!

—Anon

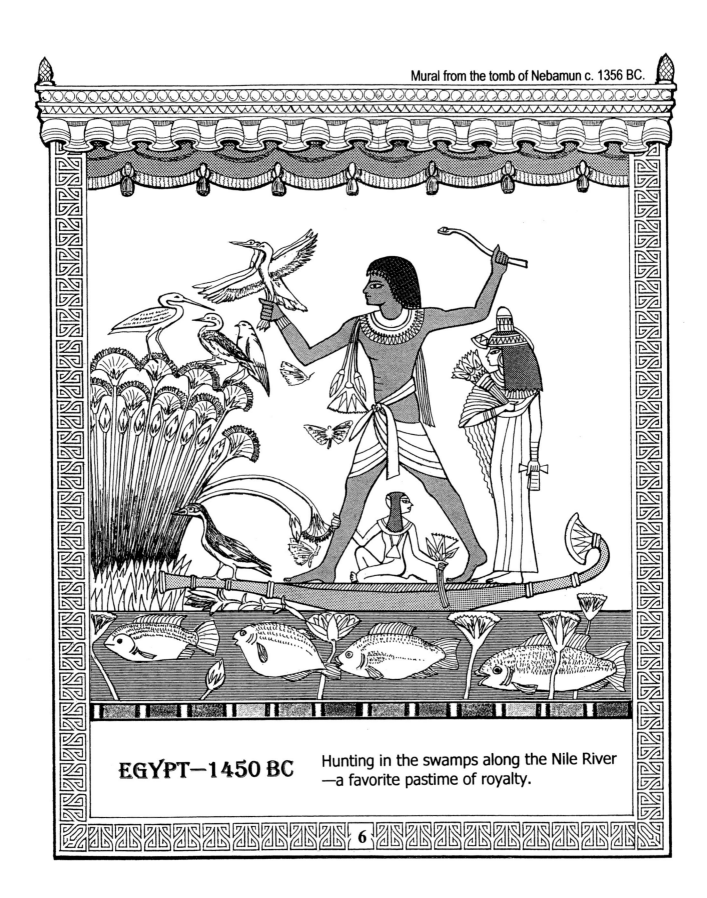

Mural from the tomb of Nebamun c. 1356 BC.

EGYPT—1450 BC

Hunting in the swamps along the Nile River —a favorite pastime of royalty.

Vision of the Pharaoh Queen

WE BEGIN THE FIRST ACT in the Theatre Sub Rosa with the incredible story of the only woman who ever ruled Egypt as a pharaoh. Her name was Hatshepsut—and she literally stood the male-dominated Kingdom of Egypt on its head.

Princess Hatshepset was born in about the year 1501 BC. Her birthplace was along the Nile River in the City of Thebes. This was an exciting time and place to be alive—at least for a princess. Thebes was the location of the central administrative offices of the government and the focal point of religious activity during a period of time that historians call "the New Kingdom."

This phase of Egyptian history witnessed the unification of Meroe (the ancient name for Egypt) with Nubia—a kingdom to the south in the 16th century BC. The unification resulted from the military exploits of Pharaoh Amosis whose mobile army of charioteers defeated the nomadic tribes from Asia Minor and the Hyksos overlords who had occupied the Nile Delta. However, Egyptian generals didn't stop at the traditional border of Northern Egypt. Instead, they pursued the Hyksos overlords into their own ancestral lands in the Sinai Desert. They continued chasing the nomads into Palestine in the Middle East. Thus, the territories that were dominated by the Egyptian military continued to penetrate deep into the ancestral homelands of their enemies.

It was at this point in time that the Egyptian military gained control over the political and religious affairs of the kingdom; and they established a military order with a new priesthood and new "warrior" deities. That is to say that they invented new gods for everybody to worship—gods that were suitable for the psychological and religious dominance of a military state. New Kingdom pharaohs were glorified as personifications of the Phoenician warrior-god Baal, Seth, or Mentu. They acquired great power and wealth as leaders of a career caste of charioteers and archers. On a more positive note, the harems of military leaders

(A relief painting from the tomb of Puah-hotep at Saqqara, c. 2450 BC showing the artist Niankhptah receiving a libation—after a drawing in Aldred, 1980, f. 47.)

Punting in Paradise

Egyptian temple and tomb murals often portray royalty enjoying the leisure-time activities of the Earthly Paradise or simply hunting in the swamps along the shores of the Nile River. The small boats or skiffs that were used in this activity were called "punts;" and the method of using poles to push the boats through the swamp reeds was called "punting."

Mastermind of Secret Discovery

Hatshepsut (c. 1478-1457 BC) was the only Queen of Egypt who succeeded in taking on the prestige and authority of male rulers— the Pharaohs. She used this power to send explorers and merchants to the Lands of Punt—the New World. Her royal statue (left) shows her dressed in the costume of Pharaoh. It was found in her Temple along the Nile River at Deir el-Bahri near Thebes.

included princesses from conquered territories and from distant trading partners as far away as the Aegean Sea. This influx of foreign influence gave the military organization and the government a broader more international complexion; and it contributed to a more cosmopolitan environment to the ethnic character of Thebes. It was in this thriving, multicultural setting that artists and intellectuals were inspired to dream about new lands across the seas. They also envisioned new freedoms and prosperity for the common people.

Thebes was a huge city that stretched for several miles along the Nile River. Picture in your mind a riverside farming community with palm trees lining the streets, an abundance of two-story adobe buildings, thriving markets with people dressed in colorful robes, and a commotion of crowds, camels, and cattle all wandering about—and you have some idea of what the scene was like in the ancient City. Commerce, religious rituals, and daily life followed the progress of the seasons from the flooding of the Nile River in the springtime to the dry months of winter.

Except when the mighty River was at flood stage, tens of thousands of sailing ships and boats of every variety plied the temperate waters. These vessels transported grain, stone monuments, slaves, officials, and luxury goods between markets in Upper Egypt and the cities of the delta region north of Cairo that was nearly 500 miles away. A boat-ride downstream could take nearly a week. Going upstream against the current took almost twice as long. In marshy areas, crocodiles waited to pounce on flocks of unwary geese that migrated north with the annual flooding. It was in these lush thickets along the river's edge that the pharaohs and princes enjoyed the pastime of "punting" or hunting using slingshots, bows-and-arrows, and throwing sticks.

As the daughter of Egypt's foremost military leader, Hatshepsut often visited the new city of Memphis that he had rebuilt just south of the Nile Delta. It was near the trading center of Cairo—about a hundred miles (or 150 kilometers) south of the Mediterranean Sea. There was an enormous traffic in merchant shipping that traveled across the Sea and up the Nile River—particularly when the government was engaged in the construction of stone temples that required enormous supplies from abroad.

The Princess grew up in the company of sculptors, stonemasons, foreign dignitaries, priests, tutors, and military leaders. She marveled at the exotic plants, animals, and treasures that were imported into the Kingdom from overseas—from as far away as the Tin Isles (or England) and from the Atlantean provinces across the Ocean. Some of the supplies even came from the Phoenician colonies that were rumored to exist near the Earthly Paradise of Osiris. Egyptian sailors referred to this territory on the opposite side of the globe as "the Isles of Inverted Waters." And that was a very accurate description of the overseas colonies, because these isles actually were "inverted" (or upside-down) with respect to Egypt.

In this waning era of the Bronze Age, Egyptians were still dependent upon the constant train of Phoenician merchant ships that brought ingots

Egyptian Naval Galley
In the service of Q. Hatshepsut
c. 1500 BC

(from Culver, 1924)

Ships & Shores of the Secret Sailors

where they went & how they got there

Secret Destinations in Ancient America

The Lands of Punt

Tropical Shores and Swamps in the Underworld along the coast of the Gulf of Mexico from Florida to Venezuela

10

of copper and tin from mines in the New World. When melted together, the alloy of copper and tin produced a very hard but easily molded metal called "bronze." This metal was so important to the progress of civilization that historians often refer to this period of time as "the Bronze Age." In an Age before iron or steel were known, this easily-molded metal was the only choice for producing axes, spear-points, arrowheads, chariot axels, horse harnesses, stirrups, chisels, carving tools, and practically everything else you can imagine. In other words, the entire military, the boat-building industry, the farmers, and all the craftsmen involved in building palaces, temples, and pyramids were entirely at the mercy of the foreign supply of cooper and tin. Thus, Princess Hatshepsut grew up hearing legends about the foreign lands. She heard about the daring exploits of the seafarers who supplied the Kingdom with the essential metals from overseas. She also learned to appreciate the needs of craftsmen, merchants, and traders whose efforts assured that the supply of vital metals kept on coming even though all the local copper mines had been exhausted. It was also apparent to the young Princess that the demands of the military for bronze weapons increased the price of the metal. When the price went up, it became more difficult for the farmers and the craft workers to do their jobs and to make a living—even though there were more demands placed upon them by the military leaders. When the farmers and artists grumbled in the marketplace, Hatshepsut had compassion for their suffering.

It is commendable to think that the Princess was concerned for the welfare of Egypt's farmers and artists. However; in a warrior dominated society, showing concern for the lot of commoners was not likely to win friends among those who actually ran the government.

As a teenager, Princess Hatshepsut was married in an official ceremony to her older brother Tuthmosis II. During ancient times, brother-sister marriage was customary among the Egyptian royalty. Religious leaders believed that this was a way of preserving the "purity" of the royal offspring—who were presumed to be descended from the Sun God. The practice resulted in the increased frequency of genetic disabilities that often plagued royal families.

The Princess was raised with the expectation that she would be the dutiful wife of the next pharaoh—that is, her brother. When her father died unexpectedly, the Princess was elevated to the position of "Regent Queen" alongside her brother as pharaoh. As Regent, she was expected to administer to the essential functions of the government until he reached the age of an adult and was able to assume full command. Unfortunately, Tuthmosis II seems to have had a genetic disorder that considerably shortened his life. When he died in about the year 1478 BCE, Hatshepshut was retained as Regent for another younger brother—Tuthmosis III. However, this new arrangement was not very suitable in the eyes of the ambitious Queen. Her successful administration of the government and her association with artisans and young priests had put new ideas into her head. She was not content to uphold a system in which she did all the work while her brother got all the credit from the court historians.

It was during her tenure as Regent that the cadre of palace priests in Memphis and Thebes came to realize that Queen Hatshepsut had remarkable skills both as a religious and as a political leader. Her preference for promoting the efforts of priests, merchants, and farmers in opposition to the interests of the military was readily apparent to the priests and government administrators. There werenumerous reformists among the priesthood and civil service who believed that the Queen would be a powerful ally in their longstanding rivalry with military leaders. At some point, this growing familiarity between the Regent Queen and the palace administrators reached a catharsis. This led to the formulation of a scheme to take over control of the entire Kingdom.

In about the year 1478 BCE, the Queen and her advisers took drastic measures in an effort to entirely change the course of Egypt's destiny. They made a mutual announcement that stunned the orthodox clergy and the military leadership. The reformist priests who had gained the upper hand in Thebes announced that Hatshepsut's birth was actually a divine act of "immaculate conception."

The priests declared that Hatshepsut's birth had resulted from the union of the old Thebian Supreme God—Amun—with the Queen's mother Ahmosis. According to the account issued by the Queen's cadre of royal priests, Hatshepsut's birth was attended by a host of deities including Bes (the god of the Underworld), the frog deity Heqet, and Thoth—the recorder of human deeds. According to this new edict from the highest religious leaders, Hatshepsut was to be regarded as the incarnation of the Supreme Deity. Her brother Tuthmosis III was "set aside"—effectively negating his theoretical title of "pharaoh." Immediately, Hatshepsut was formally elevated to the position of Pharaoh Queen.

Before the orthodox clergy could marshal their forces, the change in leadership was announced to the entire Kingdom. It was a done deal—a fait accompli. Probably, the most outraged generals fled to the foreign outposts in order to avoid their own arrest for treason. Many malcontents simply swore allegiance to the new leader while conspiring in secret to undermine her regime.

Hatshepsut's younger brother, the pretender to the throne, was bewildered by his sudden demotion and by the mere thought of a woman officially running the government. The fact that she had been elevated to the status of a "God" was beyond comprehension. However, Tuthmosis was at this point in time too young to have any say in the matter. The entire religious establishment had been undermined by rebellious priests, the offices of administration had been taken over, the least trustworthy military units had been sent to the provinces; and the public was informed of the New Order—before anything could be done to stop it.

Many of the military leaders were incensed by this usurpation of political power from traditional male control. Fundamentalist priests, whose authority had been undermined by the reformist clergy, were equally incensed. However, most of the government officials, the intellectuals, and a majority of the priests were excited by this opportunity to take command of the government. They easily gained the support of the commoners and business leaders who had resented military authority because it was so arbitrary and so contrary to the needs of commerce.

Thus, the takeover of the Egyptian government and religious centers by the reformists was a success—but it was one with an uncertain future. Since Hatshepsut's rivals included most of those who had positions of authority in the military, there was always the risk that her supporters might be quietly "eliminated" from the scene or that she might be poisoned—or simply disappear. Her advisors, therefore, had to carefully select her personal guards from among the younger soldiers who were still somewhat open-minded. They also had to plant spies in the camps of the military leaders in order to monitor the scheming of the opposition.

One of the Pharaoh Queen's first commands was the prohibition of all military activity beyond the national borders. The Kingdom of Egypt was mostly peaceful during her reign; and that resulted in a vast reduction in the operations and prestige of the military. Most of the generals resented this limitation on their theater of operations. Not only did they enjoy the thrill of fighting in hand-to-hand combat with inferior armies in Palestine, they had grown accustomed to gathering up the booty that was left upon the battlefields or in the unprotected foreign cities. In other words, not only was their independence restricted under the new regime, their profits were also severely curtailed. Queen Hatshepsut added further insult to injured prides of her generals by putting she the military to work on civil service projects. She ordered the soldiers to rebuild the canals, restore the facades of temples, and repair the public buildings whose maintenance had been neglected during decades of warfare and conquest in foreign nations.

The Queen's emphasis upon public service and commerce were the direct result of her cosmopolitan education in Memphis and Thebes. Her contact with foreign traders led to a realization that increased commerce and tourism could serve as better methods than conquest in promoting peaceful international relations. As part of this effort to promote peaceful enterprise, Hatshepsut ordered the construction of a new temple complex along the central Nile shore at Deir el-Bahri.

The Queen's Temple Complex was called *Djeser-Djeser*—meaning "The Splendor of Splendors." It was a magnificent structure whose design was intended to impress and to inspire visitors from at home and abroad for many centuries to come. There was an avenue of sphinxes lining the pathway that led from the boat landing up to the monument. The most striking feature of the building complex consisted of three massive stone terraces that were lined with colonnades on both sides of a central ramp. It was an innovative architectural style that seems to have inspired many Greek and Roman architects in subsequent centuries. Pairs of recumbent lions flanked the central ramp. They served as granite guardians to the awesome spiritual powers and secrets that were contained within the mysterious chambers. There were separate temples of worship for the gods Amun, Hathor, and Re—but none for the militaristic gods that were worshipped by the Queen's rivals.

New World Voyages to the Lands of Punt

Hatshepsut's grand building plans vastly increased the demand for trained stonecutters, sculptors, architects, and smiths. It also increased the dependence upon foreign trade. The greatest demands were placed upon the Minoan seafarers of Crete who were responsible for importing most of the foreign supplies of copper and tin.

Perhaps to guarantee the supply of vital metals, or perhaps to lower the cost, Hatshepsut contemplated the practicality of sending an Egyptian fleet to the overseas source of the Minoan metals. Of course, the precise location of the Minoan mines was a closely guarded secret. But the Queen's advisors had their own means of infiltrating the Minoan merchant marine in order to learn the sources of the vital metal. There was at least a general understanding among seafarers that the Minoan metals came from the Underworld. This was a region on the opposite side of the globe from Egypt that among the Aegean sailors and Minoan traders was known as the Realm of Hephaestus—the God of Metals.

Among Egyptian priests, the overseas isle of Osiris was known as *Sekhet-Hetepet*—or the "Fields of Peace." There was no question among the priests or the intellectuals in Egypt that such a place existed. Indeed, it was common knowledge among seafarers that there were lands across the oceans; and myths about the overseas lands had been a popular topic of papyrus books and poets.

The most important issue facing the Queen was not the actual existence of overseas lands; her greatest concern was the religious doctrine that condemned sailing overseas to the "Forbidden Territories." Indeed, most priests believed that *Sekhet-Hetepet* was the Earthly Paradise. That is, the Fields of Peace were presumably reserved for deceased pharaohs, male military heroes, and the concubines who provided the men with female companionship, wine and music. By having herself consecrated as both a Pharaoh and as a Deity, Hatshepset sought to overcome the theological bias against women as well as the prohibitions against voyages to the Underworld.

It was a cunning ploy that seemed to work. As long as the ruler and religious leaders supported the project, the commoners who were used to following orders simply did as they were told. However, there were quite a few orthodox priests who regarded the idea that the usurper queen intended to send an expedition to the Abode of the Dead as a sacrilege or an abomination. Yet, according to the inscriptions that were left on her temple wall at Deir al-Bahri, that is precisely what the Pharaoh Queen's expedition accomplished.

According to the inscription, Hatshepsut actually claimed that she was *compelled* by her faith in God—the God Amun—to sail across the seas. In other words, she was not to blame for breaking the archaic rules of the orthodox religion. The inscription indicates that the Queen had a vision while praying to Amun. It was Amun who instructed her "to bring the treasures from the Land of Punt back to the Temple at Thebes."

Precisely what that meant was an issue of some uncertainty and speculation. It still is. Modern historians haven't the foggiest notion of where "the Land of Punt" was located. Nor do they have any idea what the Queen expected to gain when she got there. All that we know for certain is that the Land of Punt was someplace overseas and far away from Egypt.

Regardless of where Punt happened to be located, the priesthood, it seems, had no choice but to accept the Queen's rationale that she was simply acting upon a direct instruction from the Supreme God. Nor would the military have any recourse but to cooperate with the enormous undertaking. Furthermore, any Minoan spies who happened to observe the enormous shipbuilding efforts at Coptos on the Nile River and along the Red Sea might tend to dismiss the project as "a flight of fancy" on the part of vain monarch. Would they have ever suspected that the Pharaoh Queen might have her eyes set upon their hoards of New World metals?

Hatshepsut faced the challenge of overseas voyaging with great deliberation and skill. She commanded the construction of a fleet of naval vessels that were suitable for overseas exploration, and she instructed her subordinates to supervise the training of crews and the manufacture of items for trade. We know from the inscription at Deir el-Bahri that the Queen's expedition carried metal blades and axes. These were the common items of trade with primitive societies. It seems evident from this clue that the expedition was headed for some distant colony that was far *beyond* the customary trading partners of Egypt that were situated in Somalia, Babylon, and along the East Coast of Africa. Indeed, the inscription at Deir al-Bahri informs us that "never in the past had such exotic foreign goods been brought back to Egypt." In other words, the plants from Punt were not the ordinary kind of trade items from the East Coast of Africa; they were totally new to Egypt.

Pharaoh Hatshepsut's fleet consisted of several vessels that were about 160 feet in length. The hulls consisted of a keel, ribs, and a skin of cedar planks that were held together with pegs and cordage. We know what they looked like from accurate stone carvings that have been found in Egyptian temples. These vessels carried a single cotton or woven flax sail; and they had two steering oars mounted on both port and starboard sides at the stern. In case the crews had to maneuver in the harbor or proceed against the wind, they were equipped with long oars and galley slaves. They also carried a contingent of archers and sailors for defense against pirates or cannibals. Officers were sheltered beneath a tent that was drooped over a long cable that extended amidships about eight feet above the deck. This cable helped to support the weight of the bow and stern. It was a sleek vessel with the kind of hull curvature beneath the waterline that is similar to that of a modern-day yacht.

The traditional interpretation of a mural at Deir el-Bahri is that the Egyptian fleet sailed to the Land of Punt via the Red Sea. This was just the beginning of a journey that probably took the expedition down the East Coast of Africa to the Southern Cape. From this point, the ships would have been in an excellent position to hop on the South Atlantic Current that sweeps northwards along the West Coast of Africa as far as the Cape Verde Islands. At that point, the current turns west into the mid-Atlantic Ocean. The current and trade winds stream west at a pace of more than one nautical mile per hour—sweeping ships westwards towards Brazil and the Caribbean Sea.

There is a second opinion, however, regarding the interpretation of the Egyptian mural in the Queen's temple. According to Charnon Simon (1990), the fleet sailed directly from Cooptos via the Nile River. If that is so, then either the expeditionary force sailed across the Mediterranean Sea towards Punt; or they used an ancient canal linking the Nile River to the Red Sea. In any case, there were most likely multiple voyages to Punt throughout the span of Hatshepsut's reign. The first of these expeditions was under the command of a trusted subordinate—Admiral Neshi.

Arab maps by al-Idrisi in 1154 and Ibn Said in 1250 indicate the existence of a large island directly west of the Straits of Gibraltar. This island was situated someplace across the Atlantic Ocean. The Arabs identified this island as *Ansharus* or "Far Land." Some scholars regard this as a fantasy representation of the mythical Isle of Atlantis. However, even that mythical island was woven into the fabric of Egyptian legends. According to the Greek philosopher Plato, his uncle had heard about Atlantis while visiting Egypt. So we have multiple clues that the Egyptians were familiar with lands across the seas; and there are subsequent maps from Arabian sources relating to the secret isles of the Far West.

It seems most likely that Punt was a Phoenician trading base that was situated somewhere near the equator on mainland west of Europe. It might have been on the coast of Mexico, Florida, Cuba, Venezuela, or Brazil. It was certainly at a location that was convenient to both oceangoing merchant ships and native trading canoes. The natives usually stuck pretty close to shore. Columbus encountered native trading canoes in the 15th century. He stated that they carried produce, copper axes, and textiles.

Major New World copper sources included the Antes Mountains of Peru (that is, the Andes) and Isle Royale in Lake Superior. Both sites at one time had millions of tons of so-called "native copper" or pure copper veins in the earth. Miners excavated the metal from these sites using Phoenician technology (hammer stones, chisels, and fire) between 3000 and 1000 BCE. The copper was brought by canoe to the Caribbean Sea and the Antilles Islands by way of the Amazon River, the Orinoco, and the Mississippi. Mexicans and Peruvian natives also made use of the copper trade. They acquired bronze tools from Phoenician merchants and they learned techniques of producing the copper alloy in their own smelters.

The Gulf of Mexico was a region that the Egyptian navigators referred to as the "Inverted Waters" or the "Heavenly Ocean." The intellectuals and the astronomers in Egypt realized that this was where the sun seemed to be located during the hours of nighttime. It was common knowledge among the enlightened priests that earth was a sphere, that it rotated on its axis, and that it revolved around the sun. However, in order not to frighten the uneducated public, murals depicted earth as a disc supported on pillars at the center of the universe. Meanwhile, the Goddess Nut held up the sky. The sun was depicted as a deity that sailed across the sky in a heavenly ship—the *Barque of Millions of Years*. It was so named because astronomers believed that the sun had existed for an eternity.

Queen Hatshepsut announced the success of her overseas expedition by proclaiming her sovereignty over "the Lands of the Setting Sun." So it is written in hieroglyphs at the Temple at Deir al-Bahri. Since this western real estate was situated across the Atlantic Ocean in the Underworld region of Inverted Waters, it is clear that the hieroglyphic inscription refers to the New World.[1]

It is not surprising that modern-day archeologists have found evidence of contact between ancient Egyptian mariners and the native peoples of the New World. In 1545, the Archbishop of Brazil astonished Vatican officials when he reported that Egyptian hieroglyphs had been found on ancient ruins near the Atlantic coast. An amateur archeologist named Carl Stolp found a lengthy hieroglyphic inscription in southern Chile; and a stone carving of a griffin-sphinx was found near Cuzco, Peru. A Mexican archeologist, Miguel Gonzalez, excavated two Egyptian artifacts near San Salvador in 1914. These were statuettes of the Goddess Isis and an unknown pharaoh. The Mexican historian Mariano Cuevas reported in his *Historia de la Nacion Mexicana* (1940) that:

> In the presence of these artifacts, it is a real possibility that Egyptians lived in the ancient city or that it was an Egyptian colony. Their influence in our country (Mexico) could have resulted from immigration—if not by Egyptians then by peoples in contact with Egypt.

Mexican archeologists who excavated ancient pyramids at the ancient metropolis Teotihuacan noted that native artisans portrayed the Sun God with the same kind of hand-held incense burner that is commonly seen in Egyptian artifacts. Ancient Mexicans built pyramids that are similar in design to the stone pyramids of Egypt; they used the Egyptian "ankh" symbol in art; they had amphoras like the common ceramic wine vessels used in the Mediterranean region; and they carried these amphoras using the same kind of net-slings that were used by Egyptian laborers. Some

---

[1] See Thompson, 1996, 70-90. R.A. Jiarazbhoy, *Ancient Egyptians and Chinese in America*, 1974, 13, mentions the hieroglyphic inscription of Hatshepsut's claim to the Lands of the Setting Sun.

ancient Mexican stone carvings from the Olmec culture have similarities of shape and style to Egyptian relief carvings; some of these carvings even have the stylized beard that was commonly used for statues of the pharaohs. The hardened metal tools that native Mexican artisans required for making many of the incredibly intricate New World stone carvings probably came from Egyptian or Phoenician merchants.

Considering that there were enduring contacts between Egyptian smerchants and the natives of Central America, it is hardly surprising that two New World plants, tobacco and cocaine, were found in the mummy of Pharaoh Ramses II. He was one of the most important pharaohs who lived in Egypt during the 12th century BC—only a century following the reign of Hatshepsut.

In the 19th century, excavating Egyptian tombs was a popular enterprise of French archeologists who were anxious for the kind of headlines that followed in the press whenever great art treasures and gold were recovered from the ancient burials. It was on one of these occasions that Muslim laborers found maize kernels (or New World corn) in an ancient sarcophagus. In addition to obtaining pure copper from New World mines and surface deposits in Upper Michigan, the ancient mariners probably imported quantities of furs, feathers, copal incense, and dyewoods from the Coast of Mexico.

On the way back to Egypt, Hatshepsut's fleet stopped at numerous ports along the African coast. They replenished their fresh water supplies, and they traded for additional merchandise that was suitable for markets in Thebes. In this manner, the fleet obtained quantities of ebony wood, the incense called myrrh, ivory, panther skins, and baboons—all of which appear on the mural at Deir el-Bahri. Historians have focused their attention upon these easily explainable imports; and that has resulted in the mistaken impression that the Queen's expedition sailed no farther than the nearby country of Somalia along the East Coast of Africa.

Midway through her reign, in about the year 1463 BC, Queen Hatshepsut lost the services of her favorite advisor—Senemut. We don't know for certain the cause of his demise or why he was never buried in his own tomb. On the other hand, it is quite evident that his association with the Pharaoh Queen put him on the "hit list" of her rivals. Clearly, the assassins were closing in on the royal household.

Hatshepsut's reign officially ended in 1457 BC. This date follows shortly after an invasion by nomadic tribes from Palestine in the region of the Nile Delta. The military was apparently caught unprepared; or else, they were willing to encourage an invasion as part of their scheme to embarrass the Queen and thus to undermine her authority. There was no official announcement of her death; nor was her tomb ever occupied. At least, it wasn't used for her burial. Archeologists excavating at Deir al-Bahri found a pile of wooden fertility statues. There has been some speculation that these symbols of the male phallus were intended as an insult because of the Queen's decision to play the role of a male leader. In any case, it was in about 1457 BC that Queen Hatshepsut virtually disappeared from Thebes along with many of her loyal supporters.

Historians inform us that desperate merchants, religious leaders, and governors all called upon the military to save the Kingdom from the nomadic invasion. The leading general was none other than the Queen's own brother, Tuthmosis III. He took over command of the country as the new Pharaoh. Then, he mobilized the army; and his forces managed to defeat the invaders with incredible ease.

Of course, Tuthmosis didn't stop at the traditional border of Egypt. Among cheering generals and charioteers, he ordered the invasion of foreign countries; and he renewed the practice of collecting tribute and booty from conquered enemies. He became very popular among the soldiers and among the fundamentalist priests who had suffered humiliation during the Queen's reformist administration. The new Pharaoh launched reprisals against the Queen's supporters; and he ordered his henchmen to erase from all the monuments any references that had ever been made to the existence of a female ruler in Egypt.

All that survived from Hatshepsut's reign were a few hidden sculptures and several murals at Deir el-Bahri. It is clear that the male-dominated hierarchy succeeded in neutralizing the influence of the Pharaoh Queen upon the course of Egyptian Civilization. As far as the fundamentalist priests were concerned, Hatshepsut and her voyages to the Land of Punt would remain secrets forever. They simply never happened.

What do Historians Think?

Where was the Land of Punt?

Nobody really knows for certain. One writer, Henry Culver who is a scholar on the subject of ancient voyages, has suggested that the "Land of Punt" was simply a designation for a place that was "very far away."[2] It was probably connected through legend to the overseas paradise of Osiris, Isis, and Bes—the very Underworld deities that figured so prominently in the life of the Pharaoh Queen. She was also a very practical leader who realized the potential value for her own people that might be gained by a direct route to the mineral wealth of the Underworld. Her claim that she was "inspired by a vision" seems to be a clever ruse to mislead her rivals.

During the Bronze Age, America was the primary source of cheap, Minoan copper. It is true that the Island of Cyprus (whose name means "Copper Island" in Greek) at one time served as the principal source of copper in the Mediterranean Region. There was also an island that was called "Copper Mountain"—until miners flattened the mountain in order to extract the last ounce of metal. When supplies of the vital material grew scarce, the regional metal traders—the Minoans and Phoenicians—were

---

[2] Henry Culver, *Ancient Ships*, 1924, p. 9. Regarding the Land of Punt: "The exact location of this elusive country has not been determined by the Egyptologists. The name was probably generic, conveying the meaning of a far-off land sometimes suggesting one place, sometimes another."

forced to find supplies that were far away across the seas. Several maverick scholars have effectively established the vital link between the Egyptian demand for copper and the extensive mining that was conducted on the Upper Peninsula of Michigan and at Isle Royale in Lake Superior.[3]

Most traditional historians have assumed that the Egyptians were not capable of ocean sailing; and they have speculated that Punt must have been located not very far away. The common assumption among orthodox historians seems to be that the Country of Somalia—just south of Egypt on the Red Sea—was the Land of Punt. However, that seems unlikely since Somalia was a usual port of call among merchants sailing on the Red Sea. The idea that this nearby country would be the source of "new and wonderful imports never before seen in Egypt" (as the inscription at Deir al-Bahri says) does not agree with Somalia as the source. Egyptian traders had no difficulty in obtaining goods from Somalia—nor was there any reason for calling it "the Land of Punt." As it is situated just south of Egypt, it is not really very far from Egypt—so the idea of Punt being a "far away place" doesn't agree either. Also, cheap metal tools like those that were carried by the Egyptian Expedition to Punt hardly seem like the kind of items that would have had any appeal to the merchants living in the port cities of Somalia. These kinds of items were produced locally—so there was no need to import them from Egypt. Another feature of the mural at Deir al-Bahri are the native villages of domed houses and reed houses built up on stilts to keep them above floodwaters. These are the kinds of buildings that Spanish explorers found along the coast of Florida, Louisiana, and Venezuela in the 16th century.

The Norwegian ethnologist Thor Heyerdahl believes that the Egyptians sailed directly west to the Caribbean Sea. While he was engaged on a tour of Peruvian museums in the 1930s, Heyerdahl noticed that numerous ceramic pots of the Moche culture were decorated with illustrations of reed boats. He also noted that boats made from totora reeds were common on Lake Titicaca in southern Peru. Since Heyerdahl was also familiar with reed boats that were portrayed on Egyptian murals, he suggested that ancient Egyptians might have sailed to the New World from the North African Coast. Historians generally scoffed at the notion that any Old World voyagers, much less the Egyptians, might have beaten Columbus to the New World. Indeed, many insisted that it was impossible for ancient mariners to sail across the Atlantic Ocean

If history teaches anything at all, it teaches us that it's never wise to tell a Norwegian that something is "impossible!" It's a surefire inspiration for the old Vikings to invest considerable amounts of cash and time to prove that they can do the impossible.

Well, Heyerdahl jumped at the opportunity to prove his point. He contracted with a team of Nile boatmen to build him a reed boat after the fashion of the ancient reed boats of the pharaohs. Then, he towed his ungainly reed boat to Morocco in 1969; and he sailed out onto the Atlantic

---

[3] See for example Fred Rydholm's book on Ancient Mining in the Upper Great Lakes, 2006.

Ocean accompanied by a crew of starry-eyed volunteers. Before long, the tortora reeds grew soggy; the bow slumped into the water; and then the boat promptly sank. The orthodox historians were overjoyed—so overjoyed, in fact, that they issued a premature proclamation claiming that the sinking of Heyerdahl's flimsy boat, the Ra, proved they were right— that primitive reed boats were incapable of crossing the ocean.

However, the Norwegian skipper simply chalked up this one failure to the ledger of life experience; and he vowed to make another try. *National Geographic Magazine*, which covered the first attempt, was equally anxious to follow the progress of the second effort. All around the world, the practical-minded people and the dogmatic scholars argued over the outcome of this real-life experiment of ancient boatbuilding technology.

This time, Heyerdahl picked an experienced team of Peruvian craftsmen to build his vessel. The Peruvian version of a reed boat proved to be much more durable than the one that had been manufactured the previous year in Egypt. In 1970, the reed vessel *Ra II* succeeded in making the crossing from Morocco to the Caribbean. Orthodox historians were stunned—particularly because of the widespread publicity provided by the staff of *National Geographic Magazine*. Heyerdahl proclaimed a "victory" for his crew and for the theory of Egyptian seafarers crossing the ocean. The best that academic historians could muster was a stinging retort saying that: "all the Norwegian had proved was that reeds could float."

Consequences for New World Exploration

In spite of the official repudiation of Hatshepsut's fame by the ancient Egyptian authorities, legends of her voyages across the Atlantic continued to tantalize Egyptian rulers and merchants. In the 12th century BC, Pharaoh Ramses II boasted of expeditions to the "Inverted Waters"—that is, to the Gulf of Mexico. In 1280 BC, a mural in the Tomb of Userhet near Thebes shows the Pharaoh drinking from a vessel holding what is called "the Water of Paradise." Such a statement could only refer to sacred water that had been brought back from the Earthly Paradise—from the Underworld. From such humble beginnings there emerged legends in Arabian folklore of a "Fountain of Youth"—in of all places—Florida! In the 6th century BC, Pharaoh Necho commissioned a Phoenician expedition to circumnavigate Africa. While that mission might seem like a straight forward assignment, there has been some speculation (particularly on the part of R. Buckminster Fuller, 1992) that the mariners sailed the long way around Africa by way of Indonesia and the Canadian Northwest Passage. In other words, they managed to circumnavigate the earth. Several ancient Greek scholars shared in that assessment. This occurred some two thousand years before the Europeans finally convinced Magellan to seek his destiny by a voyage round the world.

We have noted that several inscriptions regarding the Pharaoh Queen and several of her statues managed to survive the purge that was conducted under the auspices of Tuthmosis III and Akhenaten. It is therefore evident that at least some of the Queen's loyal followers hid her images and kept her legacy alive in spite of the risks. Those who were so engaged in preserving the legacy of overseas voyaging were members of secret societies that included alchemists and astronomers. They characterized the Atlantic Ocean as a "Two-Ways River" in secret books of mysteries called "Books of the Dead." This testimonial to the ancient voyagers who must have crossed the Atlantic Ocean in order to learn the secret of the "two ways current" is a clue to the achievements of the ancient mariners that has escaped the understanding of modern scholars.

Egyptian contact had an enduring impact upon Native American societies. Perhaps the most important consequences were the contributions to native communications and economic systems. We find that Mexicans used the same kinds of inkwells, paper, paper books, and hieroglyphs that were common in Egypt. Although most of the Mexican and Mayan words and symbols were unique, we occasionally encounter identical words in both societies as is the case with the use of the word *Re* for "the serpent-eye of the sun." There are other surprising cultural similarities such as the practice of cutting holes in the skull to relieve pressure on the brain, use of bronze-tipped mace as a weapon, use of copper ox-hide ingots as currency, similar embalming practices, and similar mummification rituals. One Mexican statue found at an archeological site shows the body of a deceased individual s wrapped in strips of cloth like those used for Egyptian mummies.

Where was the Land of Punt? In order to solve the puzzle of this intriguing name, "Punt," we need look no further than the illustrations in the Book of the Dead or in the murals of Egyptian tombs. These murals and illustrations depict the joys of pharaohs who anticipated hunting in the marshes of the Underworld. Usually, the exciting hunt for waterfowl took place from a platform on the deck of a small boat called a "punt." This type of boat could be quietly moved through the tall reeds using a pole to push against the bottom of the marshland. The means of poling the boat forwards was called "punting." In other words, the "Land of Punt" was simply a cryptic reference to the kind of hunting that pharaohs could expect to enjoy in the Earthly Paradise. Egyptian seafarers found "Punt" in the marshlands of Florida, Louisiana, and Venezuela.

Queen Hatshepsut was not alone among powerful rulers who longed to explore this Never-Never Land across the seas while they were still living.

If Hatshepsut was very lucky, perhaps she realized that her reign in Egypt was doomed before it was too late. Perhaps, at the last moment, before the henchmen of her brother came knocking at her door, she managed to slip away to her refuge across the seas. In any case, the legends of her refuge persisted for centuries; and they resurfaced in Jerusalem to inspire a future king named Solomon.

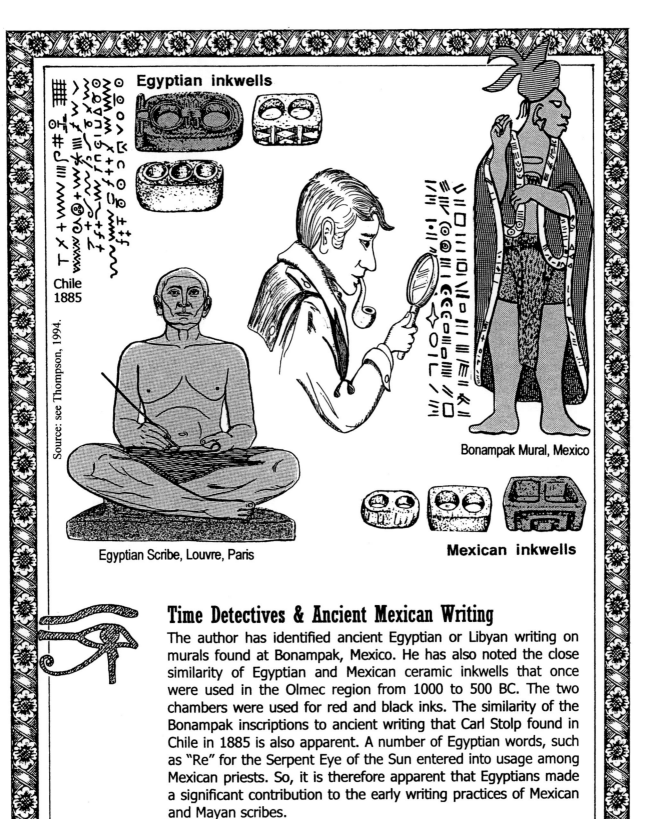

Egyptian inkwells

Chile 1885

Source: see Thompson, 1994.

Egyptian Scribe, Louvre, Paris

Bonampak Mural, Mexico

Mexican inkwells

Time Detectives & Ancient Mexican Writing

The author has identified ancient Egyptian or Libyan writing on murals found at Bonampak, Mexico. He has also noted the close similarity of Egyptian and Mexican ceramic inkwells that once were used in the Olmec region from 1000 to 500 BC. The two chambers were used for red and black inks. The similarity of the Bonampak inscriptions to ancient writing that Carl Stolp found in Chile in 1885 is also apparent. A number of Egyptian words, such as "Re" for the Serpent Eye of the Sun entered into usage among Mexican priests. So, it is therefore apparent that Egyptians made a significant contribution to the early writing practices of Mexican and Mayan scribes.

23

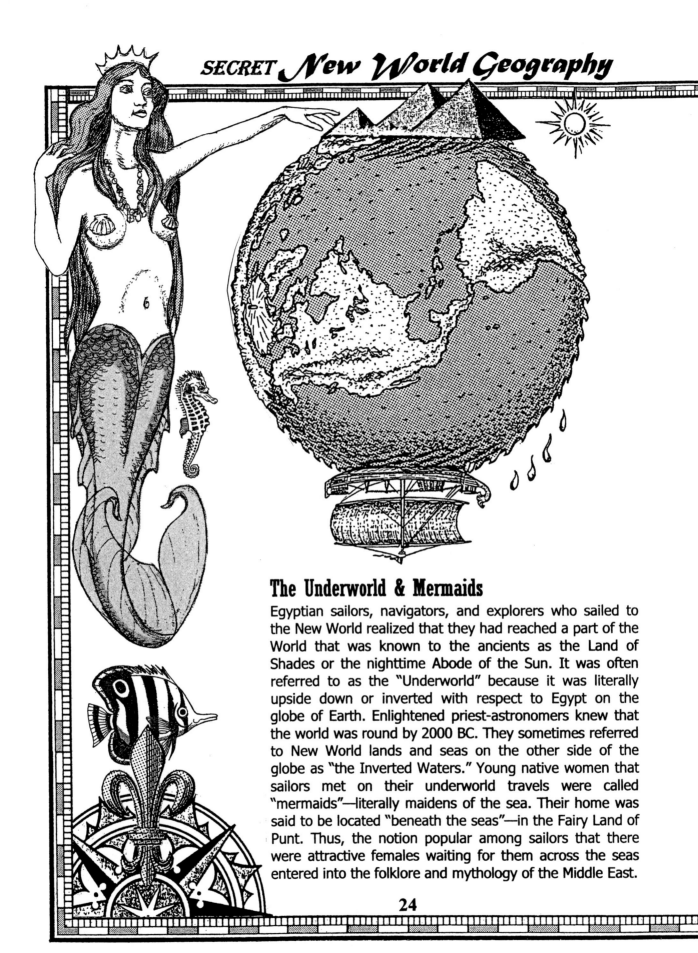

The Underworld & Mermaids

Egyptian sailors, navigators, and explorers who sailed to the New World realized that they had reached a part of the World that was known to the ancients as the Land of Shades or the nighttime Abode of the Sun. It was often referred to as the "Underworld" because it was literally upside down or inverted with respect to Egypt on the globe of Earth. Enlightened priest-astronomers knew that the world was round by 2000 BC. They sometimes referred to New World lands and seas on the other side of the globe as "the Inverted Waters." Young native women that sailors met on their underworld travels were called "mermaids"—literally maidens of the sea. Their home was said to be located "beneath the seas"—in the Fairy Land of Punt. Thus, the notion popular among sailors that there were attractive females waiting for them across the seas entered into the folklore and mythology of the Middle East.

24

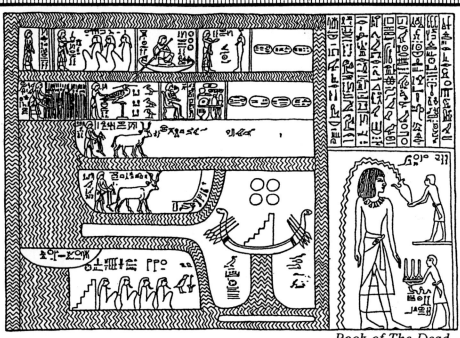

Book of The Dead

(Papyrus painting after *Book of the Dead*, British Museum, London; from Thompson, 1994, 72.)

(A relief stone carving presently in the Metropolitan Museum of Art, New York; from an illustration in Thompson, 1994, 72.)

The Earthly Paradise

Travel to an Earthly Paradise or Underworld by ship was a common theme in ancient Egyptian religious books—sometimes called "Books of the Dead." Often, this realm was pictured in papyrus paintings as an idylic land of rivers, swamps, farming and hunting or "punting." It was called Sekhet-hetepet meaning "Fields of Peace;" and it thus entered Roman mythology as "the Elysian Fields" and later Christian theology as "the Earthly Paradise." Egyptian scribes referred to the "Two-Ways River of the Ocean" that served to conduct the souls of the dead across the Atlantic Ocean to Paradise (in the New World). This indicates a vital understanding of ocean currents that mariners used to speed travel to America.

The Round Earth

A four thousand year-old stone carving from Saqqara, Egypt, confirms that priest-astronomers had knowledge of the roundness of Earth. This theological abstraction portrays the concept of Earth at the center of the universe with the winged disc of the sun traveling across the sky of the Upper World. In the Under World is the Land of Darkness and the Nether Regions of the Goddess Nether (or Netter) and the God Set (Satan).

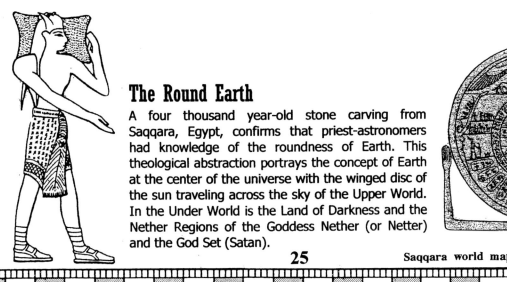

25

Saqqara world map

Evidence of Contact

Egyptian Anubis
or Jackal

Florida Jackal
from Key Marco

Mexican Ankh

Mexican amphora
with net sling
after *Vatican Codex*

(After photographs in Cuevas, 1940; from Thompson, 1994, 84)

stone carving found at Mitlatoyuca, Mexico

from Cuevas (1940)

Mexican
"Mummy"

Egyptian Statuettes in El Salvador

In 1914, the Mexican archeologist Miguel Angel Gonzalez found two Egyptian artifacts (above, left) at a site near Acajutla. These carved stone sculptures were uncovered in the course of a routine scientific excavation—so there is no concern for the possibility of a deception. A stone carving of a mummy, wrapped in a fashion that was customary of Egypt, was found near a village in Mexico (above right).

26

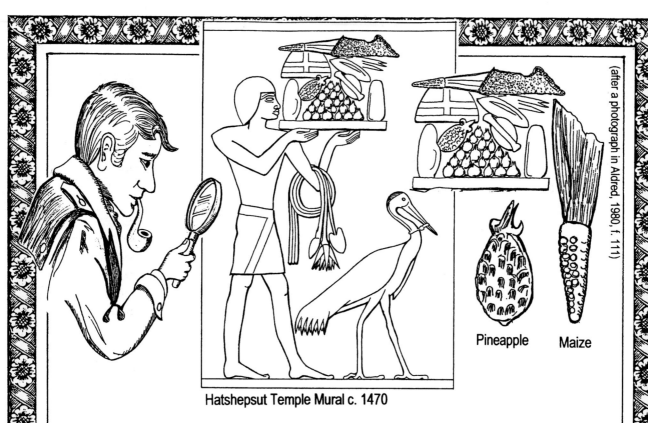

(after a photograph in Aldred, 1980, f. 111)

Pineapple   Maize

Hatshepsut Temple Mural c. 1470

Time Detectives & New World Plants in Egypt

The author has identified an ear of corn (or maize) and a pineapple on a mural from Hatshepsut's Temple at Deir el Bahri (dated to c. 1470 BC). Since maize and pineapples are typically regarded as "New World plants," the presence of these imports provides conclusive evidence of significant contact between the Old World and New World peoples. Nearly a hundred years has passed since Muslim field workers found maize kernels in an Egyptian sarcophagus. This discovery prompted the French plant historian Alphonse de Candolle to declare that: "the Arabs were trying to confuse Western historians." German scientists a few years ago identified tobacco and cocaine in the mummy of Ramses II (c. 1279-1212 BC). So it appears that there was a considerable flow of New World plants into Egypt following Hatshepsut's expeditions to Punt.

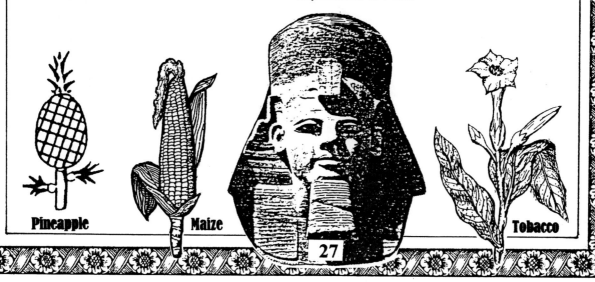

Pineapple   Maize   Tobacco

27

Templum Salomonis

ISRAEL—953 BC

King Solomon's Temple in Jerusalem is ranked among the Wonders of the Ancient World.

Solomon's Heirs

AN ORDINARY SLINGSHOT in the hands of a daring visionary changed the course of history. The shooter's name was David; and his "child's toy" proved lethal against a giant named "Goliath."

Biblical scholars place this event sometime around the year 1013 BC. According to the biblical tale, the peace-loving Hebrew tribes were confronted by neighboring warlords and their band of giant thugs who were leading the Philistine army. It seems that at the time, all the Jewish men were willing to accept the humiliation of slavery as the only alternative to certain death. However, David stepped forward and offered to challenge the champion of the Philistines. Jewish elders were puzzled by this bold offer which seemed hopeless—David being a mere shepherd boy and Goliath being so big and menacing. Nevertheless, they praised the lad's courage; they arranged for the duel; then they prayed to God.

The Bible is explicit regarding the outcome of this confrontation: God intervened that day in the affairs of mortals. It has become an enduring legend that is invoked whenever an oppressed people are confronted by what seems to be an insurmountable foe. Goliath strode forward; he walked casually while demeaning his gallant opponent. He was suitably clad in rusted armor; and he carried a sword with which to slice his pathetic opponent from head to toe.

The shepherd was not nervous. He believed that God was present to shield him from his foe. Besides, he knew that it wasn't necessary for him to actually kill his opponent with the slingshot: all he had to do was to get him off balance. He loaded his sling with a small, smooth stone just as he had done countless times before when hunting small game. Then, he hurled that stone at his adversary—striking squarely in the forehead. Goliath tripped, and he toppled to the ground. He was only dazed by the missile; but he was helpless to stop the shepherd boy from taking his own sword to chop off his head. David raised the trophy. At once, ten thousand Hebrew warriors screamed their battle cry; and they stormed forward with the furor of a great hurricane.

Solomon's Seal
Mexican Motif
Uxmal 1200 AD

Illustration from a 16th century print.

ℳastermind of ℒecret 𝒟iscovery

Handsome, randy, and wise, King Solomon of Israel was known throughout the Middle East. His reign lasted from 961 BC to 922 BC. He is shown here entertaining the entourage of the Queen of Sheba (modern-day Yemen).

When the day had ended, the survivors of the Philistine Army were fleeing to the hinterlands. David was promptly celebrated as the new "King of the Jews."

This was the beginning of a reign that lasted for forty years. The Kingdom of Israel grew in size as nearby cities either joined voluntarily or they succumbed to the might of the Hebrew Army. According to the chronicles of royal scribes, the Hebrew soldiers were always victorious. The reason given for this success in battle was that they had a secret weapon: they followed the Will of God. It wasn't "a fair fight" in human terms—setting mere mortals against a Hebrew army that could invoke earthquakes, plagues, and lightning in its arsenal of weapons. But according to the biblical story, God sets the rules; and God selects the victors. All that God required for this divine favor was loyalty, countless prayers, and the seemingly endless sacrifices of sheep and oxen.

King David was supremely grateful for all the supernatural assistance. As a gesture of appreciation and loyalty, he began an enormous building project to erect what he called "The House of The Lord." It was just the beginning. He also instructed his son, Solomon, to supervise the planning and construction of a suitable temple to house the Ark of the Covenant which was a portable altar that contained the Tablets of Moses.

In future generations, this incredible stone edifice would become famous as "Solomon's Temple."

Like all building projects that involved cutting and transporting huge blocks of stone, David's architectural plans required enormous resources of slaves, craftsmen, and metal tools. Since the Jews had risen to their apogee of cultural development at the dawn of the Iron Age—they were no longer dependent upon Phoenician supplies of tin and copper from the distant mines across the seas. There was plenty of iron ore available in nearby Turkey to the north. However, what David needed in order to give the "Lord's House" the suitable kind of interior that it required was plenty of gold. What David had in mind was a building in which the interior walls were literally covered with thick sheets of gold. Whenever priests entered carrying their torches to offer prayers to Jehovah, they would be dazzled by the incredible light shows of dancing flames that were bouncing between the golden walls.

Solomon became King of Israel in about the year 965 BCE. At this point in time, the Grand Temple was still only a vision while the realities of political organization demanded immediate attention. In order to govern the Kingdom effectively and to obtain building materials and supplies from abroad, Solomon needed to devise a foolproof method of managing a diversity of semi-independent tribes and diverse ethnic groups. It finally dawned upon him that: 1) he was wealthy; 2) he was very attractive to the ladies; and 3) he had an enormous sexual vitality.

The strategy that he devised was to divide the Kingdom into twelve districts. Then he married the daughters of all the governors in each district; he married the daughters of the most influential merchants; and he

Judean Cargo Vessel
c. 1000 BC—500 AD
(from Thompson, 1994)

Ships & Shores of the Secret Sailors

where they went & how they got there

☆☆☆☆☆

Secret Destinations in Ancient America

The Lands of Ophir

Solomon's allies, the Phoenicians brought him gold from mines in California, Panama, Peru, and Haiti (Hispaniola).

married all the princesses that he could attract from the neighboring kingdoms. Because of this profound strategy, all the governors of Israel were related to him by marriage as were all the neighboring kings. Thus, he had a direct channel of communications with all the ethnic and political factions in the region. It seems hardly surprising that Solomon was able to rule so effectively.

Before long, the Bible tells us, Solomon had brought into his household at least 700 wives and numerous concubines. In addition to becoming renowned throughout the Kingdom for his "insuperable wisdom," practically everybody living in the Middle East called King Solomon—"Uncle."

Among Solomon's favorite wives was the daughter of the Egyptian pharaoh. Along with her dowry, Solomon was given the secret sailing directions to an overseas land that was rich in gold, gems, and spices. Of course, the location of this Isle was a secret. It was a secret whose origins, according to Middle Eastern folklore, stretched all the way back to the overseas expeditions of Hatshepsut—the Pharaoh Queen.

New World Voyages to the Golden Paradise

Among Solomon's closest friends was the Phoenician ruler King Hiram of Tyre. Hiram governed an ancient metropolis and seaport that was located along the Mediterranean Coast of Lebanon. He also had connections with Phoenician merchants sailing throughout the world. Ever since the worldwide decline in the demand for copper, the Phoenician merchants sought to develop new products for overseas commerce. Chief among these new commodities were red and purple dyes, a gemstone— lapis lazuli, turquoise, Mediterranean amber, textiles, and gold. The sources of all these materials were regarded as commercial secrets. Indeed, they had to be kept secret from commercial rivals since the livelihood of the Phoenician maritime nation was wholly dependent upon their monopoly over the transport of valuable commodities.

The Phoenicians were also master shipbuilders, sailors, and navigators. These skills had been developed as a result of experimentation, and more importantly—from the inspiration of foreign inventors with whom they had ongoing contact. Early on, they learned the secrets of primitive telescopes or "spyglasses," and they learned how to use the magnetic compass. This device consisted of a magnetized steel needle that was coated with grease (or wax) and floated in a brass cup.[1]

As Solomon was so busy with his many international affairs, his twelve governments, and his many wives, it was essential for him to give someone else the responsibility for mounting expeditions to the Land of Gold. King Hiram was glad to oblige his enchanting Son-in-Law. He

---

[1] The compass was known to the Hellenistic Greeks by 900 BC and later to the Vikings circa 1000 AD. The device was seldom mentioned by Christian mariners due to the concerns raised by Church authorities that the device was "demonic" in nature.

expected to gain handsome profits by managing the mining and transportation arrangements for Solomon's gold. The first issue for the new partnership was selecting a suitable name for the distant isle. They settled on "the Land of Ophir"—which was a name they chose to honor the grandson of Noah.

Hiram selected the port of Ezion-Geber on the Red Sea as the base for building his new treasure fleet. The vessels were over a hundred feet in length. They were made in the Phoenician style with a keel, ribs, a skin of overlapping cedar planks, two steering oars at the stern, and a single mast. Ever since the invention of iron, the Phoenicians had experimented with the use of nails as well as wooden pegs for holding the wooden planks to the ribs of the ships. These vessels were loaded with stores for many months at sea in addition to stone ballast along the interior of the hull. The hull sloped gently both fore and aft—making it easy to land on a sandy shore for loading cargo. They were fast and maneuverable; they had strong flax and leather sails; and they could be rigged in a "lateen" fashion for sailing into the wind or as a "square-rig" with the wind astern. In calm weather, the crew and galley slaves could propel the vessels with oars.

The treasure fleet seldom sailed with fewer than ten ships. Hiram figured that they needed at least this many vessels in order to guarantee protection against pirate attack. They also needed adequate space for extra trading goods that were transported on each expedition.

They sailed many times. Accounts in the Bible record a few of the expeditions.[2] They headed first to a Far Eastern port that is only identified as "Tarshish." It was another secret city where Hiram's vessels sailing from Ezion-Geber had a rendezvous with a second fleet from Ophir. Tarshish was a midway point in the transoceanic trek of treasure from the New World to the Middle East. By splitting up the sailing routes and the duties of the sailors, Hiram hoped to protect his secret sources.

We learn from the Bible that it was at Tarshish where the vessels from Ezion-Geber obtained cargoes of sandalwood, spices, elephants, apes, and peacocks—in addition to the gold from Ophir. This assortment of goods and animals suggests that the mysterious port was situated someplace in Thailand, Burma, or Indonesia. The 13th century traveler, Marco Polo, was among those who searched for the location of Tarshish in this region. He concluded that Hiram's transfer point was located along the coast of Java.

Every three years, Hiram sent his fleet to Java to get the gold of Ophir. The Phoenician trade route was in effect a virtual pipeline of valuable metal that was sucked right out from King Solomon's Mines and sent it on its way to Hiram's clan in Lebanon. This flow of New World treasure fueled Phoenician mercantile enterprises throughout the Mediterranean region. A small portion of that gold ultimately found its way to Solomon's Temple. The Bible reports that Solomon obtained "400 talents of Ophir gold"—estimated to be over a ton of pure gold ingots.

---

[2] References to Ophir in the Hebrew Bible (the Old Testament) can be found in 1 Kings 9:28, 10, 11; 1; 22:48, 1 Chronicles 28 & 29; and 2 Chronicles 8:18, 9 & 10, Job 22.24, 28.16, Psalms 45.9, and Isaiah. 13 .

Even though the location of Solomon's Mines remained a secret during the King's lifetime, clues regarding the whereabouts of the Mother Lode have emerged over the passing centuries. It wasn't at all difficult for Greek and Roman geographers to trace the course of Hiram's fleets to Southeast Asia. The 2nd century Alexandrian geographer named Ptolemy deduced that Tarshish was situated on a huge island someplace beyond India. He called this island "Taprobana." The name is a combination of the Latin words for "main" and "route." The implication was that this island was strategically located "on the seaway" or "on the main route" to an unknown continent across the seas. On Ptolemy's map, Taprobana is situated directly south of India. For a long time, Europeans confused this huge isle with Ceylon (which is a *tiny* island south of India). However, the relative size of the island and its location suggest that Taprobana was intended as a schematic representation for Sumatra, Java, or Australia. It might also collectively represent all three of the major Southeast Asian islands—as they were all "on the route" to Ophir.

Another Roman map, by Pomponius Mele in the first century, has a text indicating that Taprobana is a midway point between East Asia and South America. According to the Roman geographer, Taprobana was "the principal entry-point to *the Other World.*" When we realize that "the Other World" was a Roman name for South America, then it becomes clear that Taprobana served as a way-station for mariners sailing towards South America from the Orient. Both Columbus and Amerigo Vespucci used this same expression—"Other World"—in reference to South America. So, we are on a firm footing to conclude that Solomon's Isle of Gold was located in South America.

Taprobana (that is, Java or Sumatra) was an important Island for several reasons. First, because it was located in the Tropics southeast of Asia, the harbors along its coast were always open regardless of the seasons. Second, because the location was midway between India and the Spice Islands (or "East Indies"), there were always merchants with valuable cargoes traveling in both directions. Thus, it was an excellent location to obtain spices, incense, drugs, textiles, dyewoods, and exotic plants and animals. And Third, the chain of islands between Java and New Zealand provided way stations and navigational markers that led ships towards the South Pacific Current. This current heads southeastwards along the coast of New Zealand. It cruises along at a rapid pace of over a knot-per-hour. Vessels riding this current are swept relentlessly towards the Antarctic Current; and from the Antarctic Seas, they are promptly carried by the South Atlantic Current northwards along the coast of Chile and Peru. This was the quickest way for merchants to sail across the Pacific Ocean to the region of the world's richest gold deposits in the Andes Mountains of Peru.

Solomon's miners established a colony near the Peruvian citadel of Sacschuaman (which is in the vicinity of modern-day Cuzco). From this base, teams of miners with ample military escorts proceeded to chisel and burn their way through the veins of gold that they followed deep into the bowels of the mountains. In exchange for supplying the Phoenician miners with food and water, the Peruvians gained a portion of the gold in addition to imported metal tools and textiles. They also learned Phoenician secrets of alloying copper and tin to make bronze; and they acquired a variety of metal casting techniques that were employed for manufacturing weapons and jewelry. Within forty years, most of the accessible gold deposits had been scoured from the Andes; and the Phoenicians sailed for home. Besides bronze casting technology, they left behind a few Phoenician inscriptions, a number of natives who had learned the Old World techniques of cutting stone, and miles of empty subterranean mineshafts.

The heirs to Solomon's great enterprise were many. Although the Kingdom of Israel began to disintegrate following his death in 925 BC, the Temple stood for many years as a symbol to the power of God, the skill of the masons, and the ingenuity of the architects. The Jews had come to regard the Temple and the Kingdom as the ultimate expression of God's creative power. But it was only an illusion. What truly lived on was the legend that had grown throughout the Mediterranean Region regarding the Secret Isle of Gold and King Solomon's Mines.

The legend of Solomon's gold and the Land of Ophir endured for many centuries. At the dawn of the Renaissance, in the 15th and 16th centuries, mariners were still looking for "the Lost Mines" of King Solomon. Roman merchants sought the location of the mysterious isle; Jews and Phoenicians searched for Ophir; Hindu voyagers and Muslim sailors tried to find it; even the Venetian traveler writer, Marco Polo, added his opinion about where the Mines of Solomon might be found. Of all the legends that inspired the ancient mariners, the biblical story of Solomon's Gold was the most compelling and enduring reason for sailing across the seas to the New World.

Jesus in the Land of Solomon's Mines

Among the many thousands of descendants of the prolific King Solomon was the son of a carpenter whose name was Jesus of Nazareth. He grew up in Palestine amidst the turmoil caused by Roman legions, merchants from all across the globe, and rebellious Jewish who resented the occupation of their homeland by officials of the Roman Empire. The legend of Solomon's Mines was of particular importance to Jesus because his uncle, Joseph of Arimathea, made his living by procuring metals for the Roman Army.

A large percentage of the metal supplies reaching the Roman Empire came from across the Atlantic Ocean and the Baltic Sea by way of harbors in the British Isles. Therefore, securing naval control of the British Isles was a paramount concern of Julius Caesar. During the 1st century BC, he led an invasion of Albion (or "White Land" which was the old Roman name for England). It was also called the "Tin Isle" because miners extracted a considerable amount of the metal from the earth. Subsequently, England became a strategic base for the Roman Navy. It was also an important trading center whose harbors were frequented by merchants sailing on the sea routes between Gaul (or France) and Thule. Romans identified the Scandinavian countries of Norway and Sweden as "Thule;" the overseas provinces of Nova Scotia and Newfoundland were called "Ultra Thule"—meaning that they were extremely far away to the North.

It was not uncommon for metal merchants to visit the tin mines of Albion; nor was it uncommon for them to accompany expeditions that sailed to the northwest—which was the route to Ultra Thule. Their primary objective was to obtain comparatively cheap supplies of copper and gold. Although most tools, weapons, and armor in the Empire were made from forged iron, bronze was still a vital metal for casting the fittings for wagons and chariots. Bronze was also important for casting the ornamental artworks that had become "essential" accoutrements in the more wealthy households; and it was vital for minting coins that were used to "pay" for the services of the Roman legionnaires.

Roman voyagers who sailed to Ultra Thule traded cheap iron tools for native copper nuggets. These nuggets, which the natives were able to collect from surface deposits in Upper Michigan, were carried in Canoes down the St. Lawrence River to the harbors of Newfoundland and Nova Scotia. The trade had endured for centuries; and it was still going on when the earliest French explorers reached the Gulf of St. Lawrence in the 16th century. In addition to copper, Roman merchants obtained valuable furs.

As the nephew of a metal merchant, it would not have been unusual for Jesus to accompany Joseph on one of his voyages to the west. That he actually did so during his adolescent years is not entirely a matter of speculation. There are passages in the Bible that suggest the lad had visited *Hades* and had spoken with Satan. Romans regarded Hades (or Hell) as the Realm of the Dead—or the Underworld. And that is precisely where metal merchants sailed to obtain copper—they sailed to the Isle of Shades or the Underworld. This was also later identified as the biblical Land of Gog-Magog and the home of Hephaestus who was the Greek god of metals. It was also a region of exceptional fishing—which the young Jesus, a veteran fisherman, would have found quite tempting.

Like most metal merchants and smiths, Joseph of Arimathea was a member of a secret organization of alchemists, astronomers, and mystics. Such individuals often led very mysterious lives; while their experiments and speculations about the Unknown Universe placed them on the very edge of intellectual development. They were also engaged in potentially dangerous or heretical thinking. Their lives were often in jeopardy due to the prevailing prejudices of dogmatic religious leaders. Jesus fit right in with this crowd of innovative thinkers. His philosophical and spiritual interests transcended the harsh limitations of mortal governments and fundamentalist priests. Jesus was very much the sort of person who might join a secret society where he could expand the horizons of his mind with the assistance of learned elders. There is even some indication that his association of disciples was actually a secret society that engaged in practices that today might be regarded as transcendental, magical, alchemical, or mystical. Consider for example the accounts of Jesus "performing miracles," "healing the lame," "restoring the sight of the blind," "bringing the dead back to life," "walking on water" or "transforming water into wine." The New Testament is a chronicle of the role that faith and magic can play in mortal existence.

Even at the event of crucifixion, there are indications that Jesus and his disciples were not playing entirely by the rules of ordinary men. The Bible recounts that Jesus was not treated in the customary manner with respect to the kind of punishment that was administered to usual thieves. Typically, soldiers broke the legs of those who were crucified in order to speed up their deaths. However, Jesus escaped this indignity because his disciples appealed to the Roman administrator, Pontius Pilot, to grant them an exception. They claimed that Jesus had "died" shortly after drinking a potion of bitter wine. Such a declaration by the Disciples did not require further investigation by a Roman administrator who had no desire to interfere with the outcome of the magical enterprise. Therefore, Pilot authorized the early removal of Jesus from the cross.

The Disciples promptly took Jesus to a tomb from which he soon "disappeared." It sounds a lot like magic was involved in this enterprise. A week later, after holding one last feast with his compatriots, the Blessed Teacher was enveloped in a mysterious cloud from which he ascended into Heaven.

According to various theories, the story of Jesus did not end with the crucifixion. One theory has Jesus sailing off to Albion in the company of his uncle, Joseph of Arimathea. In this alternative version to the departure of Jesus from Jerusalem, he is accompanied by his wife or mistress—Mary Magdalene. Adherents of the Mormon Faith believe that Jesus still had a ministry to complete in the New World. Presumably, he sailed across the Atlantic Ocean for perhaps the second time; and he preached the Gospel of Peace to the Native American tribes from Nova Scotia to Mexico.

The idea is not quite so farfetched as it might at first appear. Indeed, the elders of numerous tribes have handed down legends that they were at one time or another visited in the ancient past by someone who was very special. This prophet is typically characterized as either a Blessed Teachers or as "the Son of Heaven."

Some theorists have equated Jesus with the legendary Mexican Prophet—*Quetzalcoatl* (or "Blessed Twin"). He was renowned among the Toltecs during the 12th to 14th centuries. It seems that the Prophet denounced human sacrifice; and he carried a Holy Book that had many stories that were similar to the Old Testament Bible. Another candidate for the honor of "Jesus in the New World" is the legendary Algonkian Prophet by the name of "Glooskap." Missionaries and pioneers in the New England region noted that numerous Native American tribes had a particular reverence for the cross—even to the extent of calling this cross the symbol for "the Son of God."

What do Historians Think?

Modern historians are totally baffled by the whereabouts of the biblical Mines of Solomon. On the other hand, practically all the orthodox historians insist that neither Sololmon nor any other Jew could possibly have sailed to the New World ahead of the official fifteenth century hero—Columbus. Thus, the New World is the last place on earth where they would ever look for the lost mines. Most don't even bother to look beyond a few marginal sites in Africa and Asia. Any clues to the contrary are ignored—leaving half the earth, as well as all the dogmatic intellectuals totally in the dark.

This prevalent attitude in academia is totally repudiated by the preponderance of the evidence.

After the Spanish Conquistadors under Francisco Pizarro invaded Peru in the 1530s, the Spanish historian Joseph de Acosta was convinced that the Spaniards had come upon the lost site of King Solomon's Mines. This seems to make sense considering that Peruvians had more gold than anybody else on the planet; and the gold that they had was of much better quality. Also, the gold working technology that their jewelers used to craft the metal was unsurpassed by jewelers anywhere else in the world. They used the same kind of "lost-wax" casting process that was known in the Old World; and they used fine filigree trim. They used electric gold plating (with copper wires and jars of acid); they made crowns with gold disc dangles; and they made gold-copper alloys that were identical to the alloys produced by Old World craftsmen.

The Spaniards also found the empty mine shafts that the Phoenicians had left chiseled into the depths of the Andes Mountains. The Inca natives claimed no knowledge of these tunnels; nor were they familiar with the kinds of flammable chemicals that Phoenician miners had used to literally "melt" the rocks. Elsewhere in the region, archeologists and explorers found Phoenician inscriptions as well as ceramic portraits of the ancient mariners. Clearly, there were Semitic-looking people in ancient Peru.

Spanish priests were among the first to suspect that Jesus or the Apostles had been to the shores of the New World. The evidence of a Christian presence in the New Land was unmistakable. Everywhere that they traveled, the Jesuit missionaries found that Christian beliefs, symbols, and practices had been integrated into the native religions. For example, the Aztecs celebrated a kind of "communion"—with the blood of sacrificial victims sprinkled over consecrated bread.

There were also legends about an Irish monk named Brendan who had sailed to islands in the West where he had encountered Catholic churches and priests using the Latin Bible. It was therefore not at all inconsistent for the missionaries to believe that Jesus had preceded them to the shores of

Mexico. Keep in mind that among devout Christians, there was a belief that nothing was impossible—where God or Jesus were involved.

In all fairness to modern scientists and historians, we would be remiss to assume that all the examples of early Christian practices in the New World were evidence of a visit by Jesus of Nazareth. Many Christians and numerous missionaries sailed across the seas—so it becomes rather an impossibility to separate out precisely who did what and when—whether it was the Prophet, himself, a Disciple, or simply an anonymous friar who hopped on a ship sailing west. Some Spanish missionaries were convinced that they had been preceded to Mexico by the Apostle Thomas—as a result of legends regarding the travels of this disciple of Jesus. Also, use of the cross in native art can be traced to other Old World contacts where the symbol was used to represent gold, the sun, the four quarters of the earth, or the annual flooding of the Nile River.

With respect to the numerous native tales of visits by the "Son of Heaven" or a "Great Prophet," we should keep in mind that missionaries from many religions also made trips to the New World in ancient times.

Consequences for New World Exploration

References to the Land of Ophir and King Solomon's Mines occur quite frequently in the annals of world history. So do references to Isles of Gold that may well have derived from the ancient expeditions to Peru. Although Solomon and Hiram took steps to protect the secret location of their overseas gold hoard, there was no way to prevent the word from leaking out to the friends, family, and barroom associates of Hiram's sailors. It didn't help matters that the whole episode was mentioned several times in the Bible—and then repeated in Christian churches.

We next encounter mention of the Isle of Gold in the folklore of India. Hindu legends describe an overseas land called "Patala" that was renowned for its abundant gold and orchards. Hindu geographers generally placed this wondrous island someplace south and east of the Indian Ocean—or in the approximate location of South America. These legends date to about the mid-first millennium BC. It is probably not a coincidence that this is about at the same time that Phoenician mariners were sailing past India to Tarshish (that is, Java or Sumatra) where they rendezvoused with the ships from Ophir. It was at this point in time that Hindu mariners sent their own fleet to Peru seeking a load of golden ingots.

Greek geographers referred to the Southeast Asian Region of Malaya, Thailand, Sumatra and Java as the *Chersonese*—meaning "the Golden Archipelago." This name reflected their awareness that this was the trading center through which gold flowed to Europe. Roman geographers decided that the name wasn't precise enough, so they added the term *Aurea* to give us the Greco-Roman composite name of *Aurea Chersonese* for Southeast Asia. Since Aurea means "golden" in Latin, the meaning of the composite name translates as "the Golden Golden Archipelago."

In the middle of the 3rd century BC, the Greek mariner Pytheas had a brilliant idea. He knew from the common scuttlebutt of mariners and from the popular *Songs of Solomon* that Phoenician mariners were harvesting incredible mineral wealth from the overseas isles of Ultra Thule. Thus, he proposed to disguise his own trading vessel as a Phoenician ship in order to fool the rivals of the Roman Empire. His plan was to slip past the Carthaginian naval blockade at the Pillars of Heracles (that is, at the Straits of Gibraltar), and then to follow an unsuspecting Phoenician trader all the way to the secret treasures overseas. The plot seems to have worked flawlessly. According to an account of the voyage that Pytheas wrote after his return, he first followed a Phoenician trading vessel all the way to the "Tin Isle" of Albion; then he explored the Northern Ocean as far as a region known as "Ultra Thule" (the Extreme North); and finally, he located the Baltic Isle of Amber before heading back to his homeport of Marseille on the Mediterranean coast.

Pytheas was eager to share his discoveries with the folks back home, so he wrote a complete account in a book called *The Ocean*. However, it seems that the Roman authorities had reasons of their own for preserving the secrets of the Western Isles. Probably, they already knew the location of the western sources of gold and copper; and the idea that this knowledge might be given away free in a popular book struck them as incredibly naïve. So it seems that the most damaging chapters of the book were effectively censored.

Historians have noted that only a few episodes from the "lost" book of Pytheas managed to survive. These chapters included all the most incredible stories such as the Arctic sun that never set, the icy seas that had the consistency of thick porridge, and the huge tides that were supposedly "pulled upwards" by the moon. These natural phenomena were virtually unknown to the inhabitants of Rome and Greece. They lived in the warm Mediterranean region—far from the more bizarre natural phenomena of the Arctic Regions. Thus, the more unbelievable accounts of Pytheas were presented as comic oratories in Greek and Roman theaters. In this manner, the authorities effectively discounted the tales of Pytheas as a being just "a sailor's fantasy."[3]

In spite of the official opposition against New World exploration and censorship concerning theories about King Solomon's Mines, many Greek and Roman sea captains managed to complete successful roundtrip voyages to the Western Isles. We see evidence of this fact in a considerable number of Greek, Roman, and Jewish artifacts that were left strewn along the shores of the New World. These artifacts have been found across a considerable area from New England in the north all the way to Peru and Brazil in the south. Incredibly, New World shorelines from Florida to Brazil were even portrayed with reasonable accuracy on ancient maps. Surprisingly, modern historians have overlooked these clues

---

[3] For a detailed account of the reconstructed account of Pytheas, see Peter Lacey, *Great Adventures that Changed our World*, New York: Reader's Digest, 1978, 15-19.

as a consequence of the role played by Eurocentric dogma in the way people are trained to think in academia.

Historians have been aware for decades that Old World artifacts were piled up along the shores of ancient America; but they always conjured up some sort of rationale to "explain away" the evidence. When the French historian Jean du Pouget saw with his own eyes a Roman aqueduct near Cuzco in 1890, he assumed that the Inca architects had simply invented the structure. How else could a scholar who believed that Columbus was the "first" European to reach America explain the existence of an ancient Roman structure in Peru? As far as he was concerned, that alternative, which happened to be the best explanation to fit the evidence, was simply unacceptable.

After the Mexican archeologist Jose Garcia Payon excavated a 2nd century Roman ceramic head from beneath the cement floor of a pyramid, his colleagues in academia dismissed the evidence as an example of the kind of insignificant "flotsam" that had simply washed ashore from a Roman shipwreck. Likewise, heaps of Roman amphoras that were discovered by divers off the coasts of Honduras and Brazil in the 1970s and 1980s were dismissed as the lost cargoes of ships that were "blown off course." As long as the academic authorities can conjure up the rationale that there was no deliberate contact between Old World voyagers and the Native Americans before Columbus, then any foreign artifact that is found in an ancient context can be dismissed as irrelevant. Scores of Roman, Greek, and Jewish coins have been dug up or found in fields from Venezuela to New York. Yet the orthodox historians commonly dismiss these artifacts as the discarded relics of disenchanted coin collectors.

The possibility that Greek, Roman, and Jewish mariners might have sailed to the New World in search of Solomon's Mines seems to have entirely escaped the imaginations of most certified academics. Nevertheless, there is no mistaking the shorelines of Florida, Brazil, the Gulf of Mexico, and Peru on ancient maps dating back to the Roman Era. The Alexandrian geographer Ptolemy noted the location of a harbor city called "Cattigara" on a southern mainland that was southeast of Asia. This mainland was situated across the *Sinus Magnus* or "Great Gulf" that Magellan later identified as the Pacific Ocean. In other words, this port city was located in Peru. The brother of Columbus, Bartholomew, noted that Cattigara was situated on the West Coast of the Mundus Novus—or South America. This Peruvian city was situated at 8° south of the equator. This happens to be the very same place that the Spanish historian Joseph de Acosta identified as the location of Solomon's Mines.

Both the names for the Andes Mountains and the country of Peru date back to Phoenician and Roman times. On the 5th century Macrobius Map, the northern region of the Antipodes (or South America) is called *perusta*. This name refers to the hot, dry climate. On the Albertin de Virga Map of 1414, the Peruvian coast is referred to as "Ca-paru." And on the Andrea Bianco Map of 1436, this region is called "the Land of Per." Clearly, Peru was named prior to the arrival of Pizarro in 1521. Even so, orthodox historians have insisted for decades that Pizarro named the country and that this name was originally derived from the name of a local river.

Romans sailed west to the New World seeking King Solomon's Mines. They found instead New World civilizations that were anxious to trade indigenous products, metals, and plants in exchange for Old World tools, textiles, and wines. Roman merchants brought back New World plants in addition to supplies of gold, copper, lumber, dried fish, and furs. We see ample evidence of New World plants at Roman archeological sites. Mosaic murals at Pompeii dating to the 1st century include New World pineapples. Archeologists removed *maize* or corn kernels from Roman grain silos that were built in ancient Spain. A Roman herbal or book of plants included New World pumpkins. And New World tobacco was identified in Roman-era smoking pipes that were excavated from the ruins of bathhouses near the ancient Roman City of London.

As the testimonials to the wealth of Ophir were present in the Holy Scriptures, every European Christian was indoctrinated with the importance of Solomon's Gold Mines. Columbus gained the sponsorship of Queen Isabel in part because of his conviction that he could find Solomon's Mines west of Europe. In a letter to the Queen, he proposed to use all the remaining gold to hire an army for the next Crusade to retake the Holy Lands from the Moslems. This was an important consideration for Columbus and the Queen in anticipation of the "End Times," the "Second Coming," and the "Last Judgment." All these ominous events were expected to occur in the year 1500—after which time the Great Drama of Creation would be done forever.

However, destiny didn't quite work out the way Columbus had planned. Although he insisted that he had found Ophir during his meeting in 1493 with King John II of Portugal, it turned out that the gold mines of Haiti had actually been stripped bare. Whether these mines had been found as part of Solomon's arrangement with Hiram, or whether they were the remains of some other ancient opportunist is unknown. Anyway, Columbus's efforts to extract gold from the natives proved futile.

Several decades later, Hernan Cortés and Francisco Pizarro finally managed to subdue the empires of the Aztecs and the Incas. Then, they melted down the Aztec and Inca religious relics into gold ingots which were shipped back to Spain in the early 16th century. After this hoard of gold arrived in Barcelona, Church officials declared that Columbus had indeed found the lost gold mines of King Solomon.

The mystery was solved; the race to find the secret location of Solomon's mines was finished. Well, almost finished.

During the Spanish conquest of Peru, Pedro Sarmiento de Gamboa interrogated Inca officials. One of the tantalizing stories they told him concerned the voyage of the Inca leader Tupac Yupanqui who had sailed from Peru far out into the Pacific Ocean—perhaps as far as the Philippines Islands. This expedition of Inca royalty probably took place on a Chinese fleet that was sailing on a roundtrip voyage back to Peru during the following year. Tupac reported that he had arrived at an isle of great wealth called "Avachumbi". From this isle, the Inca brought back gold, silver, a brass throne, and black slaves. The Spaniards should have realized that the important clue regarding this fabulous story was that the South Seas "throne" was made of brass.

Anyway, the nephew of the Spanish Governor was desperate to emblazon his name into the history books. And he wanted to gain a fortune that would exceed the treasures that Cortés and Pizarro had stolen from the Indians. Keep in mind that this was a time in the development of European civilization when the soldiers of Christian nations presumed that God showed favor towards his followers by bestowing golden rewards. The nephew of the Spanish governor, Alvaro de Mendaña, convinced himself that Inca Tupac had been to Solomon's Mines which he further presumed must be situated someplace across the ocean in the East Indies.

The Spanish Government funded the outfitting of an expedition which departed from Peru in 1567. After two months at sea, they came upon several small islands that Mendaña declared must be Ophir. The crews landed, and they spent the next six months searching for Solomon's Mines. Meanwhile, they battled with angry natives and bloodthirsty mosquitoes. The mosquitoes won.

There was no gold on the island; nor did Mendaña's party find any evidence that there had ever been any mining in the past. A small band of ragged and disillusioned Spaniards sailed back to Peru in 1569. In Lima, they told their disheartening story of suffering and hardship.

This kind of defeatism wasn't exactly what Pedro Sarmiento wanted to hear. As the principal promoter of the expedition, his reputation was at stake. His future benefits as a civil servant depended upon his success as an administrator—and that meant spinning the story in a positive direction. Thus, he declared that the Mendaña Expedition had been an outstanding success. According to Sarmiento's testimony, Mendaña had succeeded in finding King Solomon's "lost" Isles. Supposedly, an enormous hoard of gold was simply waiting for the next crew to arrive.

Sarmiento's deceptive praise of the futile expedition was so convincing that Spanish officials mounted another attempt to find "the Lost Isles" of King Solomon. The expedition sailed in 1595; and again, they found nothing. And there our story ends with the misnaming of the Solomon Islands—as the wishful-thinking Spaniards continued to look for gold in all the wrong places.

Roman Florida—
Land of Mystery & Legend

Subtropical Florida was the gateway for Roman merchants sailing across the Atlantic Ocean to the rich markets of the Gulf of Mexico. Following in the wakes of Phoenician mariners, the Romans encountered a land that was always vibrant with the energy of Springtime. This Underworld region was regarded as the Kingdom of Pluto and his Queen—Florida. After the Spaniard Ponce de Leon named the place where he landed in 1513—Pascua de Flores—literally "Easter Passover," the name of the Peninsula reverted to its original Roman designation of Florida—the Land of Eternal Spring.

Knowledge of the overseas paradise was concealed behind myths and legends. One version of the myth has the God Pluto kidnapping Persephone back to his homeland each year at the start of winter. Roman merchants who sailed to Mexico called the Gulf—"the Caspian Sea." Modern historians have confused this Western Caspian by a landlocked sea in the Middle East that has the same name. It wasn't until the 5th century that the Roman geographer Macrobius finally put Florida on the map.

Roman Sculpture of Pluto with Persephone being carried away to the Underworld, c. 150 AD

From Thomassin's *Recueil des Figures, Groupes, Thermes, Fontaines, Vases et autres Ornements.*

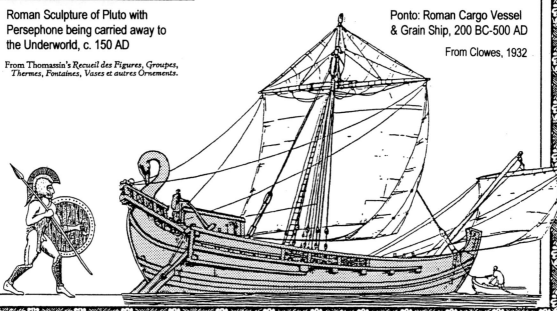

Ponto: Roman Cargo Vessel & Grain Ship, 200 BC-500 AD

From Clowes, 1932

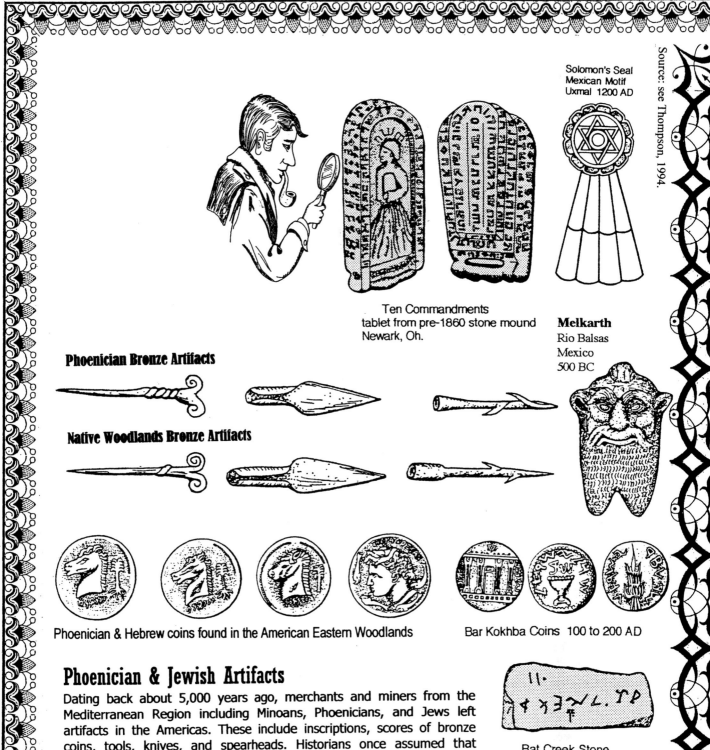

Source: see Thompson, 1994.

Solomon's Seal
Mexican Motif
Uxmal 1200 AD

Ten Commandments
tablet from pre-1860 stone mound
Newark, Oh.

Melkarth
Rio Balsas
Mexico
500 BC

Phoenician Bronze Artifacts

Native Woodlands Bronze Artifacts

Phoenician & Hebrew coins found in the American Eastern Woodlands

Bar Kokhba Coins 100 to 200 AD

Bat Creek Stone
Bat Creek, Ten. 150 AD

Phoenician & Jewish Artifacts

Dating back about 5,000 years ago, merchants and miners from the Mediterranean Region including Minoans, Phoenicians, and Jews left artifacts in the Americas. These include inscriptions, scores of bronze coins, tools, knives, and spearheads. Historians once assumed that Native Americans had no bronze tools. However, the author had identified the characteristic evidence of molten metal casting on these artifacts; and scientists at the Battelle Lab have shown that the molecular structure of sample artifacts shows that they were cast from molten bronze. Many American historians still harbor the misconception that bronze and molten metal casting were unknown in the New World until after the arrival of Europeans in the 16th century.

Evidence of Contact *in the* *New World*

Source: see Thompson, 1994.

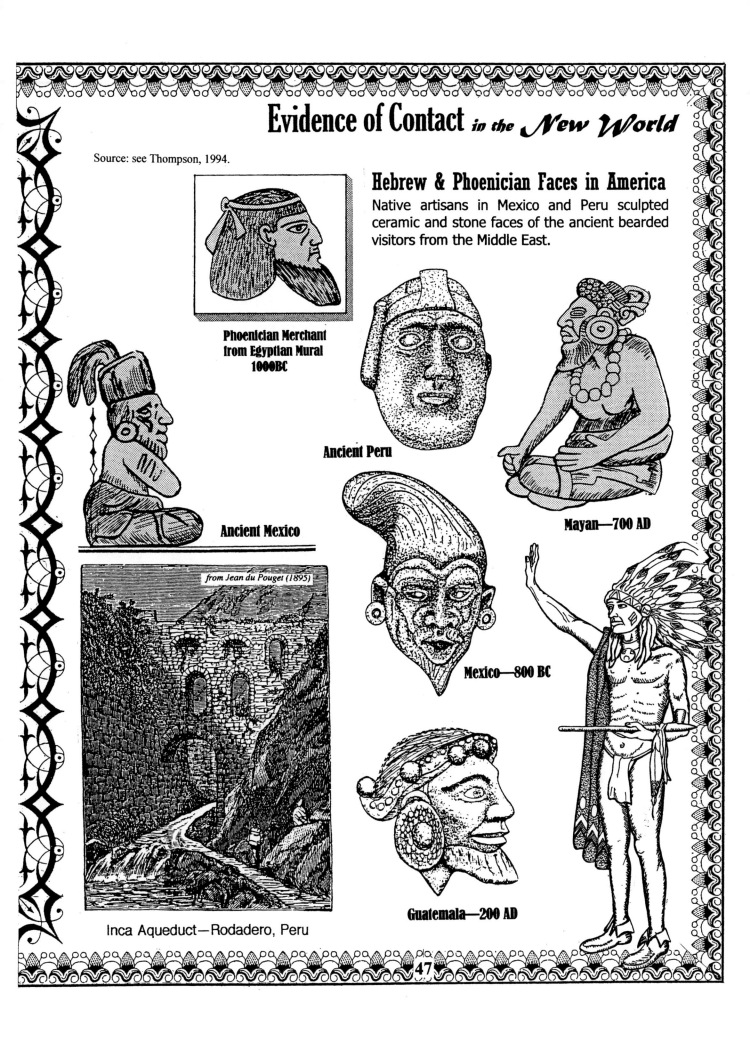

Phoenician Merchant from Egyptian Mural 1000BC

Hebrew & Phoenician Faces in America

Native artisans in Mexico and Peru sculpted ceramic and stone faces of the ancient bearded visitors from the Middle East.

Ancient Peru

Mayan—700 AD

Ancient Mexico

from Jean du Pouget (1895)

Mexico—800 BC

Guatemala—200 AD

Inca Aqueduct—Rodadero, Peru

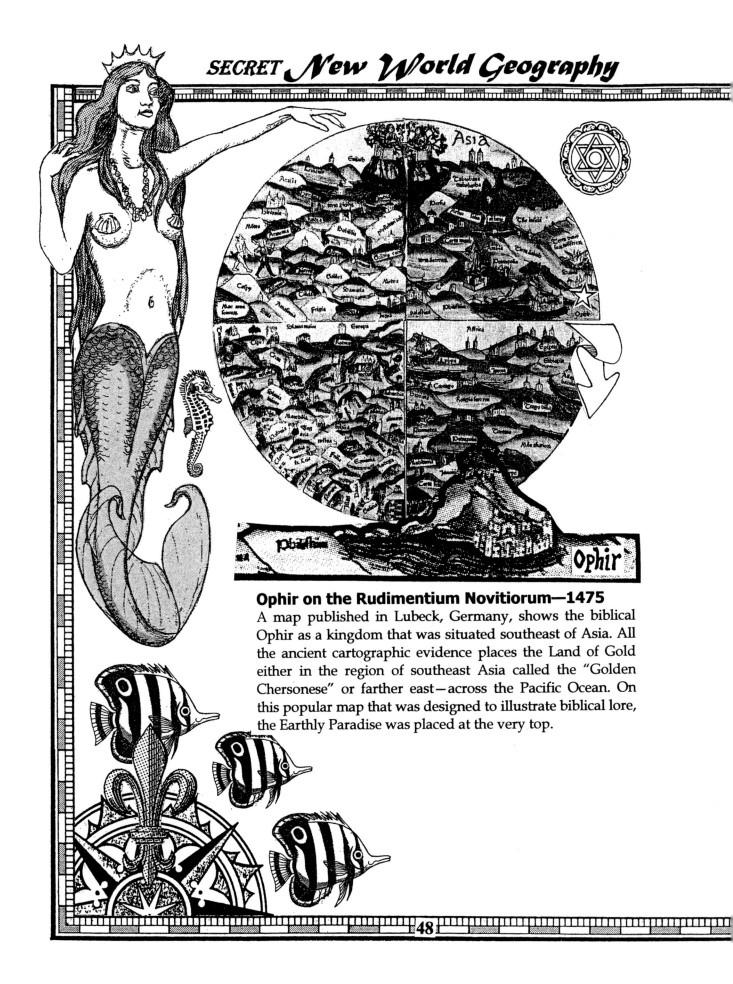

Ophir on the Rudimentium Novitiorum—1475

A map published in Lubeck, Germany, shows the biblical Ophir as a kingdom that was situated southeast of Asia. All the ancient cartographic evidence places the Land of Gold either in the region of southeast Asia called the "Golden Chersonese" or farther east—across the Pacific Ocean. On this popular map that was designed to illustrate biblical lore, the Earthly Paradise was placed at the very top.

Benedictus Arias Montanus, 1572   (From Thompson, 1996)

Benedictus Arias Montanus,
Sacrae Geographiae Tabulam,
Antwerp, 1572

The Montanus Map of Solomon's Mines

After the conquistador Francisco Pizarro revealed the location of the vast Inca gold hoard to the King of Spain, several travel writers concluded that the location of King Solomon's Mines had finally been determined. They were in Peru. The Benedictine monk, Arias Montanus, showed this location for Ophir on his world map of 1572. However, he also noted a second Ophir—that is, another location of gold mines—in the region of modern-day Sacramento. Thus, it would appear that Montanus had some knowledge of ancient gold fields that would later become famous during the 1849 California Gold Rush.

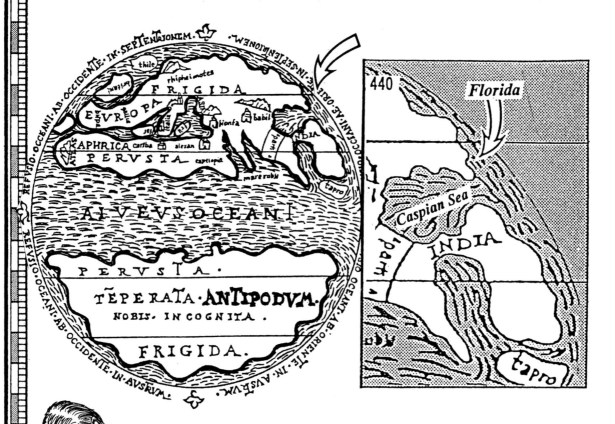

Time Detectives & Roman Florida

The author has determined that a map by the Roman geographer Macrobius shows the location of the Gulf of Mexico directly west of Europe. Romans referred to this region of Eternal Springtime as "Florida" in honor of the Goddess of Springtime, Flora. Seneca, a Roman philosopher, noted that the "Caspian Sea" was a gulf of the Atlantic Ocean; and this Gulf was said to be west of Europe. The modern-day Peninsula of Florida is shown projecting towards the southeast. Below the Gulf is an early representation of South America. It was called "the Third India," "India Occident," or "the Other World." In the Southern Hemisphere is another representation of South America. Here, it is called "the Antipodes" meaning lands on the opposite side of Earth.

After a map in the Huntington Library, San Marino, California

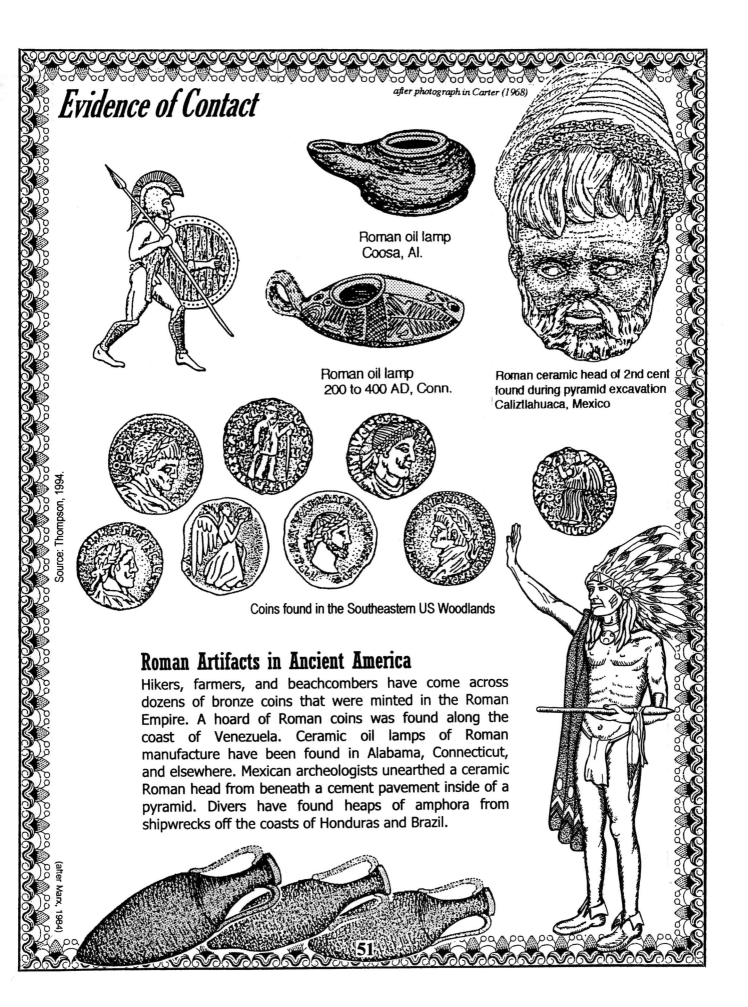

Evidence of Contact

after photograph in Carter (1968)

Roman oil lamp
Coosa, Al.

Roman oil lamp
200 to 400 AD, Conn.

Roman ceramic head of 2nd cent
found during pyramid excavation
Caliztlahuaca, Mexico

Coins found in the Southeastern US Woodlands

Source: Thompson, 1994.

Roman Artifacts in Ancient America

Hikers, farmers, and beachcombers have come across dozens of bronze coins that were minted in the Roman Empire. A hoard of Roman coins was found along the coast of Venezuela. Ceramic oil lamps of Roman manufacture have been found in Alabama, Connecticut, and elsewhere. Mexican archeologists unearthed a ceramic Roman head from beneath a cement pavement inside of a pyramid. Divers have found heaps of amphora from shipwrecks off the coasts of Honduras and Brazil.

(after Marx, 1994)

CHINA—250 BC Emperor Chi Wang stands outside his Imperial Fortress waiting for a sign from the Immortals.

Tzu Fu and the Isle of Fu Sang

DURING THE THIRD CENTURY BC, there lived in China a great emperor. His name was Shih Huang. Like most of the rulers who lived during the early years of Chinese Civilization, his childhood began amidst the simple life of farmers where his only subjects were the chickens, goats, and pigs that he had to feed and guard for his father. His closest friend was the family hound.

Shih Huang's adolescent years were more promising and certainly more exciting. He gained the attention of a powerful warlord due to his great physical strength, his mental discipline, and his agility as an archer while riding on a galloping horse. His father and his mother cried when the warlord's recruiter informed him that he was being given "an opportunity" to join the army; and everybody in the village where he lived was anxious to offer him advice about his future and how his service would reflect upon the honor of whole village. Never did the simple farmer folk imagine that within twenty years that Shih Huang would surpass in glory all his superiors in the military; nor could they imagine that he would become the king of all the military districts in the region.

As the years went by, Shih Huang found himself surrounded by countless courtiers, concubines, administrators, and priests—all of whom had advice to give him about how he should run his country. By the time he had reached his 50th birthday, the priesthood had conferred upon him the glorious title of "the Emperor—Son of Heaven;" and they had convinced him that his destiny was to live forever as the Supreme Ruler of the Earth. Such a destiny was not so difficult to imagine for a mighty warrior whose subjects worshipped him, clothed him, fed him, and entertained him as though he actually were a god.

However, in the real world, the fantasy of immortality could not last forever. Shih Huang began to notice that he could command anything from his subjects; but he could not command his own body to regain the vigor of his youth. His hair turned gray; he lost interest in his harem; and his teeth began to fall out one-by-one. When he gazed at the looking glass,

FU SANG
Magic Mushrooms

Captain of Secret Discovery

A 19th century ivory carving of a mythical Chinese seafarer provides a suitable image for the daring and cunning naval captain—Tzu Fu who sailed in the 3rd century BC. He offered to bring back the legendary Ling chih mushrooms of Fu Sang (or Mexico) for his ailing emperor—Chi Wang. He is shown here contemplating the contemporary Chinese images of the magical food of the gods (top) and the ancient Mexican mushroom plants that the natives carved in stone (bottom).

it was an aging face that he saw and not the visage that he remembered of his exciting years as a warrior. So, he summoned the priests who had beguiled him with the title of "Divine Ruler;" and he asked them to explain his predicament.

What they told him was this: There was a land far-far-away to the East called Fu Sang. This was the "Isle of Immortals," the Great Han Country, the Isle of Su Mu. It was his destiny to reside in this Earthly Paradise as one of the Immortals. All of the ancestral kings had ascended to this glorious abode following their passing from the mortal sphere of human existence. This course of events was inevitable, they insisted, unless he obtained the *ling chih*—the sacred "food of the gods"—before he died. All that he had to do was to find someone in his navy who was sufficiently brave, or perhaps very foolish, who would agree to sail across the ocean to the Isle of Fu Sang. That was the only place where he could obtain the sacred food.

New World Voyages to Fu Sang

Tzu Fu enters the stage as a minor officer in the Chinese Navy. Ordinary sailors would have been content to serve their Emperor until retirement age at which time they would have left the barracks and then taken up residence with an extended family.

However, that was not Tzu Fu's style. His expectations from life were just a little bit more demanding than those of his fellow officers. He had an insatiable craving for the pleasures of feminine company; he had a cunning mind, and he had stellar expectations for his own destiny.[1] His compatriots in the Navy must have kidded him about his and his endless dreaming about the future. But certainly, none of them ever suspected the extremes that he might consider in order to make his dreams come true.

The ordinary responsibilities of a minor officer in the Chinese Navy involved frequent escort duties when the Emperor's barge traveled on the canals or on Bohai Bay. Occasionally, Tzu Fu sailed in command of an escort vessel called a "fast junk" that accompanied convoys sailing between the ports of Northern China, Southern China, and the far-flung provinces of Southeast Asia and India. On these occasions, the officers were required to attack pirate ships or to rescue sailors who fell overboard. If necessary, they were expected to risk their lives in order to protect the huge merchant vessels with their valuable cargoes.

According to the royal chronicles, it was in the year 225 BC that Tzu Fu became aware of the Emperor's failing health. It was no secret among the admirals that the Emperor had reached his declining years; and although the Old Man himself was deluded by his status and his surroundings, practically everybody else recognized that he was actually a captive in his own castle.

---

[1] For details about 3rd century China, see Thompson, 1994, 106-135—or the latest edition of *American Discovery*.

Ships &
Shores
of the
Secret
Sailors

where they went & how they got there

**Chinese Expeditionary Vessel
c. 300 BC—500 AD**
(from Thompson, 1994)

The Lands of Fu Sang

The title "Fu Sang" for Isle of the Immortals or Isle of the Fu Sang Tree (Sequoias or Redwoods) was sometimes applied to the West Coast of North America. In the case of Tzu Fu, it was southern Mexico.

The Emperor's personal religious advisors discretely approached the naval commanders with their unusual request. What they needed, they said in confidence, was "a volunteer" to sail far away to a place called Fu Sang. This was a mysterious land that was known only from the legends of the ancestors and from the vague geography of the ancients that was called the *Shanhai Jing*—that is the Book of Mountains and Seas. Some Chinese scholars regarded this book and a map by the same name as "pure fantasy." Others claimed that it represented a geographical survey that Emperor Hwang-ti had ordered in the Third Millennium BC. In any case, the book and map indicated that Fu Sang was directly east of Japan by perhaps 10,000 miles—or 10,000 li (as they measured distances in the Dragon Kingdom). However, precisely how far away this land was—or precisely where it was actually located—was anybody's guess. The important issue was that the volunteer sailor had to find the location of the sacred mushroom of immortality and bring it back for the health of the Emperor.

Secrecy in this enterprise was essential. At the time, all the priests in China regarded this Land of Fu Sang as a sacred land. Therefore, it was forbidden for mortals to go there. Anyone who was even suspected of contemplating the effort would have been deemed a heretic in the eyes of his friends and family. Those intellectuals who were not quite so provincial in their thinking tended to regard the whole Earthly Paradise theory as a fantasy. There was a prevalent belief among those who studied philosophy and the stars that the notion of a place called Fu Sang had originated among dreamers, poets, and the people who smoked hashish.

Now, we might ordinarily think that everybody in the Navy would have been anxious for an opportunity to sail overseas in the service of the Emperor. However, there had been several typhoons lately that had wrecked a number of convoys, sailors had witnessed waves over sixty-feet high; and they barely survived. Besides, nobody in the Service had ever been to Fu Sang; there were no reliable maps showing how to get there; and there were no merchants who were even willing to confess that they had ever been to the Forbidden Lands. Anybody who offered to fulfill the Emperor's request had to be someone who was willing to suspend all rational thinking for a mission that had virtually no chance of succeeding and which depended upon magic.

It was at this most desperate moment that Tzu Fu stepped forward to offer his assistance to the ailing Emperor; and he was promptly designated as the Commander of the Expedition. All that he required, he said, was the best ship that the Navy could offer. It couldn't be too big or too little; it had to have the most resilient hull; and it had to provide adequate accommodations for the captain, crew, and a dozen marines who would have to live within its cabins for over a year. Furthermore, it had to be impervious to typhoons and seaworms. In other words, the vessel that Tzu Fu desired did not yet exist in the Chinese Navy.

The ministers and the admirals had no choice but to fulfill all of Tzu Fu's demands. They instructed master carpenters, sail-makers, and smiths to create a vessel precisely to the requirements of the junior naval officer. It would be the fastest most versatile ship in the world. Built from teak—the hardest most expensive wood—the vessel was slightly over a hundred feet in length. It carried three giant lugsails with a fore-and-aft rig that was equally suited to sailing into the wind or with the wind at the stern. There was a single rudder mounted at the stern that could be raised or lowered depending upon the shallowness of the sea. The vessel was equipped with primitive rockets, a compass, and welded iron anchors. Tzu Fu personally selected the stores of dried food. He chose his crew not from the ranks of the Navy but from the reluctant crews of merchant ships that had traveled overseas. There were no volunteers. Tzu Fu considered that anybody foolish enough to accompany such an enterprise "as a volunteer" was not mentally fit for the hazardous trip. By selecting only those mariners who were outside of the military ranks, Tzu Fu accomplished another important goal: he eliminated the possibility that any spies might accompany the expedition without his knowledge.

There was no secrecy regarding the departure of the expedition—although their destination was still a subject of conjecture. They departed from the port of Nanjing or Hangchow; and they headed out to sea towards Japan. It seems most likely that they followed the usual route of merchant seamen who sailed on the *Kuro Shio* or "Black Stream Current" that moves across the North Pacific towards the Aleutian Islands, Alaska, and British Columbia. They must have stopped on occasion at native harbors to replenish their supplies of fresh meat and water. They traded iron blades and cotton cloth for furs, home-cooked food, and for the comforts of an evening ashore with the native girls.

Among the sailors that Tzu Fu selected for his expedition, there must have been several who were competent navigators. Some of these veterans must have come this way before on merchant expeditions to ancient America's West Coast. These veterans guided the ship through the shoals and into the native harbors. They spoke the native trade languages; they knew the local chieftains; and they understood the essential protocols for gaining necessary food and hospitality. We know that this was so because the journey would have been impossible without experienced guides, the loyalty of the crew, and the generosity of the native hosts.

When they reached the shores of Mexico, the ocean current and winds reversed direction, and they needed to sail close-hauled into the wind in order to keep heading south. Tzu Fu examined the coastline with a spyglass. There were as yet no major civilizations on the West Coast in this region; but they encountered a few large villages of Mixtec and Mayan natives. Whenever the veteran pilots identified a suitable harbor near a small village, they put ashore a landing party to trade with the natives. Tzu Fu's veteran merchants were able to communicate with the natives by using a convenient "trade language," common gestures, and drawing pictures in the sand. From the trade items that the natives offered in exchange for Chinese *Ma-fen* (or hemp) and iron tools, Tzu Fu was able to estimate how close they were getting to the mysterious Isle of Fu Sang and its "food of the gods."

Finally, when they reached the Gulf of Tehuantepec near the southwestern border of modern-day Mexico, the native traders produced baskets filled with the *ling chih* mushrooms. They were so plentiful in this region that they were as cheap as a piece of fruit in the public markets.

How could he be sure that he got the right "Food of the Gods?" Well, Tzu Fu had learned from one of his confidants in the Taoist Order how to identify the sacred mushrooms. They were also known to the Chinese philosophers as "the mushroom of enlightenment." There were such mushrooms in China; but they were not the same as the kind that came from Fu Sang. The plants were called "mushrooms of enlightenment" because they produced a transcendental or hallucinogenic effect when eaten. Each type of mushroom had a different effect. The goal of eating the mushroom was to experience a vision of existence—a transcendental vision—that would enable the philosopher to see beyond the present into the future. Among Taoists, it was believed that this visionary capability was the mortal equivalent to attaining spiritual perfection. Those who attained this level of attunement were designated as "Perfect Warriors"— that is, they had reached the ultimate level of spiritual development. As "Perfect Warriors," they were entitled to wear the emblem of *Zhen-Wu* who was the Chinese Polaris—the God of the North.

Tzu Fu's confidants informed him that the Chinese priests back home would gauge the success of his mission based on four outcomes. First, he would have to return with the "fruit" of Fu Sang. This fruit was said to look like Chinese corn (or maize) but instead of being yellow, it was colored red. Second, he would have to bring back an example of the Fu Sang dyewood tree. This dyewood produced a color that was similar to dyes obtained from Sappan Tree of Asia except that it had a much deeper red color. Third, he would have to acquire a token of Fu Sang jade. This mysterious jade was said to have a deep green color intensity that dazzled the eyes of those who held it in their hands. The Taoists informed Tzu Fu that they had never seen such a stone; indeed, they had only heard of its ethereal qualities. But they didn't doubt that the stone actually existed someplace across the seas. Taoist traditions told of Perfect Warriors who had seen such a talisman in ancient times; and there was no doubting the reports from such an authoritative source. It was said of this jade that it had the capability of inspiring an immediate transcendental experience. And finally, there was the *ling chih* itself. There were old priests who claimed that they had once tasted the elixir of the gods. The effect of the plant had been overwhelming. They declared that the opening in the doorway to the Universal Spirit had been so immediate and so thorough that mortal existence no longer seemed important. Surely, the Emperor would have these priests taste the *ling chih* that was brought back to China in order to assure that the plant was authentic.

It was at this point that one of Tzu Fu's advisors made a prophesy concerning his future. The advisor was a trusted Taoist philosopher who was a practitioner of the arcane arts—that is, he made predictions concerning future events while gazing into crystals and while under the influence of powerful drugs. He informed the Naval officer that upon his return to China with the plants from Fu Sang, his life would be in jeopardy. It was the intention of the Emperor, he cautioned, to have Tzu Fu and all his crew on this mission meet with a convenient and prefabricated "accident." Most likely, they would be set upon by the Emperor's own guards in the costumes of pirates. They would simply be carrying out orders to "eliminate" a boatload of traitors. In this manner, suggested the sage, the Emperor hoped to prevent knowledge of this mission to Fu Sang from reaching the attention of the more traditional-minded priests who actually controlled the government. Once the Emperor had the elixir of immortality, he had no further use for Tzu Fu—who would then become an enormous political liability.

The sage tested the potency of the Mexican ling chih and reported that it was indeed authentic. Then he examined a token of the local Motagua jade from Guatemala; and he couldn't believe his eyes. At first, he saw his own soul reflected in the polished surface. Then, he felt himself being drawn into the gemstone in a swirling whirlpool of time and space. Tzu Fu pulled him back to reality by taking a firm hold of his shoulders. "Is it real?" he demanded to know.

"Very real," replied the sage. "In China, this gemstone would be regarded as priceless. Men would kill to own a piece of this rock."

Tzu Fu was satisfied that his expedition had reached their intended destination. He next established an observatory on land to get a firm fix on their geographical position. Since the region was not shown on any scientific map, he knew that any future expeditions to this land would have to rely upon veteran navigators and his own map to find their way back. He was determined to return some day in the future—as the sage's comments concerning his destiny in China made it clear that he had no future back in his homeland.

Several weeks were spent preparing for the upcoming voyage back across the Great Eastern Sea—that is, the Pacific Ocean. Tzu Fu set his marines to work scraping barnacles and seaweed from the hull of his ship. Then, it received a fresh coating of tongue-oil and lime. It was a proven concoction that prevented infestation by *torredos*—the dreaded seaworms that can turn a wooden hull into a sieve within a few weeks at sea. Ample cargoes of maize, peanuts, pineapples, and dried fruits were loaded aboard; and all the remaining iron tools and trade goods were distributed to the chieftains of local tribes as a goodwill gesture towards a suitable commercial arrangement in the future. Then the Commander directed the crew to hoist anchors and make way back to the Dragon Kingdom.

Their route took them west—riding swiftly on the Equatorial Current. This passage was made with the aid of astrolabes, compass, and star charts. They passed near the Hawaiian Islands, but whether or not they stopped we cannot say. Probably, they kept right on sailing as Tzu Fu was anxious to return to China. He dreaded the possibility that the aged Emperor might have died in his absence. Indeed, the one man who was nemesis might easily prove to be his key to future prosperity.

The chronicles of *Shih Chi* reported in later years that Tzu Fu returned after spending nearly three years on his Fu Sang expedition. Emperor Shih Huang was in ecstasy; and he ordered a celebration in the capital city.

Tzu Fu hastened to the palace for his audience with the Emperor. His mariners carried into the throne room brilliant green feathers of the quetzal bird, enormous dried skins of the anaconda serpent, chests full of copal incense, pots full to the brim with luscious honey, and large pieces of quartz crystal and jade. Each dazzling artifact greatly pleased the Emperor. He smiled; he laughed; he cheered. However, he was also baffled. Something was missing.

Tzu Fu clapped his hands, and servants carried in baskets of red corn and blocks of an exquisite red dyewood. The Emperor's advisors broke open the ears of corn; and they pronounced them "authentic." They carved chips from the corners of the red wood; this too, they declared was authentic. Next, the Commander produced a token of carved green Guatemalan jade from his pocket; and those standing nearby nearly swooned from the green light that flashed from its surface. He gave this to the High Priest who declared: "Our loyal Son has been to the Isle of Immortals.

However, the most important item of all was not there. Amidst all this pageantry and all these treasures from Fu Sang, there was no *ling chih.*

"Where are the mushrooms?" demanded the High Priest.

Commander Tzu humbly bowed down practically all the way to the tile floor. "Your Excellency," he pleaded, "the Immortals regard the *ling chih* as priceless. It is so valuable that they will only allow me to bring back a small chest in exchange for a suitable reward."

That rationale, of course, was a total lie. But it made perfect sense to the Emperor's Chief Councilor and the High Priest. The Emperor, who had been the most impatient person in the throne room finally spoke. "Tell me about Fu Sang and the *ling chih*" he commanded.

Tzu Fu tantalized the Emperor with tales of the wondrous magical powers of the Sacred Mushrooms. Then, he carefully outlined the demands of the Immortals. Tzu Fu carefully crafted his story from everything he could remember from Chinese history as well as from the anecdotes that had been told him by his Taoist advisers. He said that he had seen with his own eyes the ancestors of previous kings and emperors—even the legendary Hwang-ti, Kang-gi, and Yu. All this Tzu Fu made up with great cunning from his own imagination. However, all the Emperor's priests nodded in approval upon hearing so many tales that reflected their own beliefs about the importance of their ancestors and the nature of the world. With the soothing voice of a hypnotist, Tzu Fu led the venerable leader down the corridors of vanity and delusion.

This is what he said—based on official chronicles that were written shortly after the events had transpired: The Immortals required the Emperor to send as payment 3,000 young men and women. However, neither ordinary folk nor slaves would be accepted. Indeed, the standards of Paradise were very high. According to the Commander, the "Human Payment" for the *ling chih* must include the most beautiful lads and damsels of the Dragon Kingdom. And finally, they must all be skilled in some essential art or craft—such as agriculture, astronomy, and medicine.

All of these demands seemed thoroughly reasonable to Shih Huang. Therefore, he set his administrators to work immediately. They conducted interviews and auditions in order to select the most talented youths that could be found. Naturally, in order to transport the human payment all the way to Fu Sang, suitable ships were also required.

Tzu Fu insisted upon designing these vessels himself. There would be thirty new ships in the fleet; and these were ordered from the most renowned shipyards in Korea. In addition to the youths, Tzu Fu personally selected another 500 sailors as crew; and he chose several hundred marines as a precaution against pirate attack. Like the passengers, none of the crew members were very old. None were married—which assured that there were no inconvenient familial responsibilities that might interfere with their total loyalty to the mission and the Commander. All of these preparations took nearly a year; and they were monitored by a worried Emperor who grew more anxious with each passing day.

Finally, the Fu Sang Fleet departed in the year 219 BC—according to the *Shih Chi* chronicle. The very last that anybody in China remembered seeing of the "Cream of Chinese Youth" was the tops of the sails disappearing beneath the eastern horizon. They sailed the same route as before across the North Pacific Ocean. Their course of travel took them towards the Northwest Coast of the New Land where they visited the Tlingit, Haida, and Sailish Tribes; and then they proceeded south to the Gulf of Tehuantepec.

According to a 1st century BC edition of the *Shih Chi* chronicle:
> Tzu Fu found some calm and fertile plain with a broad
> forest and rich marshes where he made himself a king.[2]

The authors of the journal correctly concluded that Tzu Fu had absconded with all the wealth, all the beautiful damsels, and the entire fleet. Their assessment that he had "made himself a king" was purely speculation since nobody ever returned to tell their story. No attempt was ever made to track down the scoundrel and his followers, because nobody in China had any idea where he might have gone; and the Emperor died

---

[2] For an account of Tzu Fu (a.k.a., Hsu Fu) see Thompson, 1994, 116-117; see also George Carter, *Archeological Journal of Canada* (14:1), 14.

soon thereafter—so it was the kind of administrative debacle that most everybody in government just wanted to forget. Nevertheless, the assessment that "Tzu Fu had made himself a king" was probably accurate.

We can easily imagine the perfect ending to our story. Upon reaching the West Coast of Southern Mexico near Guatemala, Tzu Fu made a treaty with the local tribes. Of course, that had been his plan ever since he realized that the Emperor could not be trusted. The first voyage was simply a rehearsal for the grand deception. Upon their arrival in Mexico, the crew set about building a defensive palisade around a suitable hill. Probably, this location had already been surveyed and perhaps even purchased from the local Mayan tribe on the first voyage. Then, in typical theatrical style, Tzu Fu torched the entire fleet. This was done so that the new Chinese immigrants would appreciate that the move to Fu Sang was a permanent commitment.

Chinese Colony in Mexico

While the secret voyage was over, the mystery of the Chinese colony in the New World had just begun. Up to this point in time, New World shores had witnessed only a few maritime migrations of Asian refugees; while the visits by Chinese merchants were only occasional events—and they tended to be brief encounters. These migrations and visits had little impact on the course of New World civilization. However, everything changed with the arrival of Tzu Fu's fleet. For the very first time, there was an actual colony of talented Chinese artisans living near the very heart of the ancient Mayan Civilization.

The fleet anchored at some coastal village of southern Mexico such as Monte Alban, Mirador, or Izapa. It is in this region that modern archeologists have identified the emergence of a totally new artistic style dating to sometime between 300 BC and 100 BC. It has been called the "Izapan Style." This artistry is characterized by an abundance of intricate scrollwork that two archeologists, Robert Heine-Geldern and Gordon Ekholm, have identified as being "Chinese."[3]

The author's research has revealed an incredible concentration of ancient Chinese-Taoist symbolism in this region along with Chinese Kangi writing, Chinese ceramic toys, Chinese pottery, Chinese jade coins, and the sculpted faces of Chinese mariners. Human genetic research in the region has also revealed a high concentration of Chinese genetic traits among the indigenous population. This is one clear indication that there was a significant migration into the area directly from China.

Perhaps the most significant artifact of the Chinese colony is the great Izapan Festival Monument. This giant slab of inscribed limestone was carved by artisans using metal tools. Most likely, these were iron tools that the Chinese brought from their homeland. The tablet includes a portrayal of the Taoist Tree of Life at the center of a festival of priests, leaders, and

---

[3] See Thompson, *Nu Sun*, 1989, 161.

deities. Incredibly, the tablet contains ten Taoist symbols—including the Yin/Yang motif, a parasol, and the serpent/turtle emblem of *Zhenwu*.

As we have noted previously, *Zhenwu* was the Chinese Warrior God of the North. This symbol, along with the Yin/Yang motif, was a common feature of Mexican and Mayan art along the West Coast for the remainder of the development of the Mayan Civilization. It is clear from this enormous influx of Taoist symbolism along the West Coast that the indigenous peoples adopted much of the foreign religion as a result of intense, direct contact with the new Chinese colonists.

While it might be too extreme to suggest that Chinese colonists "jump started" the Mayan Civilization, this contact with foreign merchants provided essential new ingredients that were incorporated at the so-called "Formative Stage" of Mayan cultural development. In other words, the foreign cultural influence was profound; and it occurred during the early stages of cultural fluorescence when it was bound to have the greatest impact. By having access to Chinese metal tools, Taoist religious practices, Chinese architectural technology, and agricultural innovations such as rice farming, the capabilities of Mayan tribal leaders was greatly enhanced. Thus, they were able to build a new civilization in the inhospitable environs of the tropical Central American jungle climate.

According to the Chinese Chronicle written by Szuma Chien, the Tzu Fu expedition brought along the "five grains" of traditional Chinese agriculture. These included rice, millet, barley, wheat, and sorghum. Thus it is not surprising that Asian rice, barley, and millet have been found in ancient American archeological sites along with *Ma-fen* (or Chinese hemp).[4] Rice was a principal crop in Mayan jungles that were otherwise unsuitable for the cultivation of maize because the high humidity. As was true in Asia, Mayan rice farmers built canals for draining the excess water and for controlling the temperature of the rice paddies.

Tzu Fu realized the importance of astronomers in regulating the pace of a new society and in managing the times for planting and harvesting crops. The presence of Chinese astronomers at the very early stages of Mayan cultural development played an important role in the progress of Mayan astronomy. It is therefore hardly surprising that the renowned scholar, Joseph Campbell, regarded Mayan myths, religion, and astronomy as branches from Asian culture. He noted that: "The underlying mythologies of mathematical order governing the Earth as well as Heaven are the same." He further noted that the Mayan eclipse table in the *Dresden Codex* was identical to a table that Chinese astronomers produced during the Han Dynasty. Both tables predicted 23 eclipses within a 135-month period—when in fact, only 18 eclipses actually occur. In other words, both Mayan and Chinese eclipse tables were faulty; and they both contained the same errors. Campbell realized that identical patterns of errors could not occur if the original observations had been made

---

[4] George Carter has noted that millet was the oldest cultivated grain in both Mexico and China. *Canadian Journal of Archeology* (14:1), 15.

independently in China and Mexico. Therefore, he concluded that the Mayan eclipse table had been derived from a Chinese prototype.

Mayan priests were so impressed with the Taoist philosophy regarding the nature of the universe that they adopted many of the foreign practices and religious symbols. The author's research has proven that these symbols entered Mexico at the same time and place where Tzu Fu's colony was located. At about the same time, Mexicans began using a form of writing that incorporated *Kangi* symbols from China. This new writing system made it possible for the jungle tribes to communicate effectively even though they spoke a multitude of different dialects. The writing system provided a framework for political organization and military planning that was essential for the jungle tribes to overcome their enemies.

Mayan traditions identify the inventor of their writing system as a voyager from across the seas. They called him: "Itzamna." It was also said in Mayan folklore that he was the leader of what was regarded as "the little migration." While the migration from China may have been "little" in numbers, the cultural consequences were immense.

At about the time that Tzu Fu's fleet arrived from China, the Mayan tribes on the western fringes of the Olmec Empire were already in a rebellious mood. The new colony served as a catalyst for rebellion because it introduced new ideas and new hope into the region. The Chinese also brought new kinds of weapons including a powerful bow; they introduced innovative military tactics involving signal flags; and they exuded boldness and courage when confronting threats to their own security.

The American archeologist Victor Von Hagen has noted that the capital of a new Mayan Confederacy of tribes was centered at the village of Monte Alban near the Pacific Coast of Mexico. It is in this region that archeologists have uncovered the earliest use of the bow-and-arrow in Mexico; and this occurred at a time when Mayan tribes were beginning to overrun the ceremonial centers of the Olmec Empire farther north.

For all practical purposes, the Olmec regime was doomed as a result of foreign trade and colonization. All along the West Coast, Mayan tribes were drawn together as a result of the new waves of commerce that percolated through the jungle. Traders carried on their own backs assorted dyewoods, jade, tobacco, gold, and exotic plants. They also employed huge trains of slaves to cart merchandise through the jungles. This enormous volume of trade goods was brought to the harbors where it was exchanged for a variety of foreign commodities. The increasing trade precipitated the concentration of large populations that were led by fiercely independent merchants, warlords and priests. Foreign trade also brought in supplies of steel-tipped arrows and powerful composite bows. These had been the principal weapons of the Chinese military for many centuries; and they gave the Mayan warriors an advantage in combat against Olmec soldiers who were armed with spears and clubs.

Thus, commerce and foreign trade were key ingredients in the rise of Mayan Civilization.

What do Historians Think?

The profound impact of foreign colonies and trade with Chinese merchants has not escaped the attention of Western scholars—although the very notion of transoceanic influence remains a hotly debated topic. Nevertheless, the evidence continues to mount even while hidebound academics continue to procrastinate with the business of adapting their outdated paradigms to reflect the new information.

Mexican historians and archeologists have been aware for a very long time that the ancient cities of Monte Alban, Mitla, and Tollán in southwestern Mexico were extremely influential in the early development of Mayan Civilization[5]. The Zapotec culture of this region is renowned for its incredible artistry and advanced metal crafting skills that included smelting, casting, welding, and electroplating. Zapotecan artists were skilled in carving rock crystal, jade, and turquoise—a brittle material that was crafted into mosaics of wafer-thin pieces.

Although most historians insist that the native peoples lacked any knowledge of the wheel or sophisticated jeweler's tools, an inspection of the artifacts in museums that were produced by the Zapotecans clearly shows that lapidary tools were indeed used and with excellent results. Some of the round stone cups produced in the Zapotecan shops have a thickness of less than one-eighth of an inch. This incredible feat of stone carving can only be achieved using a lapidary wheel. And indeed, the marks left by such wheels can be identified on many museum artifacts. The inception of this culture is dated to around 200 BC—or about at the same time that Tzu Fu established his Chinese colony in Fu Sang.

Miguel Covarrubias, Robert Heine-Geldern, and Gordon Ekholm were among the earliest scholars who pointed out the obvious connection between the early Mayan arts of Monte Alban and the contemporary arts of China. Covarrubias noted the surprising similarities between stone tombs in Guatemala and those in Shang Dynasty China. Heine-Geldern suggested that a peculiar pattern of scrollwork seen in the ancient arts of Veracruz was derived from China. He called this "the Tajin Style."

Skeptics insisted that scrolls were common elements in the works of artists throughout the world; thus, they rationalized a convenient excuse for ignoring or dismissing evidence of transoceanic contact. However, the author has demonstrated that the scrolls are only a small part of the Taoist heritage of the Chinese colony near Monte Alban. In 1987, the author conducted an experiment to determine the origins of core symbols that served as the foundation of Mayan religious symbolism. This comparison of Chinese and Mayan art motifs provided the first conclusive evidence of significant Chinese cultural influence at the earliest stages of the development of Mayan Civilization.

---

[5] For details regarding Zapotec metal skills see Cambridge Encyclopedia, 1963, pp. 2379 & 1410.

Mexico's Asian heritage includes such unique motifs as the Scroll Eye, Scroll Wings, Speech Scrolls, and the ultimate of scroll motifs—the Yin/Yang symbol. The entire Taoist symbolism was carried to the coast of Mexico along with Chinese writing, ceramic headrests, pottery styles, and domesticated plants. The only way that such an assemblage could have occurred at the same time and at the same geographical location is through the mechanism of a major Chinese migration to the New World.

Part of the controversy regarding the existence of a Land called "Fu Sang" in America is a consequence of the mythical style of the Chinese chronicles. On the Shanhai Jing world maps, "Fu Sang" is located east of Japan on a "ring continent." This "ring continent" was a convenient way to illustrate New World continents that explorers found when they sailed in every direction from the Old World. Thus, there was the perception that the Old World continents of Africa, Asia, and Europe were all surrounded by a ring of land. Although some writers, including Henrietta Mertz and Hendon Harris, have equated the ring continent with ancient America, skeptics have insisted that the "ring continent" was only a myth. Some writers have suggested that Fu Sang was in modern-day British Columbia; others think it must have been in California or Mexico; and some regard the whole continent of North America as being the ancient Fu Sang.

Several 7th century Chinese poets referred to Japan as "Fu Sang." And this identification seems to suit most orthodox historians who want any excuse they can find for dismissing evidence of pre-Columbian voyages to America. They see in these poems about Japan a suitable alternative to Mexico. It thus is presented as a suitable place to dump any perceived threat to their concept of the Americas as being totally isolated from Old World—that is, until *after* Columbus. Nevertheless, a contemporary astronomer of the 7th century poets insisted that they were wrong. Fu Sang, he said, was located far to the east of Japan across the ocean. And this is precisely where it is shown to be located on the Shanhai Jing maps.

A Chinese chronicle written in the 5th century served to further confuse the mythical nature of Fu Sang. According to a scribe in the court of Emperor Laing Wu Ti, a Buddhist missionary claimed that he had returned from a trip to Fu Sang in the year 498 AD. The missionary, Hui-Shen, said that he had left China on a pilgrimage to spread the blessings of Buddha to the lands of barbarians across the Eastern Ocean. He visited a country that was situated 20,000 *li* (or about 6,000 miles) to the east of Siberia. That would place Fu Sang in the vicinity of Mexico.

Hui-Shen described the land as a place of giant trees, white headed birds, flying rats, a sea of varnish, and women who took "snakes" for husbands. He added that merchants paid no tax; and there were plenty horses and wagons carting around produce and supplies. Apparently, the missionary recounted his experiences to the Emperor's court at which time the scribe recorded the testimony as well as the reactions of the audience. It seems that the Emperor's guests regarded the tales as being quite humorous—if not preposterous. The idea a place existed east of China where merchants paid no tax was completely ludicrous—as were the women who took snakes for husbands.

In retrospect, it seems that there were reasonable grounds for most of the missionary's tales—particularly if we make a generous allowance for the peculiarities that result from translating between languages. The white-headed birds were probably bald eagles. The flying rats were most likely ordinary "bats." The tale about the women who took "snakes" for husbands could have been simply a misunderstood reference to native women of the Bear Clan whose husbands came from the "Snake Clan." The idea that there was a "sea of varnish" requires some creative speculation. One of the stranger sights in rural Mexico at the time of the Spanish Conquest was the native varnish industry. In many of the rural villages, the women kept large vats of copal varnish that was being cured for a variety of applications as a wood preservative. This varnish industry was most likely a consequence of contact with the Chinese who were the inventors of varnish. Hui Shen might have described these vats, with a little leeway given for translation, as a "sea of varnish." Another writer has suggested that the La Brea Tar Pits of Los Angeles might have been on the mind of the missionary when he mentioned the "sea of varnish." In any case, while the Chinese might have found this reference to be quite humorous, there is no reason to assume that it was simply a fable.

With respect to the idea that there were merchants in Fu Sang who paid no tax, the facts of the ancient Mayan economic system are perhaps quite revealing. According to anthropologist Victor Von Hagen, the Mayan merchants were not required to pay tax; and this policy was intended to promote commerce. It seems highly unlikely that a Buddhist priest could have imagined this aspect of the foreign society without having firsthand knowledge of the Mexican/Mayan economy.

The single detail of Hui-Shen's account that has been claimed as proof that he never really sailed to Mexico is the report that he saw horses and wagons. Among the academics who carry the banner of New World Cultural Isolation, there is a prevalent belief that there were no horses (or for that matter, no wagons) in the New World until after Columbus. Precisely how this notion ever came into existence—and then was promoted as unquestioned fact—has endured for decades in the dusty attics of unproven "history" in Western Academia. It is a convenient argument that is often invoked in support of the Isolationist platform. However, it is really nothing more than a fantasy of myopic thinking that serves to perpetuate an academic mistake. It is "in fact" a lie.

Most historians will readily acknowledge that there are native tribes in North America whose elders insist that "their ancestors always had horses." The accounts of the pioneers often tell of natives riding horses prior to contacts with Europeans. There were numerous contacts between natives and Old World mariners, such as the Celts, the Romans, and the Norwegians; and these were all peoples who brought along their own horses. Any of these could have been responsible for the introduction of

European and Arabian breeds into the New World prior to the arrival of 16th century Spaniards. Indeed, one Icelandic saga tells of a Nordic sailor who witnessed Celts riding horses in Vinland—that is Nova Scotia—in about the year 1200 AD. Ancient horse sculptures have been excavated in Peru; and in the American southeastern woodlands, one pioneer identified a native breed called "the cayuse" that had no obvious connection to the Spanish mounts. There is further evidence of native ponies in British Columbia, in the Outer Banks of the Carolinas, and in Argentina—where horses were so plentiful that when the Spaniards arrived in the 16th century they were hunted for food.

In sum, it must be admitted that the evidence supports the conclusion that the Buddhist priest found Fu Sang precisely as he said.

Consequences for New World Exploration

The existence of a Chinese colony along the coast of Mexico was a tremendous boost to international trade across the Pacific Ocean.

Colonies attracted trade for many reasons. They served as marshalling points for domestic goods; and these coastal markets made it easier for maritime merchants to conduct their business efficiently in one location. They were essentially the "supermarkets" of the ancient world. News about the colonies spread rapidly among the league of traveling merchants because fellow voyagers were often willing to share their "secrets" with their compatriots on the high seas—regardless of the commercial rivalries that existed between nations. This international cadre of seafarers led the land-based bureaucrats to suspect their loyalties. Indeed, Chinese officials often barred seamen from entering the cities due to fears that they might incite rebellions because of their cosmopolitan knowledge and their lack of loyalty to a specific king, nation, or creed.

Colonies provided familiar harbors and safe havens for travelers. Indeed, it was customary for ancient Mexicans to bring merchants and the transporters of goods into special houses that were provided for their convenience in every town. In this manner, the Mexican and Mayan authorities hoped to encourage both regional and overseas trade. Colonies had their own administrative organizations and military that assured standard trading practices, instruction in the trade language, standardized measures, and consistent pricing of goods. They also had tribunals that could administer a practical kind of justice that was intended to improve business relationships.

The existence of overseas colonies was generally known only to the merchants who traveled abroad; and they were understandably reluctant to reveal the secret locations of their sources of foreign goods. Indeed, it was only after the Yuan-Mongol Government of China sent Marco Polo to make an inventory of the overseas ports in the New World that the Chinese government began to gain any official knowledge of the existence of the overseas colonies.

Izapan Festival Monument
West Coast Southern Mexico
c. 300-200 BC

IZAPAN FESTIVAL MONUMENT

MEXICO

Omnibus Power Sign Symbols

China

Han mirror 100 AD

Zhou carving 800 BC

Source: see Thompson, 1989.

Mexico

Izapa, Mx. 300 BC

Mayan 300 BC

Man with Lion Dog
Uxmal, Mexico
400 BC
stone carving
Carnegie Inst.

Time Detectives & The Chinese Immigration

The author was the first scholar to identify a unique wave of Chinese cultural influence that flooded into Mexico between 500 and 100 BC. Chinese immigrants, Taoist priests, and merchants brought an unusual type of transformational symbol called "the Omnibus Power Sign." Most of the symbols on the Izapan Festival Monument (top) were derived from China. So, this appears to be a carved stone monument in West Coastal Mexico that commemorates the arrival of immigrants across the ocean. These Chinese symbols in ancient Mexico are conclusive evidence of significant cultural contact across the ocean. They were subsequently incorporated as the core of Mexican religious symbolism.

Evidence of Contact *in the* New World

China

Ceramic Toy
Houses 200 BC

Ceramic Pillow, Korea 1200 AD

Ceramic Headrest, Ecuador 500 BC

China

Source: see Thompson, 1994.

Mexico

Jade Money 300 AD
Teotihuacan, Mx.

Jade Money
Chiapa de Corzo, Mx.

Chinese Cultural Diffusion circa 300 BC

Chinese immigrants and merchants brought along their distinctive ceramic toy houses, pottery, and headrests—which are subsequently found throughout Mexico. The characteristic Chinese Yin/Yang symbol—including serpent eyes—became one of the most common symbols in Mexican art. Among the Chinese artifacts found in Mexico are two jade coins with Chinese writing. A ceramic figurine (far left) shows an ancient mariner with a characteristic Chinese beard and Lion Dog on the right shoulder.

天下圖

Map drawing after Hendon Harris, 1975.
See also Thompson, 1994, Donald Cyr, 1978.

Shanhai Jing (Map of Mountains & Seas)

An ancient Chinese map that might have been based partially on a worldwide survey conducted in the 3rd millennium BC survives in this 19th century version of a Korean map called the Ch'onhado. Known by the name Tien Xia Tu in China, it designates a region across the ocean east of China as "Fu Sang." The capital of China is at the location of the circle near the center of the map.

Serpent/Turtle

Symbol of Zhen Wu—the Perfect Warrior
Polaris or God of the North
Common in China and West Coast Mexico

c. 200 AD

Time Detectives & Mayan Writing

The author examined an ancient Mayan jade statuette and found that it was covered with Chinese writing. This artifact, called the "Tuxtla Statuette," has inscribed symbols that are identical to the ancient writing of China. The table at right shows a comparison of writing from China and from the artifact. This was just one type of writing that the natives used in Mexico. It is of great importance, because the standard writing symbols enabled merchants traveling overseas to communicate even though they couldn't speak the local dialect. Following the author's "cutting edge" research, Michael Xu and Chinese scholars identified Chinese writing on more ancient Olmec artifacts. Clearly, Mexico or Fu Sang was a place that was well known to Chinese seafarers.

A
EAST ASIA
CHINA

M
PROTO-
MAYA

Source: see Thompson, 1994.

73

ACRE—1272 AD

Secret agents Niccolò and Mafeo Polo meet with Pope Gregory at the Castle of Acre in Palestine.

Marco Polo's Brave New World

TWO EARTH-SHAKING EVENTS led up to the epic voyages of Marco Polo in the 13th century. The first shockwave that hit Medieval Europe came when Mongol armies stormed across Central Asia. The second thunderbolt struck from out of the infernal Viking lair of King Haakon IV of Norway.

In the Spring of 1261, the Nordic ruler announced his Doctrine of Norwegian Supremacy in the New Lands of the Far West. This came as quite a shock to European merchants who had become accustomed to trading for fish, furs, and copper in the Western Isles. Suddenly, all that lucrative business was halted; and the dockyards at Bremen, Calais, Antwerp, London, and Dublin were chock full of merchant ships that had nowhere to go. Heralds throughout Europe announced the Norwegian policy of treating any unauthorized mariners who were caught sailing in the Western Isles as pirates—with the assurance that they would be promptly executed.

Those were difficult times throughout Christian Europe. They were hard enough for Christians who practiced the only state-authorized religion; they were even more difficult for Jews and Muslims who were the targets of mobs and Crusader knights. Most people were impoverished serfs. They had few joys in life that alleviated the bad food and the harsh treatment that they received from their feudal lords. Few people outside the Church could read or write; and there weren't many books available for them to read anyway. The Latin Bible was one of the few books people ever saw; but only priests who could read the Latin writing actually understood the manuscript writing on its pages. Entertainment for the common people consisted of holiday festivals, dancing, drinking and carousing; but these pastimes only took place when the lords and masters excused them from backbreaking labors on the feudal estates.

Unfortunately, there was something even worse in store for the peasants of Medieval Europe. It was called "the End of the World."

Doomsday —The End of the World

The dominant theme in Medieval Europe (c. 900-1400 AD) was the End of the World. Church artists filled the minds of common folk with nightmarish images of the Biblical Apocalypse—an impending calamity of famine, suffering, warfare, disease, and devils all descending upon Europe to usher in the Final Day of Judgment. This was supposed to occur in the foreboding Year of 1300. When that failed to happen, another date was predicted.

In the waning years of the 12th century, the ruthless warlord Temujin (or Genghis Khan) replaced the Old Viking marauders as the "Scourge of Christendom." In the span of only a few years, Genghis Khan's army marched from Mongolia to Hungary—a distance of several thousand miles—conquering all the nations, tribes, and cities that stood in his path. Behind him, he left ruin, heartache, and catastrophe. It was usual for the Khan's army to simply ride into a new territory and declare that it belonged to the Mongol Lord—who was destined by God's will to rule the universe. Those who fell down to worship at his feet—he spared; those who failed to appreciate the glory and compassion of the Mongol Tyrant were put to the sword. Often, all males in a conquered territory were decapitated; and the women and children were distributed as slaves or sold to foreign countries. Some refugees who reached sanctuary in Western Europe reported that the Mongols had burned cities to the ground and had stacked the severed heads of victims in morbid pyramids.

The atrocities of the Mongol armies were "unspeakable," and so we shall have little more to say about them. However, Europeans of the Late Middle Ages began hearing rumors about the merciless invaders just before New Year's Day in the year 1200. Since Christian clerics were already expecting that Doomsday was about to occur on that very date, they presumed that the Mongols were simply a tribe of demons who were already mentioned in the Bible. They were known as "the minions of Gog and Magog." According to biblical prophesy in the Book of Revelations, the Giant Magog was in league with Satan; and the armies of Magog were expected to attack Christian Europe as part of the Apocalypse. This "Apocalypse" was explained to ordinary peasants as the Final Battle of Good and Evil. It was to be a horrific event filled with all kinds of pain, suffering, and violence; and it was destined to occur just before the Last Day of Judgment. "So it is written in the Book of Revelations," declared the Christian priests from their pulpits, and "So it shall be—Amen."

The word "Mongol" does sound a little bit like "Magog;" and the barbaric behavior of the Mongol warriors did seem like a casting right out of biblical Hell. So it is quite understandable that European priests—priests who were indoctrinated with a notion of biblical destiny—actually believed that the "End Times" were at hand. Unfortunately, many Christians, including most of the Church leaders, presumed that they were helpless to intervene in their own Destiny. Their reasoning went something like this: If the Mongols were indeed the legions of Satan, as Church scholars had concluded, then it was actually a "sin" to resist the Mongols. According to the Church Fathers, God's Will and God's "Grand Plan" called for the End of the World. Any attempt to interfere with the defeatist script of Scripture would simply make God angry and result in even more incredible suffering among the Faithful.

However, not everybody in Medieval Europe adhered to the defeatist way of thinking. There actually existed a small group of men and women who believed that they could play proactive roles in the course of world

Mastermind of Discovery
Queen Chabi of Yuan China, Marco's Patron

Marco's Boss at the Vatican
Pope Gregory X

Explorer, Writer, Spy
The Venetian—Marco Polo

Mongol Emperor of China
Kublai Khan

events. Some of these nonconformists were outspoken heretics. Typically, these naïve idealists were accused of offenses against the Mother Church in Rome; they were hunted down; and they were summarily burned at the stake. Another targeted group of outsiders were the Jews. They were a threat to the interests of the Church because they were often quite successful in business ventures. Unlike Christians, they were allowed to charge high rates of interest on loans; and the dependency that many kings and businessmen had upon international Jewish banking arrangements meant that the Jews exercised considerable influence on governments. Thus, they were effective rivals of the religious leaders who served the pope. They were constant thorns in the sides of doctrinaire bishops. They were often thrown into pits and burned by Christian mobs as a consequence of ignorance, superstition, and the incredibly stupid belief that God would reward the parishes of Europe if they were "cleansed" of nonbelievers prior to the Second Coming of Christ.

One group of enlightened thinkers attempted to institute gradual reforms within the Church itself. Many of these reformists belonged to the Brotherhood of Franciscan Friars. This is hardly surprising since the Franciscans, or "Little Brothers of the Poor," traveled about a lot administering to the needs of peasants, mariners, and merchants. From these rather ordinary folk who were on the "front lines" of medieval life, they learned quite a lot about the workings of society from a "bottoms-up" perspective. Intellectuals in the Brotherhood often engaged in philosophical debates; and they studied the writings of scholars in other religions. The most important group in the Brotherhood were "the Mystics." These were people who dreamed about a New Script for the future of the world.

The Mystics did not accept the prevailing dogma that God had already written the Last Act of the Creation Experiment. Quite the contrary, they believed that humans should be "partners" with God in the ongoing creation and renewal of the physical world. In other words, the Human Play in their eyes was still an open-ended drama. Some even entertained the notion that it was a play that was never-ending. A few daring radicals concluded that Jesus was more human than godlike, that the Sacrament was only "ordinary" bread, and that all religions were equally endowed with both revelations and superstitions.

As you can probably imagine, mystical thinking was not received with enthusiasm in the Medieval Church. It was only natural for the practitioners of the mystical or "humanistic" way of thinking to be somewhat secretive about their beliefs in order to avoid reprisals from the orthodox clergy. When Church authorities found books that expounded the humanist philosophy, they often relished burning them as an act of piety. Usually, the books were anonymous as the wayward scholars had no intention of lighting fires beneath their own feet.

One course of action that the Mystics employed was to form secret societies. It was from this need for personal security among intelligent and

Ships & Shores of the Secret Sailors

Yuan Chinese Expedition Ship c. 1000-1500 AD

where they went & how they got there

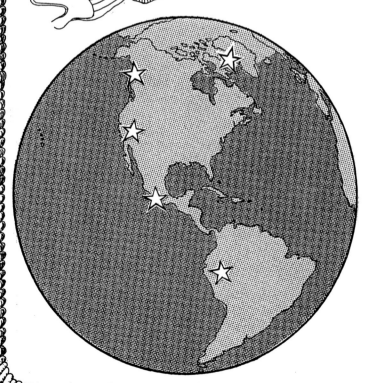

Ta Han, Tien Mu, Extreme East

Bergi—Canadian Arctic
Anian—Alaska
Quivira—Northwest Coast
California
Toloman—Mexico
Peru

enlightened people that the term *sub-rosa* (or "under the rose") finds its way into the chronicles of the Middle Ages. Presumably, meetings held "under the rose" were kept confidential; attendance was anonymous; and anyone who betrayed the names of those who were present, or what was said, could be isolated from the group and perhaps assassinated.

It was from the ranks of Mystic Franciscans that Pope Innocent IV appealed for help in dealing with the threat from Mongol invaders. History has recorded the names of only two volunteers—but there were certainly many friars who chose to work behind the scenes. The friar-agents who are known to us include John of Plano Carpini (a.k.a., Giovanni de Pian di Carpini) and William of Rubruck.

Friar John left on a mission to the Mongol enclave at Karakorum in the year 1245. He stayed for almost three years with the newly elected, Grand Khan Guyuk. Friar William arrived eight years later. Although historians have characterized both friars as being gregarious buffoons, their outward appearance was simply part of the disguise. For all practical purposes, they were very effective spies.

While touring the Mongol camps (and posing as somewhat bumbling friars), John and William made careful observations of the Mongol military organization and their strategy for international conquest. They investigated the Mongol sources of deadly rockets and guns; and they determined that these incredible weapons had been obtained from Chinese factories. At the time, such weapons were virtually unknown in Europe. John and William paid particular attention to the Mongol maps. These observations were chronicled in a 13th century manuscript that is known as *the Tartar Relation.*

At that point in time, Europeans generally had a very primitive and inaccurate comprehension of world geography. Most maps that were seen by the common people were primarily intended to reinforce the learning of biblical stories. So, they included such outdated information as the locations of the Tower of Babel, the landing site of Noah's Ark, the tramping ground of Gog and Magog, and the Earthly Paradise along the East Coast of Asia. None of this information had any practical value; but then the Church Fathers were not known for their geographical expertise. Among the Holy Fathers, prayer was considered to be the preferable method of finding one's direction through life; while the compass was scorned due to its presumed association with the demonic forces.

After examining the Mongol maps, John and William were shocked out of their socks. The Mongol world map showed "new lands" east of China across the ocean. This was the first inkling that the Franciscan spies had of the superior Mongol world geography. Using captured Chinese and Korean vessels, Persian and Song Dynasty crews under Mongol command were actively surveying mainland that was situated in what was called "the Extreme East." This region of the world was located east of Japan across the Great Eastern Sea. It seemed obvious to the Franciscan agents that the Mongol armies were planning to attack Europe simultaneously from both the East and the West. The specter of an amphibious assault from the undefended Atlantic Coast seemed to be a very real possibility.

The concerns of Franciscan agents grew more intense after the Mongols captured the enormous navy of the Song Dynasty in China. If Kublai Khan's Yuan Chinese Empire had actually been situated directly west of Europe, as most biblical geographers believed at the time, then Christian Europe really would have been "Doomed"—just as the prophets had feared. Regardless of where the Khan's Empire was situated, survival of Christian Civilization literally depended upon learning the secrets of Kublai Khan's military strategists and the secrets of their diabolical Chinese weapons. Of paramount concern to the Franciscans was gaining access to geographical information about the secret Mongol bases in the New Lands. It was at this point in time, in the year 1255, that the pope sent two of his most trusted agents from the *Cadre de Espionage* to the Far East. Their names were Niccolò and Maffeo Polo.

New World Voyages by Marco Polo and the Yuan Navy

The illustrious Polo Family enters the world stage in the pages of Marco Polo's famous book—*Discovery of the World* or simply, the *Book of Marco Polo's Travels*. This Travelogue has both tantalized and confused historians ever since it was written in 1298.

Modern historians have tended to regard Marco Polo's Book as an ordinary journal of daily sights that a tourist might have simply recorded for the entertainment of friends and family after returning from vacation. Actually, that style of writing was a very clever *ruse*. That is to say, the Book is not exactly what it appears to be on the surface. It is, in fact, a quite ingenious "spy book." In order to unravel the many clues that are contained in the Travelogue, we have to realize the important role that espionage played during the years that Marco was away from Venice.

The first clue regarding Marco Polo's status as a master spy is the fact that he didn't write the book himself. Technically speaking, he was the author. However, he didn't actually write down a single word.

In order for Marco Polo's *Book of Travels* to be produced as a public literary work, a special agreement had to be worked out between Venetian and Genoese authorities. Marco Polo was not exactly in a situation where he could say whatever he wanted to say in a publication of this nature; there was too much at stake. At the time, he was a Genoese prisoner of war following his capture in a naval battle in 1298. He was in effect under "house arrest" in a Genoese villa; and he was living in a situation that is called "duress." That is, he was compelled to give information against his will. Marco's Genoese captors wanted him to reveal all his secrets about the Far East. At the same time, Marco realized that if he did give away sensitive information that helped the commercial and military objectives of his enemies that he was likely to be assassinated by Venetian agents.

That is to say that much of what he knew about Mongol military secrets and the Mongol commander, Kublai Khan, was *sub rosa*.

The French-Italian romanticist Rusticello of Piza was given the task of actually writing the *Book of Marco Polo's Travels*. It was from his hand that the words were actually written down while the Venetian traveler verbally recounted the tales of his exploits in the service of Kublai Khan. This arrangement seemed to be acceptable to the Venetian Council which exercised authority over agents and mariners traveling abroad. By allowing Marco Polo to dictate tales about his Far Eastern travels, they offered a convenient solution that would enable him to meet the demands of the Genoese without forcing him to violate his oath not to write about what he saw in the New Lands. The Venetian authorities were informed that Marco would be held until they obtained a suitable ransom. In this case, the ransom was a book of secrets about the Far East.

Marco Polo used the first chapters of his book to tell the story of why his father and uncle traveled to China in the first place. He says that they were ordinary "jewel peddlers" who just happened to keep heading farther-and-farther east. Marco explains that they just kept going east—for thousands of miles across some of the world's most desolate and hazardous terrain—because they simply had the incredible "luck" of finding lucrative markets for their precious stones. The explanation in Marco's book seems a little far-fetched—even if we ignore the fact that Niccolò and Maffeo left Europe suddenly, right after Niccolò's wedding to a prominent Croatian debutante. We must also hold in suspense any consideration that Niccolò might have had for his reputation in Croatia for abandoning a wife who was pregnant with his child. And we must also wonder at the folly of two Christian jewel peddlers traipsing across lands that were occupied almost entirely by Muslims and Mongols—the two groups that were generally the most hated by doctrinaire Christians.

Later in the book, Marco mentions that his father happened to be good "friends" with Pope Clement IV—who was at the time the spiritual and political leader of Christian Europe. Such a friendship with the highest authority in the land hardly supports the notion that the Polo Brothers were ordinary "jewel peddlers." We are led to conclude that using the profession of "jewel peddlers" offered a convenient disguise that enabled the Polo Brothers to travel freely in territories under Mongol control. The jewels that they carried were worth a fortune—yet they could easily be concealed in the thick folds of clothing that was the customary dress of desert travelers.

Incidentally, their "friend" the Pope was also a confidant of the most outspoken and mysterious Mystic Franciscan who ever lived. His name was Roger Bacon. He was also an English scientist who took a serious interest in the arcane arts, who experimented with astronomy, gunpowder, and magnetism at a time when such activities were condemned by Church authorities; and among his most urgent pleas to his followers was for them to learn the geographical secrets of the world.

The Travelogue reveals that Niccolo and Maffeo Polo spent fifteen years in China. They didn't just simply peddle jewels. Instead, they worked their way into the highest offices of the Mongol government; and they finally gained the confidence of Emperor Kublai Khan. That's not too shabby work for a couple of mere jewel peddlers. Also, we learn from Marco Polo's book that his father and uncle were commissioned in the service of the Mongol Emperor. They were assigned duties as ambassadors to the pope; they were entrusted with the contents of a diplomatic pouch; they were given special passports as the Khan's personal emissaries; and they were delegated to obtain sacred oil from the Holy Sepulcher in Jerusalem. On the surface, this might seem like a perfectly ordinary assignment for a couple of ordinary "jewel peddlers."

However, whenever the Polo Family was involved in a mission, nothing was ever as simple as it appeared to be on the surface. There was always a hidden motive or a secret agenda that was at work behind the scenes. As a protégé of the scientist Roger Bacon, Niccolò Polo was quite aware of the role that superstition played in the popularity of sacred potions, miracles, and magical animals. At the time, Europeans were fascinated by stories about unicorns, dragons, and other fantastic creatures that were common in the romantic literature. The Polos, however, scoffed at such ridiculous tales.

The very idea that Niccolò would seriously consider that "sacred oil" from Jerusalem would have any value in relieving the Emperor's gout is simply ridiculous. Yet, Marco Polo chose to dictate this drivel to his scribe, Rusticello. Marco knew that by including a few miracles in his book, the superstitious Genoese were likely to believe everything else. Thus we see in Marco Polo's Travelogue a delicate balance of very useful information about the Far East interspersed with cunning distortions and patronizing anecdotes about miraculous cures and creatures. Frequently, Marco chose to include a humorous twist in order to make fun of those who took his book too seriously.

The Book of Travels is essentially a "spy book." Nevertheless, it contains many revealing clues regarding Marco Polo's incredible journeys to the New World. And that seems to have been the intention of the clever Venetian from the very beginning. If he had to dictate a book in order to gain his release from captivity, then it would be a book that epitomized the best he could offer in humor, sarcasm, and deception. At the same time, Marco had every intention of furthering the interests of science, discovery, and world peace—while simultaneously lambasting Europeans for their incredible ignorance and their devotion to absurd medieval superstitions.

Niccolò and Maffeo Polo returned to Venice in about the year 1269. This was shortly after the death of their friend Pope Clement IV. We learn from the *Book of Travels* that the Polo Brothers visited the Vatican. They had brought with them a letter from Kublai Khan requesting that the Pope send 100 teaching friars who could demonstrate the superiority of Christian doctrines over other religions. In retrospect, many European theologians regarded this letter as an indication of the Khan's interest in the wholesale conversion of his entire Empire to the Christian religion. In the eyes of the Church Fathers, such an achievement would be well received in Heaven as it would immediately quadruple the number of Christians in the world—and there would be lots of employment opportunities for missionaries. However, until the election of a new pope, there could be no official response to the Khan's request.

Meanwhile, Niccolò returned to Croatia where he discovered that he had a son—named in his absence, Marco Polo. His wife had died shortly after childbirth; and Marco had been raised in his wife's extended family. He was also apprenticed to a local bank where he was in training to become a rather ordinary coin counter and accountant. History would have been much different if Marco's father hadn't been a jewel peddler.

From this point on in Marco's Book, the seemingly ordinary events that follow actually reveal a pattern of activities and deceptions that were designed to conceal the lad's great secret. From the moment that he first met his father, he abandoned his humble but secure banking career for the challenges and rewards of the espionage service.

Marco immediately accepted his father's offer to spend his "senior year abroad"—not as a bank teller in China—but as a spy. His relatives were certainly dismayed by the stunning announcement that he intended to accompany his "irresponsible" father on another trek to the Far East. However, there was no stopping the adolescent's determination to follow in his father's footsteps (so to speak).

It would appear from the accounts in the *Book of Travels* that Niccolò Polo was compelled by some ill-conceived loyalty to Kublai Khan which meant that he was apparently in some haste to return to the Emperor's Court. This seems like a strange kind of compulsion for an ordinary "jewel peddler" or for a man who was supposed to be a devout Christian. Most people in Europe either feared or despised the Mongols—yet Niccolò was reportedly "anxious" to return to Mongol China.

Then, in spite of this expressed need for haste, Niccolò spent over two years in Venice; and he required an additional four years to make his way back to China. That expedition involved leading a camel train across Turkey, Afghanistan, Tibet, and Mongolia in order to reach the palace of Kublai Khan at Cambaluc (near modern Beijing). We learn from Marco Polo that during this time, he learned three new foreign languages— presumably Mongolian, Korean, and Arabic. These languages had no practical use—unless Marco was planning to spend lots of time sailing about with Korean sailors and Arabian merchants. Upon reaching Kublai Khan's summer resort at Zan-du, we learn that Marco was able to speak to the Emperor and Queen in their own Mongolian dialect; and he had complete competence in the Mongolian diplomatic and social protocols. His fluency in the language, his grace in the presence of royalty, and his mastery of Mongolian musical instruments completely charmed Queen Chabi who from the very moment they met began planning her own agenda for the young foreigner. As it turns out, even his training as a bank clerk had some value on this espionage mission to China as the Emperor promptly appointed him to the position of a roving revenue agent.

As the Emperor's personal agent, Marco was able to inquire into the most secretive operations of both the government and the military. *The Book of Travels* recounts some of the places that Marco visited and some of the reports that he supplied to Kublai Khan. According to Marco, his reports were so fascinating that the Emperor encouraged him to expand the range of his journeys. He says that he subsequently sailed to the "East Indies," to isles "40 days east of Siberia," and then to lands called "Anian," "Kondur," "Malaiur," and "Locathe." He speaks of a Land of Gold southeast of Asia that is "like Another World;" and he mentions the wonders of Japan—which was another "Land of Gold" and red pearls.

Historians have been unable to trace the locations of many of the places that Marco Polo claimed to have visited. Either the names don't fit, or the sailing directions that he gives are way off the mark. On the other hand, if we consider that the Travelogue was actually a "spy book," and if we realize that Marco had to tell his tales about the Far East without revealing Venetian secrets—then we can find clues to solve the mystery.

In the 1930s, an Italian named Marcian Rossi brought a trunk-load of documents to the Library of Congress where he hoped they would be examined by competent scholars. Among these documents were several 13th century maps along with letters from Marco Polo's daughters—Moretta and Bellela. Surprisingly, these maps have reasonably accurate shorelines for Alaska and modern-day British Columbia. The Swedish historian Leo Bagrow declared in the journal *Imago Mundi* in 1946 that these documents "were genuine." The author has identified additional "Marco Polo Maps showing the shorelines of Vancouver Island, Puget Sound, Oregon, California, Mexico, and Peru. All of these maps are authentic; they all existed in Venetian archives prior to the European discovery of New World lands during the Renaissance. And they were all at one time or another regarded as "secret maps."

In his Book of Travels, Marco Polo mentions that Chinese merchants sailed across the Eastern Ocean to countries "east of Japan" where they obtained profitable cargoes. Clearly, the Chinese were sailing to colonies or native harbors along the coast of modern-day Vancouver Island, California, and Mexico—and this was way back in the 13th century. These were the very lands that were mentioned in the Franciscan book, the *Tartar Relation*; and they were even depicted on a Franciscan map that was given to Yale University in 1964. Called the "Vinland Map," the Yale document includes the same description that is contained in the *Tartar Relation*. It says: "The Tartars confirm New Lands to the east."

When we consider that Niccolò Polo spent 15 years in China before returning to Venice, then it becomes clear that this was the initial stage for an espionage program that was carefully designed to learn the geographical and military secrets of the Mongol rulers. Niccolò returned to the Vatican in order to give his report to the Pope who was the "boss" if not the mastermind for the whole project. He also wanted to enlist the services of a younger agent who could be trained in the skills needed to penetrate the hierarchy of the Mongol Navy. Niccolò's intention was for this agent to accompany Mongol vessels sailing to the New Lands. By accompanying the Yuan Mongol survey teams, the young agent would be able to copy their maps; and he would learn where they intended to establish staging areas for an invasion of Europe from the west.

Marco's greatest ally during the years he spent in China was his Mongol patron—Queen Chabi. We learn from the Rossi documents that it was Queen Chabi who took an active interest in the lad's promotion up the ranks of the Yuan Chinese expeditionary forces. In about the year 1282, she had him assigned as her personal representative on a diplomatic mission to Sakhalin Island. This mission for the Queen was to be one of the most harrowing adventures of Marco's espionage career.

After leaving the port of Nanjing on a quiet afternoon, the sturdy junk sailed in a northeasterly direction passing by Japan. Within a few days, the weather turned nasty; and Marco's junk was caught up in a typhoon. For several days, the junk was tossed about by gale force winds and heaving waves that swept the helpless sailors northwards along the Asian coast towards the Arctic. When the winds finally diminished, the seasick crew crawled back onto the battered deck; and they managed to find succor in a desolate harbor along the coast of Kamchatka.

It was in this wintry sanctuary of jagged mountains and churning surfs that Marco Polo met one of the strangest men that he ever could have imagined. From out of the mist, there appeared a dory loaded with fur-clad men and women chattering and waving in some quaint language that was totally incomprehensible. However, there stood up in their midst a short rather chunky old man who was dressed from head to foot in ermine and sealskins. He had a walrus grin from cheek to cheek; and he shouted to Marco a greeting in Arabic. The lad was totally baffled by the appearance of this gregarious fellow who should have been riding a camel someplace in the Arabian Desert. Instead, here he was welcoming a totally unknown visitor to his humble abode in the Far North.

Marco's benefactor was a Syrian fur trader named Biaxo Sirdumap. Biaxo and his merry followers were always happy to have visitors in this wilderness—so they opened the doors of their hunting lodges; they prepared a feast; and there followed a rowdy evening of singing, dancing, and drinking. Quite possibly, someone in Marco's crew produced a pouch of Chinese *Ma-fen* (or hemp) which they smoked with tobacco.

As often happens when complete strangers meet under life-threatening circumstances, a strong bond of friendship soon developed between Marco and his Syrian host. It was not long before Biaxo, a seasoned mariner, offered to guide Marco and his entourage back to their original objective on Sakhalin Island. The Syrian also entrusted a map to his new friend showing the location of his favorite hunting grounds.

Marco was stunned: these "hunting grounds," where Biaxo got his prime sealskins, was located far to the east in a New Land that was totally unknown to Europeans. This was precisely the kind of information that the Franciscan agents wanted so desperately to obtain—and it was being freely given to them by a Syrian fur trader!

A copy of Biaxo's map was one of the documents that were found in the Marcian Rossi collection. It is the oldest map known (dating to the mid 13th century) that shows the Arctic Seas near Siberia and the Peninsula of Alaska. Biaxo called this New World land the "Peninsula of Seals"—because it was the place where he obtained sealskins. These skins and the cured pelts of the Arctic fox, sable, and bear were worth a fortune in trade with the Chinese. Marco knew that they were equally valuable in Europe.

Following Marco's successful mission to Sakhalin Island, Queen Chabi recommended him for a position as the Khan's ambassador on a series of mapping expeditions that was generally known as "the Extreme East. This was only one name for the West Coast of the modern-day American Continents. They were also known by such legendary titles as *Ta-han, Su Mu, Ta-han Tensuyu, Tien-mu,* and *Fu Sang.*

The first objective of the Yuan Navy was to chart the seaway heading eastwards above modern-day Canada. This seaway was known to Europeans as "the Northwest Passage."

In Marco Polo's era, the Arctic climate was much more mild than it is today. There is some indication in Norwegian folklore that the Eskimos (or Inuit seafarers) and a few wayward Vikings were using this route to transport furs from Siberia and Alaska to markets in the New England Region and also on to Europe. We know that Marco Polo sailed along this route as far as Baffin Island. Indeed, he mentions in his Travelogue that he sailed on one journey some "40 days" east of Siberia. This would have brought his vessel to the region of Hudson Bay. It was in this locality that Marco Polo reported an unusual phenomenon. While sailing north by compass, he says in Book I (Chapter 51) of Travels that he noticed that the needle of the compass was pointing north, while at the same time, the Pole Star seemed to have "a southerly bearing."

It is evident from this observation that Marco Polo had reached a point along the Northwest Passage where his expedition was directly north of Hudson Bay. It is in this region of the Arctic where the magnetic compass plays tricks on mariners. That is because the magnetic compass does not actually point towards the North Pole, it really points towards an invisible "Magnetic Pole" that migrates around the region of Hudson Bay. Marco's observation in the Travelogue is the first indication that European explorers were becoming confused in their direction of travel due to a phenomenon of Nature called "magnetic declination," or "magnetic variation." Chinese astronomers had become aware of this phenomenon by the 10th century; however, there was no way at the time to calculate how this "trick" of Nature might impact navigation in distant seas.

The accurate portrayal of Baffin Island on the so-called "Yale Vinland Map" probably derives from this expedition of the Yuan Chinese mariners in the 13th century. Although the origins of the map remain controversial and obscure, it is generally believed that a Swiss Franciscan compiled the document from a collection of earlier maps around 1440 AD.

While one contingent of Yuan explorers mapped the Canadian Arctic along the Mackenzie River Valley to Lake Conibaz (or Great Bear Lake); another group charted the Alaskan coast southwards past the Tlingit villages of modern-day British Columbia and on to the Haida villages of Nootka Island. This is the same island that George Vancouver renamed in his own honor in 1792. Yuan surveyors mapped the ocean gulf that is known today as Puget Sound and the Straits of Juan de Fuca. According to Marco Polo's secret code, the latitude of this gulf was 48° N—and that is right on target. His code and maps made the importance of this gulf as an access point to native exports was obvious to later explorers.

Marco Polo wrote in his journals about the products of the land, the trading practices of the natives, and the nature of the local currency. He also noted the unusual costumes, the exotic foods, and the bizarre sexual practices of the primitive people. It was also Marco's job as Ambassador to conduct the formal ceremony of territorial recognition. According to Kublai Khan's instructions, Marco's presentation of gifts such as iron tools, textiles, hemp, and bags of brass coins constituted an offer to become a trading partner of the Chinese. When tribal elders offered gifts in return, this gift-exchange was regarded as an acknowledgment of the status of the Khan as "the Son of Heaven." From that moment forward, the region was officially known in China as a "Province of the Realm." Unlike the European practice of declaring ownership of native lands—and then forcing natives to adopt European religion, customs, and clothing, the Yuan Chinese simply wanted loyal trading partners.

Marco Polo named the Northwest Coast region "Quivira Province." He settled upon this name because all the natives in this region used primitive bows-and-arrows that they carried in leather bags. In the Franco-Italian language that was used in Venice, these bags were called *quivers*. In the 16th century, the Flemish geographer Gerhard Mercator used Marco Polo's name for this region of the West Coast for all his maps of North America. He called it "Quivira Province"—indicating an awareness that it was an official territory of the Mongol Chinese.

Farther south, the Yuan mariners came upon the mouth of the Columbia River. It is quite apparent that Marco Polo's team of surveyors spent a great deal of time exploring this region of modern-day Oregon because a detailed map of the Columbia River Valley and the Willamette River Valley was among the documents that Marco Polo smuggled back to Venice in 1295. Subsequently, the Oregon map turned up in the studio of the English master geographer John Dee. Eventually, the map played a key role in the secret voyage of Francis Drake to the Pacific Northwest—but that is a tale of adventure we shall enjoy in a late chapter.

Kublai Khan's Expeditionary Forces were charged with more than just mapping new territories and conducting the ceremonies of provincial recognition. They were also expected to collect samples of the valuable exports that Chinese merchants were importing back to the Yuan Empire in violation of the customs regulations. In other words, Chinese merchants didn't pay taxes on items that they didn't declare to the harbormasters back in China.

It was also customary for the Khan's forces to be on the lookout for unusual animals that would be of some interest in the royal zoo. It is therefore not surprising that the Yuan explorers brought back some of the indigenous horses that they found in the region of Lake Conibaz in Central Canada. At the time, this region was home to the Nemepo (or Nez Perce), the Wachipones, the Lakota, and to Mongolian immigrants who had fled from Genghis Khan. The most distinctive horses from this New World breed have a unique "spotted blanket pattern" on their hind quarters. European explorers dubbed these beautiful horses "Appaloosas" because they were abundant in the Paluse region of Washington and Oregon. Horses with the "spotted blanket" markings first make their appearance on Chinese silk paintings during the Yuan Dynasty of Kublai Khan.

South of Oregon, Marco Polo's surveyors mapped a territory that seemed like a huge island. It appears on numerous Venetian maps prior to the 16th century European "discovery" of California—yet that is precisely what it represents. This geographical enigma of "Island California" is how Yuan Chinese geographers initially conceived of the West Coast of North America. At the moment, all the evidence suggests that the name "California" derives from the expeditions of Marco Polo. The name is a combination of the Latin word *cali* (meaning beautiful) with the word *fornia* (meaning island in front of a continent). In any case, the name emerges in 15th century French romantic literature in reference to an exotic island of women in the South Seas. Supposedly, the lesbian leader of this cannibalistic paradise was Queen *Califa*.

Marco Polo's name for the Gulf of California was *Mar de Vermil*— which translates as "the Vermilion Sea." Another enigma of ancient American discovery is that the Gulf of California was actually called by this name—*Mar Vermil*—for several centuries. It was only updated to "the Gulf of California" after modern geographers couldn't figure out where the ancient name had ever come from. They were baffled; and for the most part, they are still in the dark regarding the origin of this mysterious name.

The reason why Marco Polo chose this name was because the natives in this region produced a valuable red dye; it was a dye that was called in Marco's Franco-Italian language *vermilion*. This dye was extremely valuable; and it was extremely difficult to produce. Mexican peasant women obtained the remarkable vermilion ink by collecting and processing the tiny dried bodies of cochineal bugs. These bugs infest the prickly pear cactus whose ancient habitat was primarily the Sonoran Desert along the coast of the Vermilion Sea of Western Mexico. In the

16th century, an alternative name for this dye was "cochineal." This name ultimately derives from the Cochin merchants of India.

Vermilion ink was used to mark the Emperor's seal on Yuan Dynasty paper money. Marco Polo described the ink and the paper money in his Travelogue. However, he didn't say where the dye came from because that information was a secret. Keep in mind that the dye was more valuable than gold. It was not until the Spanish conqueror Hernan Cortés reached the Gulf of California in 1534 that Europeans finally learned the source of the valuable red dye that was mentioned in Marco's Book.

When the Yuan mariners reached the coast of Mexico, they found that the Toltec Empire was still in power; but it was under attack by nomadic warriors. Apparently, the rebellious Mixtec tribe had obtained a deadly new kind of weapon by trading with Asian merchants along the Pacific Coast. It was the "composite" or "laminated" bow.

The Mixtec chronicles of the 15th century portrayed how these new weapons enabled their ancestors, a band of "rag-tag" Indians, to overcome the powerful armies of the Toltecs. The Mixtex Codex (or picture book) illustrates how these powerful bows could shoot an arrow clear through a wooden shield and through the warrior standing on the other side. The Toltec soldiers, though elegantly dressed in feather uniforms, were armed only with shields, spears and *macans*. These macans were a primitive type of Mexican sword that consisted of a flat piece of wood lined with sharp glass. They were horribly deadly weapons in close combat; but the Toltec soldiers could never get close enough to their "barbarian" opponents to take advantage of their superior numbers and their military training. Indeed, as the Codex illustrates, the Mixtec warriors gathered outside a Toltec City until the local garrison assembled on the battlefield. Then, from a safe distance, the Mixtec archers let fly a deadly barrage of arrows that completely flattened the ranks of Toltec soldiers. Next, the Mixtecs collected their arrows from the bodies of their vanquished opponents; and they prepared to march on the next garrison. Within a dozen years, the Empire collapsed. When Europeans arrived on the shores of Mexico a century later, the success of the Mixtec ancestors was legendary—but the champions never learned the secret technology of the bow-makers; and so, they were virtually defenseless against the new invaders from abroad.

Marco Polo identified the West Coast of Mexico as the Province of the Toloman—that is, the Toltecs—and it appears under this name on the Flemish maps by Mercator in the 16th century.

Marco mentions in his Travelogue that he made a voyage to the "East Indies." This is probably a cryptic name for isles in the South Seas that included Australia, New Zealand and even Peru. Marco used the words "Other World," "Land of Gold," and "Land of Brasilwood" when referring to these isles. He clearly differentiated between the exotic red dyewood of Brazil and the more tepid sappan dyewood of East Asia. The term "Other World" is precisely what the Romans had used in reference to the Antipodes or South America. It is hardly a coincidence that Columbus used that very same word in reference to the new southern continent that was known as the *Mundus Novus* (or "New World") in the 16th century. At that point in time, nobody in Europe doubted that Marco Polo had already been to the Antipodes and to Mexico.

Marco Polo's map of this region, or rather the map that was produced by Persian cartographers, was inserted southeast of Asia on the world map by the Venetian cartographer Albertin DeVirga. The precise date of this map is somewhat uncertain—as the last number was blurred beyond recognition. Nobody in academia has ever questioned the authenticity of this map; but the dates given for its composition range from 1410 to about 1420. DeVirga referred to this continental island southeast of Asia as *Caparu sive India Magna*. Notice that part of this name is "paru." The western shoreline of Caparu shows a close parallel to the actual coastline of Peru. It is easy to see that the name "paru" was known to at least some privileged geographers prior to the arrival in Peru of the Spanish conqueror Francisco Pizarro in the 1520s. Modern textbooks wrongly credit Pizarro with naming the land. It was already named on Chinese maps and their Venetian copies. Considering the placement of this isle on the Venetian map, there is the distinct possibility that the land area was also intended to represent Australia.

Immediately following his voyage to the East Indies, Marco Polo's father devised a strategy to get the Franciscan espionage team back to Europe. This scheme involved using the Khan's own relatives as justification for their departure from the Yuan Empire. It was the only conceivable way to escape the Khan's strict authority. Niccolò offered the services of his son as the leader of an escort that would transport a new wife for the Khan's brother who was the Ilkhan of Persia. Three Persian barons had already made one attempt to escort the bride by way of the overland camel route called the Silk Road. However, this had failed because of the numerous rebels who blocked their passage.

Niccolò Polo suggested to the Emperor that he consider a new route by sea around the rebel forces. He stressed that his son, Marco, had proven himself an effective leader of naval expeditions; and his loyalty to the Khan was above reproach. The Khan never would have approved such a plan—but he had no choice but to grant his authorization when his desperate relatives insisted that there was no alternative.

And so, the three Venetian spies departed in 1292 from the Mongol Empire. Their so-called "jewel-peddling" enterprise had lasted nearly 35 years. Marco served as "Fleet Admiral" of the expedition which meant that he had the final say on matters of policy and destination. The actual sailing commanders were drawn from the ranks of the finest captains in the Chinese Navy. Their command consisted of 14 huge ships and about 3,000 men. Along the way, they had to battle with pirates; they endured lightning storms at sea; and they had to elude the customary undersea hazards of shoals, reefs, and shallows. According to Marco's Travelogue, six hundred men and two of the barons perished before they reached the

Persian Gulf. However, the expedition would have to be counted as a "success" because they managed to bring Princess Kogatin safely to her new home in Hormuz.

By this point in time, the Polos were loaded down with a considerable wealth in precious gems, incense, Persian rugs, spices, and assorted valuables from the Far East that they intended to sell back in Venice. They stowed this merchandise on camels and headed for Constantinople.

New World Voyages by the Venetian Navy

Upon their return to Venice in 1295, the Polo Brothers and Marco reported to the Naval Arsenal. This was the customary procedure any time an overseas traveler arrived in the region. It gave the Naval Commandant and the Council of Ten an opportunity to debrief travelers on any information that might be of importance to the State. In this manner, the Venetian government sought to preserve its prestige as the preeminent arbiter of Far Eastern goods in the Mediterranean.

Most likely, it was at this time that the Naval Commandant confiscated all of Marco Polo's maps. He was also required to swear an oath that he would not write about his travels in the service of Kublai Khan. He was also instructed to remain silent regarding any secrets that might compromise the Venetian advantages in foreign commerce. Otherwise, he was free to disclose anything that he fancied regarding the exotic societies that he had visited in the Far East. As a consequence of his oath before the Venetian Council, Marco Polo abandoned his hopes of writing a comprehensive book about Asia and the New World. Such a book would have been of considerable value to merchants and missionaries; but that was not in the cards. He also relinquished a pile of books and inventions that provided details regarding such important Chinese inventions as magnetic compasses, astrolabes, muskets, gunpowder, mechanical clocks, steel blast furnaces, metal rolling mills, printing inks, textile weaving machines, water wheels, steam engines, and other devices that improved manufacturing, shipbuilding and navigation.

These devices, all of which were regarded as "secret technologies," were placed in the hands of engineers and chemists who worked *sub rosa* within the confines of the Arsenal. Only the most trusted agents were ever allowed to monitor the ongoing experiments with Chinese inventions. Besides being concerned with the threat of technological theft, the Venetians realized that Church officials regarded many of the experimental devices as being of a "demonic nature." Rumors circulated regarding the goings on inside the Arsenal; but only those with the highest security clearance were allowed to know the full extent of the operation.

Under the auspices of the Council of Ten, secret inventions were on occasion released into the Black Markets or given to military allies. Maps of New World lands surfaced wherever it suited the commercial interests of the State. Thus, European historians are moved to comment about the so-called "sudden emergence" of Chinese inventions in Western Europe. These inventions surfaced mostly in Northern Italy. And they emerged upon the scene *fully-developed*—as though they were somehow conjured up from the furnaces of Hell. Indeed, they were invented in a sort of hell— in the furnaces and laboratories of the alchemists, the Masons, and the smiths. Only the Commandant knew the identities of the secret scientists who labored in the Arsenal.

The prohibition against writing about his travels left Marco free to discuss many of the exotic sexual practices, strange animals, and unusual natural phenomena that he had witnessed overseas. He was also under no official restraint when telling stories about the splendors of Kublai Khan's palace or the wonders of Yuan Chinese government. Thus, Marco embellished tales about the Khan's enormous harem of thousands of damsels; he elaborated on the details of the enormous birthday celebrations that were held in the Khan's honor; and he expounded upon the enormous wealth of the Khan in paper money worth. This paper fortune, Marco insisted, was worth "millions-and-millions" of gold ducats. This reference to the Khan's paper fortune is probably the source of an irritating nickname that hounded Marco Polo until his death. Wherever he traveled in Venice, he was ridiculed as *El Milione*—"the Millionaire."

Since paper money hadn't been invented yet in Europe, the notion that merchants might accept a piece of paper as having any worth at all struck Italians as being about the most absurd thing that they could ever imagine. After Marco told stories about "rocks that burned," cloth that was impervious to flames, and nuts the size of a person's head, most ordinary folks thought he was crazy. We know in modern times that Marco was simply referring to coal, asbestos, and coconuts—all of which seem quite ordinary to us. However, among the provincial Venetians, these bizarre rocks and plants all seemed like ludicrous concoctions from the imaginative mind of Marco Polo. He soon gained fame throughout Italy as the "greatest exaggerator" of all time. That title caused Marco and his family to endure great shame when he appeared in public—but it served well the interests of the Venetian Council of Ten. Marco's popular reputation as a "storyteller," meant that they could rest assured that nobody would believe anything serious that he might inadvertently say about Golden Lands overseas.

Meanwhile, the Venetian Council took serious interest in what Marco Polo had to say about the source of a valuable commodity called "brasilwood." Ever since the 12th century, port documents in Italy mentioned two very similar cargoes that were brought in by ships from overseas. One of these was brasilwood and the other was known as *grano de brasil*—or "grain" of Brasil. In both cases, the commodity was characterized as an import from a land someplace overseas that was known as "Brasil." However, nobody in Venice seemed to know where this land was located. The wood import was a cheap source of red dye; and this red dye was an essential ingredient in the wool industry. The "grain" was what Italian merchants first called the dried bodies of cochineal bugs. Indeed, the dried bugs do look a lot like grains of rice or seeds; and some Italians even tried to grow what they hoped would be vermilion trees by planting the so-called "grains" in soil. Of course, nothing sprouted.

During the 13th century, there was a heavy traffic in brasilwood from the Far East across the Indian Ocean. So, many people believed that the dyewood came from someplace in Asia. Historians have mistakenly assumed that "brasilwood" was simply another name for the prolific sappan wood of Malaya. However, the Asian dye was inferior in terms of its depth of color and its durability. Indeed, Marco Polo took great pains to distinguish the two varieties of dyewood.

In the 15th century, French authorities determined that the red dyewood was coming into Europe in ships manned by Irish crews. It is hardly surprising, therefore, that European cartographers presumed the existence of an Island of Brasil directly southwest of Ireland. Although there is no such island in that location, it serves as a clue to the secret voyages that were being made across the Atlantic Ocean to Brazil.

If we go back in time to the 13th century reign of King Haakon IV of Norway, we will immediately see why the Norse declaration of sovereignty over the Western Isles in 1261 was such a catastrophic event for the merchants of the North Sea. For many centuries, the Celts, the Basques, the Irish, and the Germans had sailed across the North Atlantic in order to take advantage of the abundant fish, copper, timber, and fur resources of the Maritime Provinces and the region that later became known as New England. If brasilwood was being brought to Europe in Irish and Norwegian vessels, as seems to have been the case, then it had to be transported through the Norse harbors in the New England region which was then called Dusky Norway or Great Ireland.

Since the Western Isles were typically reached by sailing on a route that went due north by compass bearings, there was a common misunderstanding that these isles were somehow situated around the North Pole. In fact, they were actually close to the Magnetic North Pole in the vicinity of Hudson Bay. Mariners depended upon the magnetic compass for sailing in the summer months because the Pole Star was concealed behind the blazing summer sun in the Arctic Regions. And the usual route of travel was from Scotland or the Orkneys Islands "north" to Iceland—then "north" to the New Land.

King Haakon IV and the Norwegians actually called the region of the Western Isles by the name of *Landanu* or *Nyaland*—meaning "New Land." Even though Norwegian authorities knew that the so-called "New Land" was situated southwest of Iceland, the official Norwegian maps of this time period indicated that these lands were *north* of Norway. By calling this region "New Land," Norwegian officials hoped to conceal the fact that the ancient mariners had been sailing to these isles for many centuries. These isles were actually the legendary Western Isles of the

English King Arthur that King Haakon IV hoped to claim through geographical magic.

The Norwegian claim was buttressed by a papal decree. Indeed, a grateful pope wished to reward King Haakon IV for his role in the Crusades—so the Norwegian claim was given a papal endorsement. The Vikings had come a long way from being cursed in European churches as the "Scourge of Satan" (in the 9th century) to becoming the "Champions of the Faith" in the 13th century.

Papal endorsements and geographical deception were major factors in the bogus Norwegian claim to the Western Isles. However, of even greater importance was the Norwegian Navy. During the 13th century, the Norwegians had the most powerful navy in all of Europe; and scores of armed cutters—the dreaded "dragon ships"—patrolled the coastal waters.

Following Marco Polo's return from China, the Venetian Council devised a secret plan to circumvent and to undermine the Norwegian monopoly over the Western Isles. It is even conceivable that Marco Polo was called upon once more to lead the espionage teams that were involved in this operation. During the early years of the 14th century, he was engaged in the metal trade with England. It was an appropriate disguise for a Venetian agent since the annual fleet of galleons that sailed from Venice carrying Chinese silks, spices, and porcelains sailed to ports in Flanders and then on to London.

It would have been a rather simple matter for an ordinary merchant ship heading for London to "fall behind" the fleet and then sail out into the North Sea. If by chance the vessel was intercepted and hailed by a Norwegian cutter, then the captain could plead that he was "lost" and that contrary winds or "a tempest" were to blame.

It is also conceivable that the Venetian explorers sailed directly west of the Canary Islands along a route later followed by the Portuguese. Marco Polo was already familiar with the patterns of circular ocean currents in the Pacific Ocean; so it is possible that Venetian explorers assumed that a similar mid-ocean current would carry them directly westward to Brazil.

We do know that the Venetians implemented their scheme to undermine the Norwegians, because they managed to map the Carolinas, Florida, and the Gulf of Mexico in the early 14th century. In about the year 1310, the Venetian cartographer Marino Sanudo completed a map showing a region called "Tartary." This "Tartary" was a name that Marco Polo used for Mongolia. On Sanudo's map, it was situated directly west of Europe. The configuration of the coastline includes a southeast peninsula (Florida), adjacent isles (the Antilles), and a western gulf (the Gulf of Mexico). Historians accept this map as being "genuine;" however they have completely overlooked the distinctive features of the Florida Peninsula and the Carolina coasts on this map. North of Tartary, the cartographer indicated the location of "Albania." This was a clear reference to the Colony of Albion that King Arthur had established during the 6th century in the region of Nova Scotia.

The Venetian voyages to this region were secret. We hear nothing of Marco Polo's involvement nor of any Venetian captains who announced "new discoveries in the west." What we do see from this daring and highly-effective endeavor is the Sanudo Map. Manuscript copies of this map were pasted into hundreds of manuscript copies of a document called *Liber Secretorum Fidelium Crucis*–that is, "the Book of Secrets for True Believers in the Cross." Publication of this book dates to the 1320s. With such a title, and timed to coincide with a new Crusade to the Holy Lands, the book was certain to achieve widespread circulation throughout Europe.

Those who examined the map were certain to notice the location of the legendary Albania (or Albion) directly west of England. There were many rumors circulating about this region overseas. Some people said that it was the "Isle of Avalon"—the resting ground of King Arthur. It was the "Earthly Paradise—the Elysian Fields," said the Greek sailors. It was "the Breas Ail," insisted the Irish bards, and the "Promised Land" of Saint Brendan the Navigator. Such rumors, which were doubtless encouraged by Venetian agents, were intended to encourage French, German, and English farmers to migrate across the ocean. In spite of the Nordic patrols, many of these immigrants were certain to succeed in breaching the blockade.

An enormous quantity of ancient European artifacts found throughout the New England region and the East Coast reveals that many European immigrants succeeded in eluding Norwegian patrols. Once ashore, they set up hillforts and began farming the land. Indian tribes in this locale were active trading partners—because they desperately needed the metal tools and textiles that arrived with European farmers.

It appears from the Sanudo (or Vesconte) map that the Venetian Council hoped to burden the Norwegian government with so many alien ships and farmers that it would be unable to prevent merchants from gaining access to Brazil. The attention that was given to mapping Florida and the Antilles suggests that the Venetians hoped to establish way stations at harbors in this region for ships that were hauling back cargoes of brasilwood from South America.

Unfortunately, the World Plague of 1340-1360 effectively halted the plans that the Venetians had for developing New World resources. That effort would have to wait for a better time in the future.

What do Historians Think?

Western historians have never been very enthusiastic about the legacy of Marco Polo. Perhaps there has always been an unconscious fear among the more dogmatic scholars that the public would wonder about the true identity of his "Other World," his "Land of Brasilwood," his "Land of Gold," and his "Countries East of Japan." Sooner or later, somebody was bound to question the anomalies of the history books.

Back in the 1550s, the Scribe of the Venetian Senate, John Baptist Ramusio, wrote a book about Marco Polo's voyages and the voyages of other prominent Venetians. He included a popular tale about the Zeno Brothers who had sailed to "Islands" west of Iceland in 1380. In other words, they had reached the American continent ahead of Columbus. At the time, Ramusio believed that Genoese historians were promoting the legacy of Columbus in such a way that detracted from the exploits of Marco Polo. It was his contention that the voyages of Columbus paled by comparison with the travels of Marco Polo. He even went so far as to assert that the Venetian traveler had reached the New World ahead of the Genoese hero.

Ramusio was right on target with his concern that the academic scholars of Genoa and her allies were making a concerted and a fraudulent effort to propagandize the study of history. However, his opponents were graduates of Church sponsored universities; and they pointed out that Ramusio lacked the credentials of a certified historian. They also savaged his "evidence"—claiming that a map by the Zeno Brothers was a hoax and that the inaccuracies of Marco Polo's account of the Far East had cast doubt on the possibility that the Venetian had ever traveled to China. Some suggested that the entire Travelogue consisted of stories that Polo had plagiarized from other journalists. Over the passing centuries, Columbus became something of a "cult hero" in academia. Many scholars expounded the glories of their champion as though they were cheering the home team at a sporting event.

In subsequent years, it became quite a popular pastime among isolationist scholars to trash the reputations of Ramusio, Marco Polo, and the Zeno Brothers. Meanwhile, the so-called "authorities: praised the Genoese Columbus as a superhero. He was frequently given credit for achievements that somebody else had done—such as proving the earth is round, noting magnetic variation, bringing the first maize back from the New World, etc. Being part of the Columbus Bandwagon was likened to a test of national loyalty. Those who suggested that other mariners had sailed to the New World ahead of the Genoese Champion were accused of being anti-American. Western academics virtually cheered in 1995 when Frances Wood, a former head of the British Library, once again raised the issue: "Did Marco Polo Go to China?"

The premise of Ms. Wood's best-selling book was that Marco Polo was a clever liar who never left Venice. This conclusion, made by a popular champion of the Columbus Team, was based on the fact that Marco's *Book of Travels* failed to mention the Great Wall, chopsticks, foot-binding, or the ubiquitous tea ceremony. However, historian John Larner published a definitive scholarly response regarding Marco Polo's Asian exploits. His book, *Marco Polo and the Discovery of the World* (1999), effectively said "nuts" to Ms. Wood's contrived masterpiece. The Great Wall, he noted, was reconstructed during the Ming Dynasty—long after the travels of the Venetian writer. Furthermore, Marco Polo had spent his time mostly with Mongol officials. In their company, the Chinese tea ceremony, chopsticks, and foot-binding were not such a big deal. Larner added that the presence of Kublai Khan's Golden Passport among the possessions of Marco Polo following his death was solid proof that he had acted, just as he claimed, as the roving agent of Kublai Khan.

On the other hand, it must be admitted that the *Book of Marco Polo's Travels* does contain many significant errors. These are errors that one would not expect if the Venetian had made a serious effort to accurately report *everything* that he had witnessed in the Orient. For example, he says that Japan was located 1,500 miles east of China. Now this was a huge error. Somehow, that error got incorporated into Portuguese maps in the 15th century; and they greatly confused Columbus who was seeking to reach Japan in 1493. Actually, Japan is situated only 500 miles distant from China—and the direction is not east but northeast.

Anybody seeking to find Japan, where Marco Polo said it was located in his Travelogue, would simply wind up sailing to nowhere in the middle of the ocean. While it might seem on the surface that Marco Polo didn't have the foggiest notion of where Japan was located, the reality is that it was his job as a spy to introduce a little "fog" here-and-there. By reporting inaccurate information, he was able to confuse the rivals of Venice who might try to take advantage of the sailing directions to Japan in order to set up their own maritime commerce. Come to think of it, that is precisely what the Genoese Columbus had in mind—that is, taking advantage of the Venetian report regarding the location of Japan. And Columbus wound up getting lost. That was precisely what Marco Polo had intended in the first place—to mislead the commercial rivals of Venice. In other words, his method was extremely successful. He was so successful, in fact, that even modern historians are confused by what he said in his famous Book.

In any case, the Marco Polo maps in the Marcian Rossi Collection clearly show Japan in the right location—500 miles northeast of China. The key, here, is looking at all the evidence as well as the cultural context of the times. According to an independent scholar of Balkans History, Victor DeMattei, the Venetian Council was extremely concerned about preserving commercial and military advantages. Anyone who had the far-reaching intelligence that Marco Polo had acquired would have been subject to review by the Naval Commandant and by the Council. If Marco Polo had failed in his responsibilities to the State, he could have been dealt with severely—perhaps killed or even thrown alive into a canal with a chain wrapped around his legs.

A potential breakthrough in learning the real story of the secret voyages to the New World occurred in 1933. A San Diego Italian businessman named Marcian Rossi became aware of some family heirlooms—that is, letters and maps—relating to the legacy of Marco Polo. Rossi subsequently offered one of the maps to a prominent scholar for his inspection. The map was pronounced as being "genuine;" and since it was a general map of Asia, the scholar expressed his opinion that this document from the Rossi Collection proved that Marco Polo had been to China. A number of articles on the subject appeared in a San Diego newspaper and in the New York Times. After this momentary burst of attention, the subject of Marco Polo's New World maps sort of simmered down in academia. Several years later, Rossi obtained a larger collection from his ancestors; and these documents including several more maps were loaned to the Library of Congress for examination.

Several years passed by without any report being issued by the staff at the Library of Congress. The slow response was due mainly to the controversial nature of the documents and the traditional bias in academia favoring the glorification of Christopher Columbus. However, this time, a rather curious historian from Sweden by the name of Leo Bagrow took a personal interest in the Rossi Collection.

After spending nearly ten years fighting his way through the bureaucratic bottleneck of the Library administration, Professor Bagrow finally gained access to the Rossi Collection. He was amazed by what he saw. The Collection included several letters from Marco Polo's daughters Bellela and Moretta Polo. There were also a number of maps—some of which Bellela had traced on vellum (or sheepskin), some were traced by Moretta, and a number of truly remarkable maps were in the script used by a contemporary and friend of Marco Polo—the Venetian Admiral Roger Sanseverinus. None of the maps were examples of Marco Polo's own handwriting—which is consistent with the notion that he was forced to relinquish all his original Chinese maps to the Venetian authorities.

Admiral Sanseverinus made copies of two Yuan Chinese maps directly from Marco Polo's original documents. They distinctly showed the Peninsula of Alaska. That is, there was clear documentation that Marco Polo had participated in the mapping of the New World prior to the voyages of Columbus. Of course, a number of conservative scholars at the Library of Congress did not like Bagrow's assessment that the documents were "genuine." They insisted upon including the views of skeptics in a review that was published in the journal *Imago Mundi* in 1946 (Volume V). It was the opinion of the orthodox scholars that the sections of the map showing New World territories (that is Alaska and the West Coast) must have been copied from maps that James Cook drew in the 18th century.

In order to validate or disprove that claim, the author compared the "Map with Ship" from the Rossi Collection with the maps of the North Pacific that had been produced by Captain James Cook. If the opinion of the skeptics had been true, then there should have been considerable similarity between the coastlines shown on both maps. However, there was none. Maps by Captain Cook also indicated a perpendicular strait separating the coast of Siberia from the coast of Alaska. Actually, the Strait of Anian on the Marco Polo map was at an oblique angle slanting to the east. It is apparent that this oblique angle on the map was the result of a land survey that failed to allow for the great amount of magnetic declination—up to 90°E—along the coast of Alaska. All of James Cook's maps were adjusted for this extreme degree of magnetic error *before* they were ever published. The fact that the map from the Rossi Collection did not take into account this distinctive feature of geography is a certain indication that it was not a copy made from Captain Cook's map as the historians had claimed.

Thus far, all the evidence indicates that the maps in the Marcian Rossi Collection are genuine artifacts from the life and times of Marco Polo. So, one might reasonably wonder why the documents have never been released to the public; nor have they been adequately reviewed in scientific journals. The problem is that devotion to the doctrinaire hero, Columbus, and therefore—"the status quo," has led to some desperate measures to compromise the evidence. Supposedly, the fear of a "hoax" by the Rossi Family motivated officials at the Library of Congress to request a review by the Nation's Number One Spook—J. Edgar Hoover. Thereafter, orthodox historians, at least those who were aware of the existence of the Rossi Collection, have suggested that the maps are "tainted" simply because at one time in the past they "were investigated" by the Federal Bureau of Investigation. In other words, the mere fact that a single map was long ago referred to the FBI for analysis is used as a convenient excuse for dismissing the entire Collection without further consideration. Only Derek Hayes, in his landmark book of Pacific Cartography (1999), noted that the FBI had actually reported "no evidence" of a hoax.

Are maps to be regarded as "innocent" until proved guilty in a court of scientific inquiry? Or are innuendo and heresy sufficient grounds for burning the truth and ignoring the evidence? When historians collectively seek to discredit or conceal vital clues to the mysteries of the past, they are engaging in a form of historical deception and cultural assassination. If it is true, as they say, that "the Past is the key to the Future," then we had better be quite certain that we are getting our facts straight about what really happened in the Past.

Consequences for New World Exploration

One of the more incredible aspects of Marco Polo's legacy is the startling rise of his popularity during the 15th century. Historians celebrate the beginning of a New Era of rational thinking, artistic genius, and technological advancement that is called "the Renaissance." Marco Polo's Book played a key role in the emergence of this remarkable intellectual transformation from out of the rubble of the Middle Ages.

If we carefully consider all the evidence, we realize the many reasons why Marco Polo's Book became so popular. To begin with, the Book was carefully crafted upon the principles of both the "scientific method" and "good business" practices as they were expounded in the writings of the Mystic Franciscan—Roger Bacon. Secondly, Marco's journalistic format consisted of a series of episodes involving travels to exotic lands. They were the forerunner of the modern style of adventure travel literature. These episodes, or Chapters, made the Book a convenient and enjoyable method of introducing the illiterate commoners of Europe to the joys of reading. And Third, Marco Polo's Book, and the secrets that he revealed to his daughters, served as an inspiration to the aristocratic ladies of Italy.

Following Marco Polo's death, his three daughters, Bellela, Moretta, and Fantina, were in great demand at the salons of the fashionable ladies of Verona and Florence. These Cities became known as the "hothouses of the Renaissance" because it was in this region where the earliest flames of the New Era began to leap upwards. It was the common practice in Northern Italy for the men to engage in business activities while the women attended to domestic affairs. However, the men didn't want their daughters to just sit about the home and do nothing worthwhile. Instead, they encouraged the interests of their wives and daughters in socializing and learning about music, the arts, and the world—as these would give them social skills that would eventually make them more attractive as dining partners or as potential wives. So, the salons gained the full support of the business leaders who must have hoped that they would keep their wives "out of trouble" while they attended to business. Well, they were dead wrong about keeping them out of trouble.

The women's salons were a place where the older ladies instructed their protégés in the social graces. They also indulged in bedroom politics, the unveiling of erotic art, and the reading of avant-garde poetry. In this setting, the "Three Sisters" of the Polo Family were a big hit. They gained popularity because they revealed the secrets of their father's New World voyages to "Forbidden Lands;" they described the strange beasts that he encountered; and they exposed scandalous details of the exotic sexual practices that he had witnessed in the South Seas. In their words, the mermaids came to life; the gala parties of the Khan inspired their wildest fantasies; and their father's exploits among cannibals, pirates, and Indians made them tremble with vicarious excitement. And wherever they traveled, the ladies marveled at how much the Three Sisters reminded them of the "Three Graces" of Greco-Roman mythology. It was as though the spirits of a bygone era—the era of the Greek Goddesses had come forth to inspire them to dream about the Future.

Many of the aristocratic Italian ladies were eventually married off to the princes and business leaders of Northern Europe. This practice invariably placed them in positions of great social, cultural, and political influence. The Medici Family ladies in particular counted among their husbands many dukes and several kings. Two of their children were popes. Wherever they went, they set about transforming the medieval behavior of their spouses into the civilized manners that the New Age required. Even more important, they taught their subjects how to read.

The emergence of the Renaissance in the 15th century was no accident. It was the gift of a creative spirit that was nurtured in the artist studios and the salons of Northern Italy.

It is no coincidence that printing presses came into common use throughout Europe during the early Renaissance; nor is it a coincidence that Marco Polo's Book was selected for widespread publication. It became, literally, the "Guide Book" of the Renaissance.

Marco Polo's Book was a testimonial to the bureaucratic genius, the technological wonders, and the commercial excellence of the Yuan Chinese people. This was a culture in which there were no "End Times." Indeed, the term *Yuan* that Kublai Khan had chosen for the name of his Dynasty meant "the Beginning of the Universe." At the time, Chinese society was an amalgamation of many cultures, many ethnic groups, and many religions. Thus it reflected the universal commercial enterprise that was a centerpiece of the Mystic philosophy. It was also the central theme of the secret cadre of European business leaders and intellectuals who actively promoted the publication and distribution of Marco Polo's Book.

In 1428, Prince Pedro of Portugal arrived at Venice seeking to obtain a copy of Marco Polo's Book—and any old maps that might be lying around at the Senate. The Chronicles of Venice reported that the Prince left with his arms full of useful documents. These would eventually play a vital role in the Portuguese effort to reach the Spice Islands and China ahead of their traditional European rivals—the Spaniards and the Genoese.

Columbus, John Cabot, Giovanni Verrazano, and practically every other hopeful explorer read Marco Polo's Book in hopes of learning the secret routes to the Orient. The fairytales about "Lands of Gold" that Marco Polo had intended to deceive Venetian rivals nevertheless served to inspire the efforts of New World explorers for several centuries.

Among the many Chinese inventions that the Polos brought back to Venice were muskets and mechanical clocks. Perhaps these two devices played a greater role in changing the landscape of history than anything else. Mechanical Clocks were the nemesis of the traditional Church control over Time. As long as church bells announced the passing hours, and monks monitored the falling sands in hourglasses, there endured the illusion that the priesthood had some vital role in controlling the hours and the days of God's Creation. The notion that Time would eventually "run out" like the sand in the hourglass was simply an analogy that was derived from the quintessential medieval device for keeping track of the hours.

However, the way that people thought about Time changed drastically the moment that mechanical clocks began ticking in Northern Italy. Soon the "infernal invention" spread throughout Europe. Many clock towers arose from the guildhalls—making it dramatically clear that Time was no longer "in the hands of the Church." It soon became apparent to everybody that Time and Destiny were in the hands of business leaders. At this point in the New Era, the hourglass became practically useless. Time no longer "ran out;" instead, it went on forever.

Before long, people began carrying "time" around in a vest pocket.

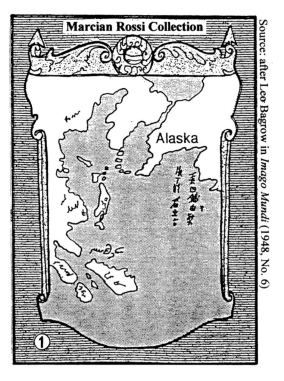

Marcian Rossi Collection

Alaska

Source: after Leo Bagrow in *Imago Mundi* (1948, No. 6)

presently in the Library of Congress Map Dept. Archive; see Thompson, 1994.

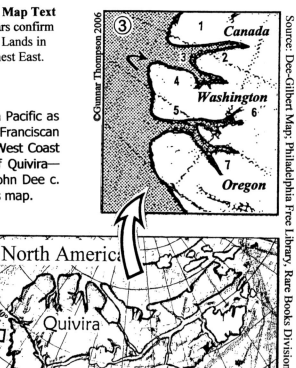

After a map in the Yale University Library

Yale Vinland Map c. 1440

Alaska

Sea of Tartars

NW Coast

East Indies

CHINA

California

Indies

*YV Map Text
Tartars confirm
New Lands in
Farthest East.

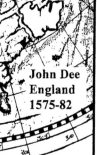

③

Canada

1

3

2

4

Washington

5

6

7

Oregon

©Gunnar Thompson 2006

Source: Dee-Gilbert Map: Philadelphia Free Library, Rare Books Division

Marco Polo's Maps

1) Marco's 1295 map of Alaska (Anian) and the North Pacific as copied by his friend, Admiral Roger Sanseverinus; 2) Franciscan map c. 1440 showing Mongol/Chinese discoveries of West Coast regions from Alaska to California; 3) Marco's map of Quivira— Puget Sound & Columbia River Valley as copied by John Dee c. 1575; 4) Marco's "Island California" as copied on Dee's map.

North America

Quivira

40°

40°

John Dee
England
1575-82

Island California

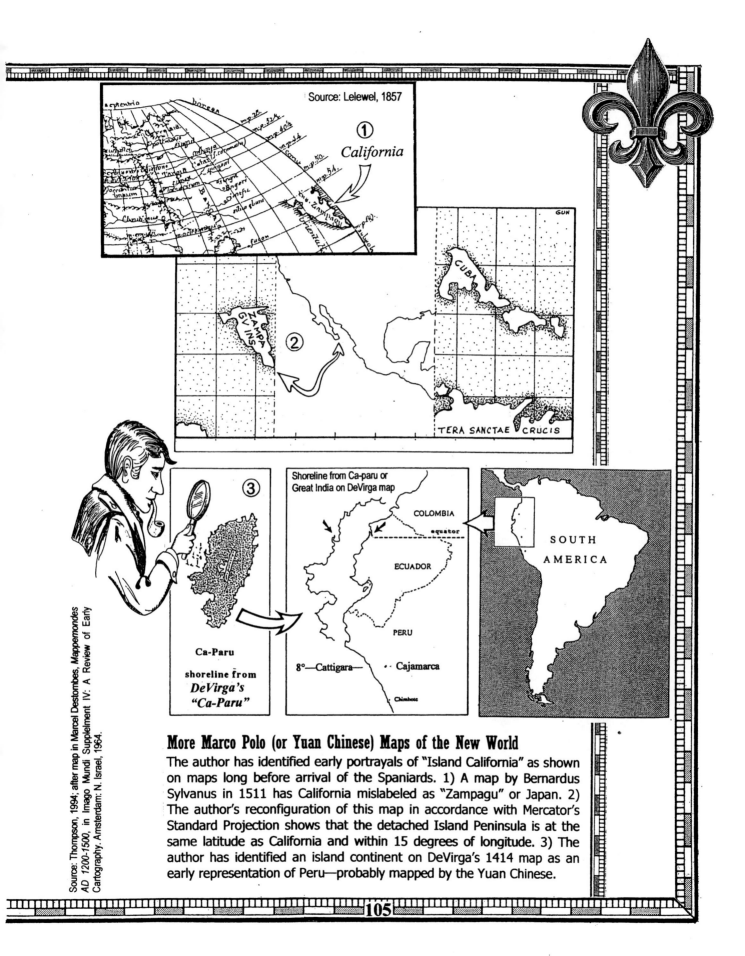

① California

②

TERA SANCTAE CRUCIS

③

Ca-Paru

shoreline from
DeVirga's
"Ca-Paru"

Shoreline from Ca-paru or
Great India on DeVirga map

COLOMBIA
equator
ECUADOR
PERU
8°—Cattigara— · Cajamarca
Chimbote

SOUTH
AMERICA

Source: Thompson, 1994; after map in Marcel Destombes, *Mappemondes AD 1200-1500*, in Imago Mundi Supplelment IV: A Review of Early Cartography. Amsterdam: N. Israel, 1964.

More Marco Polo (or Yuan Chinese) Maps of the New World

The author has identified early portrayals of "Island California" as shown on maps long before arrival of the Spaniards. 1) A map by Bernardus Sylvanus in 1511 has California mislabeled as "Zampagu" or Japan. 2) The author's reconfiguration of this map in accordance with Mercator's Standard Projection shows that the detached Island Peninsula is at the same latitude as California and within 15 degrees of longitude. 3) The author has identified an island continent on DeVirga's 1414 map as an early representation of Peru—probably mapped by the Yuan Chinese.

The Three Polo Sisters & the New World Discovery Seminars

Marco Polo's daughters, Bellela, Moretta, and Fantina toured the salons of Italy where they kept alive the legacy of his New World discoveries. Pictured above is a gathering of young intellectuals near Florence, Italy. The three Sisters evoked the spirit and vitality of the Greco-Roman fairies known as "The Three Graces" (below).

Three Graces after a painting by Francesco Cossa c.1500

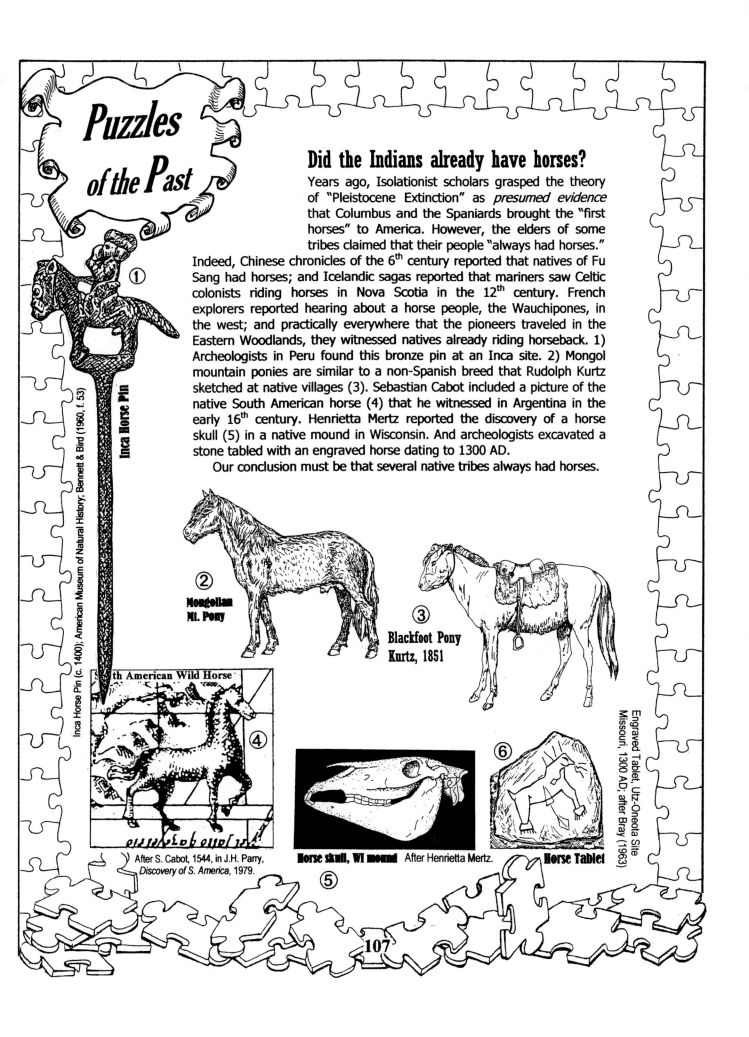

Puzzles of the Past

Did the Indians already have horses?

Years ago, Isolationist scholars grasped the theory of "Pleistocene Extinction" as *presumed evidence* that Columbus and the Spaniards brought the "first horses" to America. However, the elders of some tribes claimed that their people "always had horses." Indeed, Chinese chronicles of the 6th century reported that natives of Fu Sang had horses; and Icelandic sagas reported that mariners saw Celtic colonists riding horses in Nova Scotia in the 12th century. French explorers reported hearing about a horse people, the Wauchipones, in the west; and practically everywhere that the pioneers traveled in the Eastern Woodlands, they witnessed natives already riding horseback. 1) Archeologists in Peru found this bronze pin at an Inca site. 2) Mongol mountain ponies are similar to a non-Spanish breed that Rudolph Kurtz sketched at native villages (3). Sebastian Cabot included a picture of the native South American horse (4) that he witnessed in Argentina in the early 16th century. Henrietta Mertz reported the discovery of a horse skull (5) in a native mound in Wisconsin. And archeologists excavated a stone tabled with an engraved horse dating to 1300 AD.

Our conclusion must be that several native tribes always had horses.

① Inca Horse Pin

Inca Horse Pin (c. 1400); American Museum of Natural History; Bennett & Bird (1960, f. 53)

② **Mongolian Mt. Pony**

③ **Blackfoot Pony Kurtz, 1851**

④ South American Wild Horse

After S. Cabot, 1544, in J.H. Parry, *Discovery of S. America*, 1979.

⑤ **Horse skull, WI mound** After Henrietta Mertz.

⑥ **Horse Tablet**

Engraved Tablet, Utz-Oneota Site Missouri, 1300 AD; after Bray (1963)

107

Puzzles of the Past

How did the rag-tag Mixtecs conquer the mighty Toltecs?

At about the same time that the Yuan Chinese and Marco Polo were traveling along the Mexican coast, in the 12th and 13th centuries, a band of so-called "Northern barbarians" took on the soldiers of the Toltec Empire.

These ancestors of the Mixtec or Aztec peoples of Central Mexico boasted that they had a new kind of weapon—a powerful bow that could shoot arrows through shields and through the warriors standing on the other side. This was not a Mixtec invention; it was a device that was obtained through trade and never made by the local tribes as they lacked both the materials and technology. However, they used the weapon effectively in battle against Toltec soldiers who were armed only with the traditional weapons: spears and a sword-like *macan*—or mace. As shown in the *Mixtec Codex*, below, the barbarians simply marched from village to village. They decimated the local garrisons by launching arrows from their powerful (Mongol?) bows while still out of range of their opponents. Marco is shown (above, left) armed with a laminated Mongol horn bow. Because it was short and powerful, it was an effective weapon for use on horseback. This is the kind of weapon that enabled the Mixtec barbarians to defeat the armies of the Toltec Empire.

MARCO POLO

Mixtec Codex courtesy of the New York
Public Library, Rare Books Division

108

Puzzles of the Past

What inspired the origins of Indian Horse Culture?

When Marco Polo traveled along the West Coast between 1280 and 1290 AD, he called the region "Quivira Province" because all the indigenous peoples were familiar with the bow and arrow. They all had "quivers" for carrying this equipment. Most weapons were locally made; others were obtained through trade. By the 13th century, the Nez Percé (or Nemepo) and other tribes had learned or acquired the technology for making laminated bows from the horns of mountain sheep. These short, strong bows made it possible to hunt from horseback. The tribes that moved out onto the Plains of the West—developing a nomadic culture based on hunting buffalo—already had horses. What they needed to launch this cultural transformation was an effective weapon. Wherever the European pioneers traveled, they remarked that the natives already had a well-developed "Horse Culture." The influx of Mongol immigrants who were seasoned riders and breeders gave Plains Tribes many Mongol traits.

Thus, it was Native ingenuity and horses, not Columbus, that launched the march of the Native Americans across the Western Plains.

After Russell Curtis Painting, c. 1900

Plains Indian with Horn Bow

Mongolian rider

Karl Bodmer painting, courtesy of Smithsonian Institution Bureau of American Ethnology

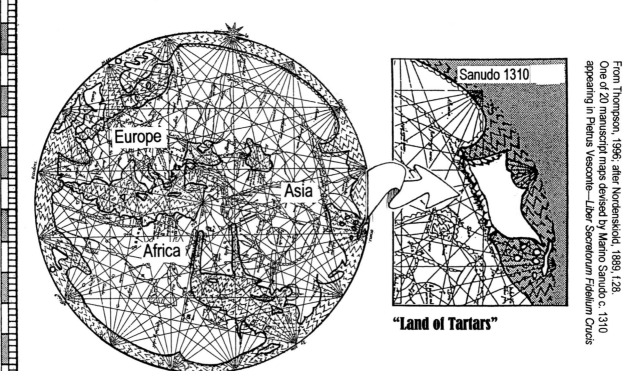

Sanudo 1310

"Land of Tartars"

From Thompson, 1996; after Nordenskiold, 1889, f.28.
One of 20 manuscript maps devised by Marino Sanudo c. 1310
appearing in Pietrus Vesconte—*Liber Secretorum Fidelium Crucis*

Marco Polo's Florida & Mermaids

While Marco Polo was still alive, and while he was engaged in the metals trade of the North Atlantic, a Venetian cartographer named Marino Sanudo prepared a map of Marco Polo's Far East that looks a lot more like Florida and the Antilles. This rather primitive map seems to represent a Venetian survey of the Gulf of Mexico—which was preliminary to building an overseas transport of valuable brasilwood (or dyewood) that came from the tropical forests of the region. Marco Polo's mention of the promiscuous young women of the "Other World" led European geographers to include images of mermaids on their maps of Florida and the South Seas.

Marco Polo

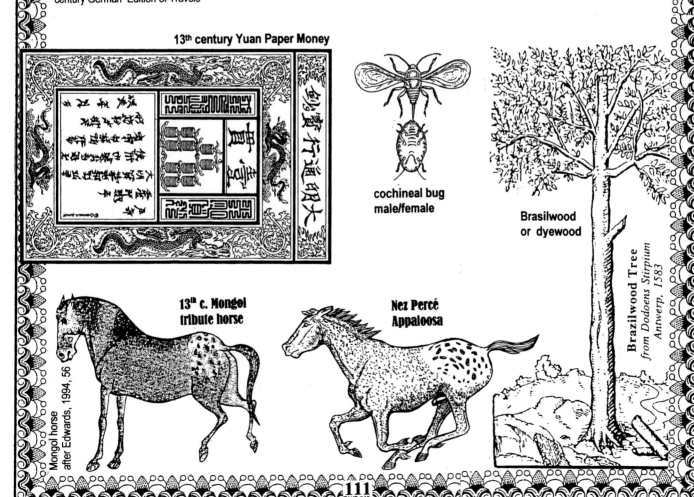

New World Imports in Yuan China

In his Travelogue, Marco Polo mentions that Chinese merchants engaged in voyages to countries *east* of Japan on expeditions lasting a whole year each way. The only countries east of Japan would have to be in the New World—along the West Coast. Marco mentions three imports from this region: red pearls, vermilion dye, and brasilwood (or dyewood) which he differentiates from the locally grown sappanwood. Vermilion dye came from cochineal bugs that inhabit the prickly pear cactus of the Sonoran Desert along the shores of the Gulf of California. In Polo's time, this gulf was known as "The Vermilion Sea"—because it was the source of a dye that was more valuable than gold. The Chinese used the dye for the emperor's stamp on formal documents and paper money. In about the year 1300, just after Marco's voyage to Canada and the Oregon coast, the Chinese artist Chou Meng-Fu painted a horse on silk that has been identified as an Appaloosa—a breed first developed by the Nez Percé Indians.

Marco Polo in the Far East
After an illustration in the 15th century German Edition of Travels

13th century Yuan Paper Money

cochineal bug
male/female

Brasilwood
or dyewood

Brazilwood Tree
from Dodoens Stirpium Antwerp, 1583

13th c. Mongol tribute horse

Mongol horse after Edwards, 1994, 56

Nez Percé Appaloosa

From *American Discovery* by Gunnar Thompson (1994).

NOVA SCOTIA—1230 AD

Unauthorized sailors from Scotland reach the shores of Norway's Forbidden Colonies.

Friar Nicholas and the Search for Avalon

BRAZEN NOSE is the name of a street running through the City of Oxford. It is also the first clue to solving a profound mystery that has haunted the English countryside for the past seven hundred years. Along this street in the Middle Ages, there lived a secretive English wizard. During both days and nights, he conducted such fearsome experiments that the earth trembled and the air erupted in a thunderous roar.

The Wizard's name was Roger Bacon.

Of all the friars who joined the ranks of the Franciscans, none has ever caused more mischief nor engineered more distress for his superiors than the illustrious Roger Bacon. Although his middle name was surely "Trouble," it may also be said in his favor that none have achieved greater notoriety as a scientist and as a philosopher than Friar Bacon.

Most often, he operated behind the scenes in the plots and scheming of a secretive group of Franciscans who are mentioned in the marginal notes of history as "the Mystics." He was identified early in life as a lad who was inventive and imaginative. His tutor, a gentleman who was equally on the edge of brilliance and insanity, was the renowned Grosseteste. The mentor was also a Franciscan and a professor at Oxford—which serves to explain how Friar Bacon wound up in the quiet student dormitories that lined the campus. Grosseteste's name is translated literally as "Big Balls"—and he had a reputation to suit his equipment.

We can credit Grosseteste for leading the young Bacon down the pathway to hell—that is, if you take the paranoid perspective of the orthodox priests who condemned Bacon's books, his experiments, and his philosophy. Don't be deceived by the modern-day popularity of the English Franciscan that gushes forth from the lips of the tourist guides at Oxford. The old friar was at one time declared to be "Enemy Number One" of the medieval Church. It would be a fair assessment of the English gentleman's contribution to history to say that he led the conspiracy of intellectuals who completely rewrote the Destiny of Western Civilization.

The Boss—King of England
Edward III (b. 1305, r. 1327-1377)

Mastermind of Discovery
John of Gaunt, Duke of Lancaster (-1399)

Monk, Womanizer, Spy
Nicholas of Lynn (c. 1305-1370)

The Clerk—Spy Manager,
Poet, Astronomer, Moralizer
Geoffrey Chaucer (1343-1400)

Mystics transformed a mule that was wallowing in the muck of the Middle Ages into the roaring lion that emerged in the Renaissance. The way that this shift in the fortunes of European society is presented in the history books, it often seems like pure magic. However, it was actually the result of women and men risking their lives, working in secret and under the most difficult circumstances—just so we could enjoy the wonders of science and the freedom to explore and to discover the real universe.

For Grosseteste and his protégé, Roger Bacon, science and technology were the keys to the future. It is to their credit that they persevered on this path in spite of the threats from orthodox clergy. Indeed, the leaders of the Church regarded their experiments with gunpowder and magnetism as evidence that they were in league with Satan. Many generations later, after the importance of their work was revealed to a grateful society, the names of these alchemists would become renowned. Grosseteste is praised in England for advancing scientific learning; Bacon is remembered as the "inventor" of gunpowder and the champion of the scientific method.

Friar Roger didn't actually "invent" gunpowder. He simply experimented until he was able to settle upon a suitable recipe of saltpeter, charcoal, and sulfur. The trick was making a stable concoction from locally available materials that didn't blow up unexpectedly. And that was Roger's contribution to the development of a substance that was of critical importance to the military security of European nations. In the Middle Ages, the greatest threat was from the Mongol hordes that were invading from the East. Since Church authorities generally regarded anyone who conducted such experiments as being "an alchemist" and thus a disciple of Satan, the Good Friar had to be very cautious. Nevertheless, rumors about his "Brazen Nose" experiments spread throughout Oxford Shire.

It so happens that gunpowder is useless without some sort of a suitable container. So Friar Roger also experimented with tubes that were cast from molten brass. These "tubes" were the first cannons that were ever made in Europe. They were quite noisy, and they made a lot of smoke. When the Friar lit a match and touched it to the fire-hole, his cannon made a horrible sound that was a lot like a sneeze. However, the "Ha-choo!" from Bacon's cannon startled and shook the neighborhood. It was from this characteristic noise that Roger devised the cryptic name Brazen Nose (literally, the "brass nose") for his secret invention.

Historians at Oxford are well aware that Roger Bacon conducted experiments in his "Laboratory-Garage" on the University Campus. Indeed, the complaints from neighbors regarding the flashes of light, acrid smoke, thunderous noise, and shaking earth were all too numerous to ignore. However, precisely what it was that the Oxford tinkerer and his youthful assistants was concocting has escaped their imaginations. That is because the Wizard conducted all his tests *sub-rosa*. There were no chronicles of these experiments nor did any stunning headlines concerning new discoveries get posted on the campus bulletin boards.

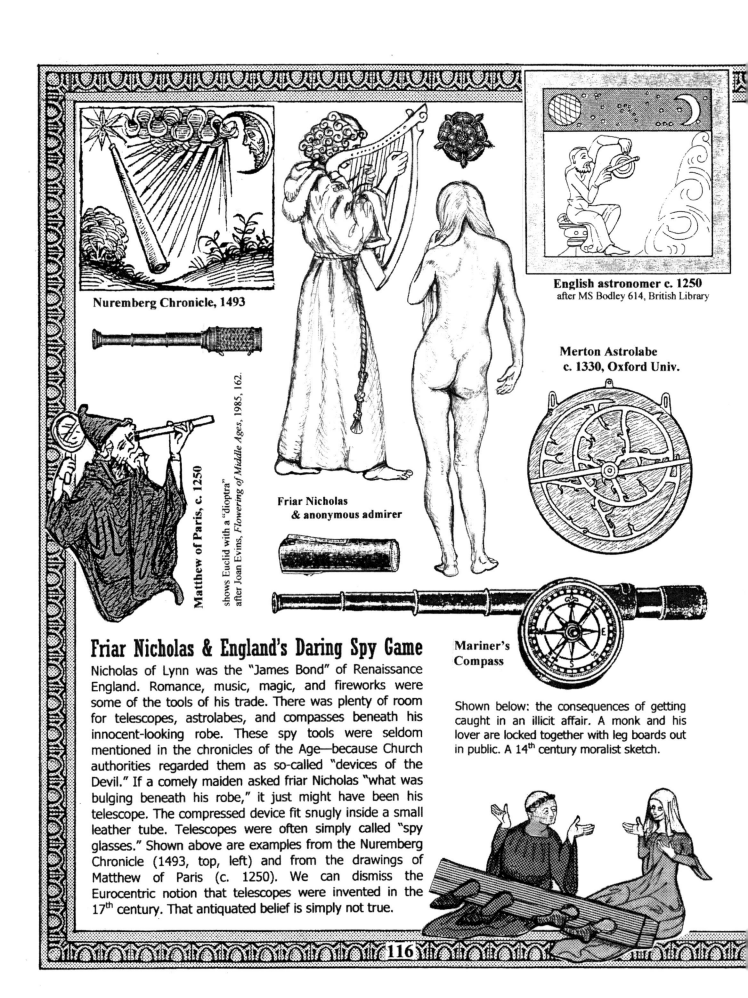

Nuremberg Chronicle, 1493

Matthew of Paris, c. 1250
shows Euclid with a "dioptra"
after Joan Evins, *Flowering of Middle Ages*, 1985, 162.

Friar Nicholas & anonymous admirer

English astronomer c. 1250
after MS Bodley 614, British Library

Merton Astrolabe c. 1330, Oxford Univ.

Mariner's Compass

Friar Nicholas & England's Daring Spy Game

Nicholas of Lynn was the "James Bond" of Renaissance England. Romance, music, magic, and fireworks were some of the tools of his trade. There was plenty of room for telescopes, astrolabes, and compasses beneath his innocent-looking robe. These spy tools were seldom mentioned in the chronicles of the Age—because Church authorities regarded them as so-called "devices of the Devil." If a comely maiden asked friar Nicholas "what was bulging beneath his robe," it just might have been his telescope. The compressed device fit snugly inside a small leather tube. Telescopes were often simply called "spy glasses." Shown above are examples from the Nuremberg Chronicle (1493, top, left) and from the drawings of Matthew of Paris (c. 1250). We can dismiss the Eurocentric notion that telescopes were invented in the 17th century. That antiquated belief is simply not true.

Shown below: the consequences of getting caught in an illicit affair. A monk and his lover are locked together with leg boards out in public. A 14th century moralist sketch.

116

Lacking any documentation regarding what took place in Bacon's Garage has left modern historians completely "in the dark."

It might have been a simple matter for one of the Deans to peek behind the Garage Door; but quite frankly, they didn't want to know what ungodly brew they might happen to see. The fearsome noise and rumors that Bacon's accomplice was Satan were sufficient to keep most simple folk and faithful Christians away from his door. We also know from abundant clues that the Kings of England were already involved in some nefarious activities that were intended to undermine the intelligence capability of Roman spies. So, it is quite possible that guards were posted to keep ordinary townspeople and inquisitive clergy away from the door.

The important issue for us to keep in mind is that Oxford University was a willing accomplice in the secret dealings of the kings and the alchemists. And this unholy alliance occurred long before the modern era of "public disclosure" concerning military funding. Having such men as Grosseteste and Bacon on the college campuses was vital to the nurturing of fertile minds and thus to the cultivation of new recruits. Those students who were curious about magic, astronomy, medicine, and chemistry were pushed gently over the edge of accepted doctrine; and they were initiated into the ranks of educated heretics. Over time, the English royalty demanded a portion of the gold that found its way into the coffers of the wealthy Church officials. Agents of the kings promptly deposited a good measure of the loot to Oxford clerics who were engaged in secret research. This was the beginning of government grant-funded research; but you won't read about it in the history books.

From time-to-time, the kings turned to the Mystic Franciscans to undertake more than just laboratory assignments. The venerable 16th century English Historian Richard Hakluyt noted that a certain Friary (or friar's dormitory) had become notorious by the 14th century as a "Den of Spies." This Friary was located northeast of London at a place called "King's Lynn." It seems that this Friary provided accommodations only for members of the secret brotherhood of Mystic Franciscans.

In those days, the Franciscans were often called "Grayfriars"—because their attire consisted of a simple gray cloak with optional sandals. It was an ideal outfit for secret agents because there was plenty of room beneath the cloth to hide the assorted paraphernalia that is typically needed on espionage missions. Franciscans were also called *Minorites*, or "minor" friars, by their Church colleagues. This inferior title derived from their minimal level of training in doctrine and their lack of involvement in the management duties within the offices of Church government.

Ordinarily, the Minorites were poorly supervised; and they were able to operate freely wherever they traveled. Bishops and priests tended to turn up their noses at these "Little Brothers of the Poor" who were typically regarded as being both intellectually and socially inferior. This institutional bias was a great asset to English Minorites in the Secret Service, because the other clergy tended to leave them alone.

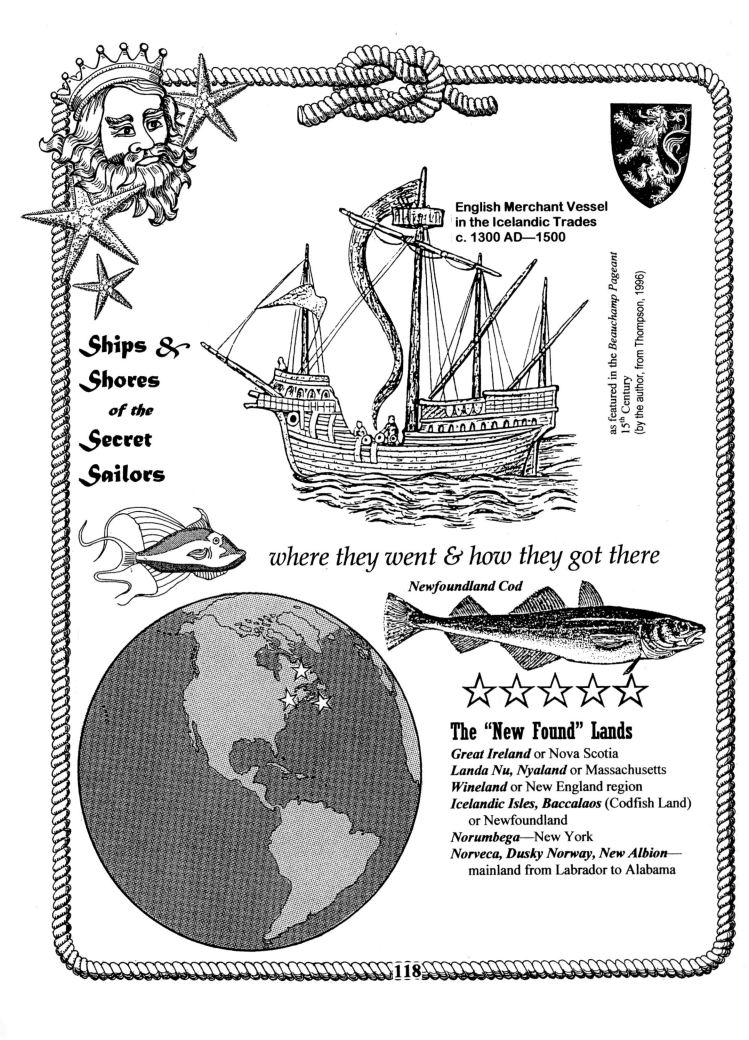

Ships & Shores of the Secret Sailors

English Merchant Vessel in the Icelandic Trades c. 1300 AD—1500

as featured in the *Beauchamp Pageant*
15th Century
(by the author, from Thompson, 1996)

where they went & how they got there

Newfoundland Cod

The "New Found" Lands

Great Ireland or Nova Scotia
Landa Nu, Nyaland or Massachusetts
Wineland or New England region
Icelandic Isles, Baccalaos (Codfish Land)
    or Newfoundland
Norumbega—New York
Norveca, Dusky Norway, New Albion—
    mainland from Labrador to Alabama

The extraordinary friars at King's Lynn played a particularly important role in the foreign intrigues of King Edward III. At the time that the boyish prince was crowned in 1327, the Kingdom was in dire financial straits. Both Edward's father and grandfather had engaged in foreign wars in an effort to extend their domains to the shores of Wales and Scotland. Such conflicts were very costly. Indeed, they made demands upon the royal purse that were far beyond the resources of the Nation. The barons and businesses were taxed to the hilt; the kings had demanded contributions from wealthy clergy; and still, there was not enough money in the Land to pay for the all the troops that were needed to suppress rebellions. So, the Edwards did what everybody else did in those days: they obtained loans from Venetian and Florentine banks.

However, there was a ketch—or a secret arrangement that was part of the deal. Eventually, the details are bound to percolate to the surface in spite of the best efforts to keep the arrangements *sub rosa*.

It seems that the Venetians wanted the assistance of the English Crown in a little problem they were having with the Norwegians. As it turns out, the Medici Company had an interest in a certain dyewood that was only available from the Western Isles. Ever since King Haakon's Declaration of Supremacy in 1261, access to these Isles had been very difficult because of the fierce Norwegian cutters that tended to intervene in merchant shipping. The Venetian agents who held the "purse strings" to Edward's loans asked him: "Would it be possible for his agents to assist in a little skullduggery and some hazardous international espionage?"

"Of course," replied the King. "That's a good job for the Minorites!"

Minorite Voyages to the Icelandic Isles

In about the year 1360, a strange and anonymous book surfaced in England. It was called in Latin *Inventio Fortunatae*. This translates into English as "the Discovery of the Fortunate Isles."

Now, this is a really intriguing title. The so-called "Fortunate Isles" refers to lands that the Greeks and Romans said were situated far to the west across the Atlantic Ocean. Essentially, this was the name that was given to the Earthly Paradise—the Elysian Fields. It is really unusual that someone would write a book about "discovering" these mythical isles in the late Middle Ages, because most European cartographers believed that they had already identified the mythical isles of Greco-Roman legend as the Canary Islands that are situated just to the northwest of Africa. However, that mistake was based upon the notion, also mistaken, that there were no more lands west of Spain before reaching China.

So, it seems that the European concept of world geography was all confused; and this was largely due to mistaken notions that the Bible was more important than actual experience when it came to understanding geography. The Bible seemed to indicate that there were only three continents; and this misconception led to the cockeyed notion that China was west of Europe. According to the devout geographers, there were no mythical isles called "the Antipodes;" and there were no other so-called "New Lands" to find. And that misconception of the medieval geographers brings us back to the intriguing title of the mysterious book. It would appear that the anonymous author was making a claim that he had actually found the *real* Fortunate Isles. In other words, he was making the declaration that there was in fact mainland west of Europe. It wasn't China; it wasn't a so-called "New Land;" it was actually a whole continent that had been known to the ancients. It was in fact a whole continent that Europeans had "lost" as a consequence of their own geographical ignorance and the blinding effect of Church dogma. The author deemed this discovery to be so vital that he had decided to write a book about what he had found. He wasn't about to reveal his name; because he understood that such a foolish act would only lead to his own elimination; and the folks who he wanted to enlighten about the nature of the universe would be none the wiser.

The Book, *Inventio Fortunatae*, was known to the Bristol merchant John Day. He had acquired a copy sometime in the 1480s; and this acquisition was apparently deemed to be so important that rumors spread as far as Spain that he had obtained a copy of the anonymous book. It was not long before a "Spanish Admiral" wrote to him requesting to borrow his copy of the *Inventio*. There has been some speculation that this "Admiral" was Columbus; but it now appears that another Spanish mariner was also curious about the western mainland. John Day responded to this request by saying that his copy of the book had been lost.

Nevertheless, we know that Columbus managed to obtain a copy. Probably, this occurred prior to his voyage west of Iceland in 1477. This was a time when the Genoese mariner was contemplating involvement in the risky maritime trades that were taking place between ports in Scotland, Iceland, and Nova Scotia. In any event, Columbus discussed this book with his son, Ferdinand, on one occasion; and Ferdinand mentioned in a biography that he wrote about his father that the *Inventio* had played an important role in the voyages that Columbus had led to the west.

We also know from the writings of Bartholomew Las Casas that a copy of the *Inventio* was among the possessions of Admiral Columbus when he died. Las Casas was a priest who got the assignment of writing a coherent history about the Columbus discovery of China. He collected all the documents that could be found pertaining to the 1492 Voyage; and it was at this time that he mentioned the mysterious book. However, from this point, the book seems to have disappeared.

The *Inventio* was also mentioned as a source for portrayals of the Western Isles and the Northern Regions on maps by Johannes Ruysch in 1502 and by Gerhard Mercator in 1569. So, there is no question at all that such a book did exist in the 14th century; and it certainly played an important role in the expeditions of 15th and 16th century explorers.

The English historian Richard Hakluyt pieced together the clues regarding the author of the book and its contents in the 16th century. As a Professor at Oxford University, Hakluyt was in a position to learn from the Deans about the folklore of the University and its distinguished alumni. He noted that Merton College had once had a factory in the 14th century; and this factory had been used for the production of a specially adapted version of the Arabian astrolabe. These brass instruments were very precise, very complicated, and very difficult to master. They were the principal tools that were used in early navigation and mapping. So, it seems that the Deans of Merton College were involved in some secretive effort to supply tools for mapping and navigation. They also used the facilities of the College for training Minorites in surveying skills.

At the same time, Oxford counted among its more accomplished graduates a certain friar named "Nicholas of Lynn." Apparently, this Friar Nicholas was a Franciscan in his younger years; and he later joined the Carmelite Order. So it would appear that he either had difficulty with making commitments to a particular Order; or he was somewhat opportunistic in choosing his associates. He was called "Nicholas of Lynn" because he resided for a considerable time at the Franciscan Friary of King's Lynn. This was the same dormitory that was also the notorious hangout for the King's cadre of espionage agents. That residence gave Friar Nicholas quick access to the sea—thus facilitating missions overseas on behalf of King Edward III. According to the official records of Oxford University, Friar Nicholas wrote an instructional manual concerning the use of astrolabes. This manual included eclipse tables that were of importance to overseas navigators needed the information for estimating longitude. And this was an essential task that enabled the construction of accurate maps showing territories that were far away.

So what was so important for Merton College to map in secret?

The clincher in Hakluyt's study of the clues came from the works of a 14th century English poet, Geoffrey Chaucer. According to Chaucer, the Oxford Minorite, Nicholas of Lynn, was an accomplished musician who was also skilled with an astrolabe. That struck a note with what Hakluyt had learned from the folklore at Oxford. A student-friar named Nicholas was also renowned for his angelic voice. Chaucer wrote that Friar Nicholas was so attractive and so skilled with the lute, and his voice was so melodious and seductive, that he was a big hit with the ladies—even the married ladies. In his own poetry, Chaucer expressed his irritation towards a "man of the cloth" (that is, the *gray* cloth) who used his musical skills, his charming personality, his godlike Grecian appearance, and his innocent status as a Minorite to take advantage of gullible young ladies.

We can read all about the womanizing friar Nicholas in the *Canterbury Tales*. Probably, Chaucer had no idea that Friar Nicholas was also using these same qualities to achieve his mission as a spy. During his travels on behalf of the English spy master, Prince John of Gaunt, and the King, the Minorite's life was in jeopardy whenever he was confronted and questioned by the Norwegian guards. He also had to be careful about whom he trusted since not all the Minorites at Oxford were part of Prince John's private espionage service.

Clues regarding the secret English scheme to map the Western Isles began to emerge even before the ink was dry on the friar's book. According to a letter that Gerhard Mercator wrote to his friend John Dee in 1577, it was a Dutch travel writer who first became aware of the English plot. Mercator mentioned that he had obtained a copy of a book called *Travels in the North*. This was another travelogue that a writer named Jacob Cnoyen had produced in about the year 1365. Cnoyen's manuscript was of great interest to John Dee because of his duties as both a spy and a geographer for Queen Elizabeth. Thus, Dee sent Mercator an urgent letter asking for a copy of the book. However, by the time that his letter arrived in the Low Countries (the Netherlands), the book had been loaned out once more and subsequently lost.[1] At least, that was the rationale Ortelius used in his dealings with the English. The truth of the matter may never be known with any certainty; however, the simple fact is that neither the English nor the Dutch fully trusted each other. At one point in time, the English accused Mercator of being a spy; and John Dee was always reluctant to provide him with copies of charts from the newly-surveyed territories.

Nevertheless, the tale that Mercator related in his letter to John Dee is quite revealing concerning the role of English Franciscans in the huge and dangerous effort that involved the mapping of overseas Norwegian Territories. We learn from Mercator that the Duch traveler, Jacob Cnoyen happened to be visiting the Court of the Norwegian King in Bergen in 1364. It was in this old Viking City that he came upon a group of pilgrims from the Western Isles. They explained that they had come from a region that they identified as "Dusky Norway."

Most likely, the pilgrims were on their way to Trondheim. It was customary in those days for pilgrims to travel great distances in order to visit the shrine of Saint Olaf. He was a former King who had played an instrumental role in the conversion of Viking warriors to Christianity. At the time, "Dusky Norway" was a general term for the provinces of the so-called "Northern Isles." Since mariners customarily sailed by compass bearings due north of Iceland on their way to the overseas provinces, it was presumed that these regions in the vicinity of Labrador, Newfoundland, and Nova Scotia were situated near the North Pole. Actually, they were due west of England. So, it would be more accurate to refer to these as the "Western Isles." There is also some indication that Norwegian authorities knew that the isles were situated in the Far West—and they hoped that by calling them "Northern Isles" to thereby confuse the kings and mariners of rival nations. So the confusion that we sometimes encounter when we look at the old maps was intentional.

---

[1] The letter from Mercator to John Dee is in the British Library. See E.G. Taylor, A Letter Dated 1577 from Mercator to John Dee, in *Imago Mundi*, (13), 1956, 56-68.

One of the pilgrims was a priest who showed Cnoyen a rather impressive astrolabe. According to the priest, this was a gift from an English Franciscan from Oxford who was visiting the Western Isles. At the time, in the middle of the 14th century, there was nothing unusual about English friars visiting either Norway or the overseas provinces. Indeed, the popularity of the new Christian religion spread like wildfire— so Church authorities in Norway were desperate for all the priests and friars who were willing to come. However, the fact that the friar was also a Franciscan who came from Oxford University leads us to the inevitable conclusion that he had sailed to Dusky Norway with the intention of making a map of the Western Territory. Mercator must have been suspicious regarding the motives of the friar's trip abroad.

Apparently, Jacob Cnoyen was also suspicious; and he conducted further investigations into the activities of the English Franciscans in the Nordic Isles. His testimony was summarized in Mercator's letter to John Dee in 1577. And here's what he had to say:

> The priest who had the astrolabe related to the King of Norway that in 1360 AD, there came to these Northern Islands an English Minorite from Oxford who was a good astronomer, etc. Leaving the rest of the party who had come to the Islands, he journeyed further through the whole of the North, etc., and he put into writing all of the wonders of those islands, and he gave to the King of England a book which he called in Latin *Inventio Fortunatae*. This book began at the last climate, that is to say in Latitude 54°N; and it continued all the way to the North Pole.[2]

Cnoyen must have inquired about the Western Isles, the *Inventio Fortunatae*, and the shenanigans of the traveling English friars by interviewing a number of independent sources. Indeed, Mercator's letter to John Dee included numerous intriguing details that could not have been known to the pilgrims in Norway. According to Cnoyen, the *Inventio* described huge isles surrounding a magnetic mountain (the Magnetic North Pole), swift Arctic currents and glaciers, temperate lands, and incredibly—forests of brasilwood. He also mentioned that the pilgrims in Norway had come from an overseas colony that he identified as the very same *Avalon* (or "Isle of Apples") that King Arthur had established in Nova Scotia during the 6th century.

The annals of Oxford University reveal that hundreds of Franciscan friars were trained at Merton College during the early 14th century. This training took place at the same time that a factory at the college produced such surveying and astronomical devices as magnetic compasses, telescopes, and astrolabes. This occurred shortly after the orthodox authorities in the Franciscan Order had condemned the writings of Roger Bacon and had placed him under house arrest in France. As part of this

---

[2] *Op cit* Excerpt from Mercator's letter to John Dee, 1577.

horrendous effort to erase from memory the heretical teachings of Grosseteste's disciple, they burned all the manuscript copies that they could find of books that Friar Bacon had written.

A mere thirty years after Bacon's death, the Deans of Merton College were operating training programs at full tilt. They were teaching young friars in the astronomical and surveying skills following guidelines that Roger Bacon had established before his arrest. The Deans also managed to produce a copy of Friar Bacon's prohibited text, the *Opus Majus*, which had been condemned as a threat to Christian doctrines. Among the more frightening tenets of Bacon's philosophy for building a new world order was the urgency of making a scientific map of the globe. By making such a map, he stressed, intelligent Christians could promote the mutual interests of both business and the reformed Church. It's no wonder that the orthodox clergy regarded Roger Bacon as the supreme threat to their authority. On the other hand, his philosophy of a reformed Church had an enduring appeal among the intellectuals of the British Isles.

Although all of the manuscript copies of the *Inventio Fortunatae* are presumed to have been lost, the English Franciscan map of the Norwegian Provinces ultimately found its way to Venice. The map of New World territories along the East Coast from Labrador to Brazil was included in the World Commercial Map that Albertin DeVirga produced sometime between 1410 and 1420. On this map, the Norwegian Provinces are identified by the word "Norveca"—which simply means Norwegian Territory. There is also a label beneath a crown that reads *Norveca Europa*. This symbol and the legend identify "lands belonging to the Crown of Norway." It is important to note that the cartographer did not use the designation of *Engronelant* (or "Greenland") which at that time would have indicated that the northern land was the Arctic Isle of Greenland. This "Norveca" was something entirely different. In the Declaration of Supremacy which Haakon IV issued in 1261, this province in the Northwest was referred to as *Landanu*—or the "New Land."

This New World map includes coastal land areas that are very similar to New England, Florida, the Gulf of Mexico and the Antilles Islands. The Gulf of Mexico is identified on this map as *Mar Caspium*—or "the Caspian Sea." This is the same name that the Romans used for the Western Gulf of the Atlantic Ocean—that is, the modern-day Gulf of Mexico. The Roman writer Seneca had said that this "gulf of the Caspian" was directly west of Spain; and it opened directly onto the ocean. This is not a reference to the tiny Caspian Sea of the Middle East.

So we can be certain that this land area is an early representation for America's East Coast. It is shown on this 1414 Map as a continent reaching out from the northwestern side of Norway. So, it appears from the existence of this New Land on the Albertin DeVirga Map that the English succeeded in mapping the East Coast; and thus they succeeded in meeting the requirements of the Venetian bankers who held the financial axe over the heads of English kings.

So, it would seem that the Venetian strategy of undermining Nordic supremacy in the North was going quite well. Their objective was to regain access to the Western Provinces. Prior to Haakon's Embargo, trade with the colonies was a thriving business. Christian settlements along the East Coast consisted mostly of small villages that were built up around trading posts and hillforts. Numerous carraks, cogs, and knorrs sailed into the nearby harbors. These were usually small vessels under a hundred feet in length; they were built with keels and wooden hulls with oak planks arranged in a clinker fashion; they carried a single mast with a cotton or flax sail; and they had a steering-oar mounted on the starboard side near the stern. Merchants brought rum, beer, cordage, cloth, and iron tools to the provinces; they hauled back to European ports cargoes of dried fish, whale oil, furs, copper, tar, and wine.

Such excursions typically went unreported in the journals of the Middle Ages because few people could write; and those who did know how to write seldom wrote about such mundane subjects as the comings-and-goings of merchant vessels. On occasion, disputes between Christian kings were recorded because they served to document settlements which had some bearing on the future relations between nations. There are a number of such documents from the 14th century that tell of English poachers being apprehended by Norwegian patrols in the waters south of Iceland. In the 15th century, the Harbormaster's Log of Bristol tells of ships hauling back cargoes of dried fish—which must have been taken from someplace near the Grand Banks of Newfoundland. Vessels that fished in those regions invariably landed in Dusky Norway to replenish water supplies and to enjoy the hospitality of the local trading posts.

On occasion, European vessels ran aground off the Nova Scotia coast; and the inhabitants succored the crews. One tale that endured in the 14th century Icelandic sagas told the story of a merchant named Bjorn who crashed his ship along the shore after being driven far to the west by a storm. Irish immigrants who were living in the New Land rescued Bjorn from the surf. Later, Bjorn mentioned that his rescuers were riding horseback when they came to his aid.

According to a Spanish Franciscan who visited Nova Scotia in the middle of the 14th century, there were colonies of Irish immigrants in the region. He further reported in a document called *el Libro de Conocemiento* (that is, the *Book of Knowledge*) that the Irish called their province "Ibernia." This was simply an Old Irish variation for Ireland. It was a common practice for immigrants to name their new homelands after the place that they had left behind. Often, they had some compassion for future historians by adding the word "new" or "great" as an indication that this was the second homeland. Nova Scotia was also known as *Irland Mikla*—or "Great Ireland."

On the Viladestes Map of 1413, the Island of Ibernia is situated *north* of Iceland and *west* of Norway. In other words, it is in about the right location for Nova Scotia—if we take into consideration the routes of travel and the effects of magnetic error on compass directions. We can be certain that this northern isle of "Ibernia" was not a mistake for Ireland, because the Viladestes Map also includes the distinctive Land of Irlanda (that is, the *real* Ireland) in the right location immediately west of England. Here's what the Spanish Franciscan had to say in *the Book of Knowledge*:

> Being in Irlanda, I sailed in a ship bound for Spain. We went with those on that ship on the high seas for so long that we arrived at an island called Eterns, and another called Artania, and another called Citilant, and another called Ibernia (*that is, the Ireland of the North*). All these islands are in the part of the world where the sun sets in the month of June. They are all peopled, well supplied, and with a good climate.
>
> In this island of Ibernia, there are trees, and the fruit that they bear are fat birds. These birds are very good eating whether boiled or roasted. . . .
>
> Know that this Island is outside the seven climates. The king of this island has for his device the same flag—gold with a black lion—as the king of Noruega (*Norway*).
>
> After this, I departed from the Island of Ibernia in a ship. We voyaged so far over the Western Sea that we sighted the Cape of Finnisterre (that is, End Land—which is the northwest cape of Spain).[3]

As was the case with the English Franciscan who wrote the *Inventio Fortunatae*, the author of the *Book of Knowledge* chose not to give his name to the manuscript. What we see in these two somewhat similar geographic accounts is a desire on the part of the authors to emulate Marco Polo's paragon of travel journalism. At the same time, both friars appreciated the importance of maintaining anonymity. Marco Polo already held the title of "the World's Greatest Liar;" and he needed no competition from the humble friars of the North Sea. Thus, they managed to keep their contemporaries as well as future historians mostly in the dark.

One place that didn't remain in the dark was the location of the old Viking colony of Wineland. Situated in the temperate and fertile meadows of modern-day New England, the region was featured on hundreds of manuscript maps that were included with copies of a new English Geography Text, *the Polychronicon*, by Ranulf Higden (circa 1350). The geographer who produced Higden's somewhat schematic maps indicated that "Wineland" was northwest of England—thereby challenging the Nordic claim that the Western Isles were situated around the North Pole.

This refreshingly new perspective of the overseas isles—the "isles of opportunity"—was continued in the 15th century by a printed map called the *Rudimentum Novitiorum*. This map was printed in editions of thousands of copies in Augsburg and Lubeck between 1475 and 1485. It

---

[3] From Clements Markham, Ed., *The Book of Knowledge*, Hakluyt Society, London, 1912.

identified *Vinland* or *Winland* as an island country in the northwest. At the same time, copies of a standard "route map" of Nordic territories circulated in North European ports. These route maps indicated the best sailing route or "highway" from Scotland to Bergen, then to Iceland, Gronlandia, and on to Winlandia (the Nordic colony near Cape Cod). Clearly, there was a concerted effort to facilitate the traffic of North European merchants sailing to the Western Isles. And there was a particular effort to direct merchants towards the Old Vinland Colony. In 1073, the historian Adam of Bremen reported that Vinland was noted for its wines. It was still a vibrant trading center in the 14th century. And wine grapes were still growing everywhere when the French explorers arrived in this region of the "New World" in the 16th century.

Of course, wherever there is trading, the lords of the manor are certain to demand their share of the profits. Norse tax collectors extracted a huge fortune from the owners of trading posts and hillforts. According to a letter from King Peter of Cyprus that was recorded in Menzieres' *Songe du Vieil Pelerin* (1369):

> The King of Norway had an enormous realm. Parts of his domain were in the ocean far from Norway and beyond Godeland. His emissaries that he sent on ships to collect taxes from his subjects required three years to complete their rounds and return home again.[4]

By "Godeland," King Peter probably meant the region of modern-day Massachusetts that was at one time known as *Vinland det Gode* or "Wine Land the Good." European hillforts, farms, and trading posts extended far up the St. Lawrence River, the Hudson, and the Potomac. Considering the vast size of the Nordic possessions and the income from taxes that flowed into the Church coffers as well as into the King's treasury, it is hardly a wonder that the Norwegians wanted to keep this bonanza a secret.

However, the English friars managed to survey the lands from Greenland in the north to Brazil in the south. Each team of friars recorded the astronomical data, latitudes, and eclipse measurements for a small section of land. Once all of these sectional maps were assembled back in London, in Prince John's headquarters, it was possible to construct with reasonable accuracy a composite map showing the entire East Coast of the New Land. And this is what we see reproduced on the Venetian, Florentine, and Genoese maps that were issued between 1447 and 1457.

These maps essentially show what has been referred to as the "Toscanelli geography"—and they are the same kind of maps that guided Columbus to the Caribbean Sea in 1492. The Florentine and Genoese Planispheres (or oval maps) feature a new wilderness mainland directly west of Europe. This mainland was deceptively shown as a vast eastward

---

[4] King Peter's letter is mentioned in Frances Gibson, *The Seafarers: Pre-Columbian Voyages to* America, Philadelphia: Dorrance & co., 1974, 179.

extension of Asia. Probably, this distortion resulted mainly from a desire on the part of mapmakers to keep peace with naïve Church authorities.

Western Refuge of the Templar Knights

There stands in the City of Newport, Rhode Island, a distinctive round stone tower. It measures roughly thirty-feet across; and it stands nearly ten meters high. Built of chiseled blocks of granite on the side of a hill, it has a commanding view of the harbor down below. The most distinctive feature of this building is the use of Roman arches to span the distance between eight massive pillars.

This is not the sort of structure that you might erect in a weekend. Indeed, the tower must have taken a dozen skilled workers several months to build. They had to cart the stones from a distant quarry (with the aid of horses); they had to chisel the stones to fit the required shape of the arches; and then they had to assemble the building blocks without the whole building collapsing in a pile of rubble. This is not a Viking structure—as there is nothing remotely similar to it known from Norway. The Tower is most like the medieval baptisteries that are found in French churches or perhaps the ancient Roman mausoleums that were built on octagonal bases of stone columns supporting Roman arches.

A wide variety of theories have been advanced in an effort to explain the origins of the Round Stone Tower. Besides being touted as a "Colonial windmill," it has been identified as a "Celtic church" and as a "Chinese lighthouse." Radiocarbon dates that have been obtained from organic material contained in surface mortar span the centuries from 1300 to 1700 AD. It may well have been used as a windmill; but it certainly wasn't originally designed for that purpose. A Colonial Deed to the land indicates that the Tower was already standing when the first European pioneers moved into the region in the late 1600s.

The structure was clearly built as a fortress—although it is by no means a castle. As considerable work was involved, as well as the involvement of highly-skilled masons, we can conclude that whoever built the tower had a highly-trained, highly-organized, and very dedicated team of laborers. They were familiar with the building traditions of French masons; but they were not from the class of refined engineers who constructed medieval cathedrals. The structure is primitive in many respects, but it is very sturdy—suggesting that it was designed primarily for defensive purposes.

One theory that seems to account for all of these factors is the theory that Templar refugees built the structure in the 14th century. In 1312, the French king and the pope announced the official condemnation of an organization that was known as the "Knights Templar." This was a brotherhood of Crusader Knights who rose to prominence as suppliers and landlords for Christian armies heading to the Holy Lands. Over time, they achieved great political and economic power. Their holdings and influence rivaled those of the pope and the King of France. All the sovereigns of Europe owed money to the Templar Bank; but none were so far in debt as King Philip IV of France. When Philip accused the Templars of sacrilege and underpayment of taxes, all those kings who owed money became like a pack of wolves around a wounded lamb. In 1302, all the Templars living in France were arrested and tortured before being barbecued. By 1312, the pope joined in the frenzy; and Templars throughout Europe were taken before tribunals and accused of crimes against the Church.

Many fled to a secret refuge across the seas in the New Land.

What do Historians Think?

No one in academia seriously questions whether or not a book called *the Inventio Fortunatae* once existed in Europe. Only Mercator's letter to John Dee offers a few delectable details regarding what it may have said.

Meanwhile, orthodox historians have condemned the *Inventio* as being mythological; and thus it is supposedly unworthy of consideration by "serious" scholars. However, if we take the time to weave together the clues from various sources in addition to the *Inventio*, then we can begin to make some sense out of the enduring mystery.

In 1964, the historian Tryggvi Oleson insisted that the *Inventio* was nothing but a fable and that the Minorite's tale of travels to the so-called "Polar Regions" was self-incriminating. Oleson quickly grasped what he believed was an obvious flaw in the Minorite's story—and that was the claim that he had encountered people living near the North Pole and that the region had a temperate climate. Since it was obvious to Oleson that there are no people living at the Pole, if we exclude Santa, and the climate in the Polar Regions is frigid, then it was readily apparent that the whole story was fictional.

Having thus dismissed the *Inventio* as a fairytale, Oleson didn't bother to consider the possibility that the Minorite's account of travels in the "Polar Regions" actually referred to the Magnetic North Pole of Hudson's Bay and not the Geographic Pole of floating ice. If the Minorite intended to describe lands near Hudson Bay, then he was actually speaking about a habitable land with a temperate climate.

Another outspoken critic of early voyagers to the Western Isles is the Palo Alto historian Kirsten Seaver. She has been particularly critical of the English historian Richard Hakluyt who identified the mysterious Minorite as an Oxford professor—Nicholas of Lynn. According to Ms. Seaver: the anonymous author of the *Inventio* has always been described in the ancient accounts as "a Franciscan." She adds that: Oxford University records indicate that Professor Nicholas of Lynn was a member of the "Carmelite Order." This discrepancy between memberships in different religious orders is given as the rationale for concluding that the Oxford Professor called "Nicholas" could not possibly have been the same "Nicholas" who was identified by Hakluyt as the author of the mysterious book.

It has not occurred to Ms. Seaver that Friar Nicholas might have belonged to one Order as a youth and then joined another Order as a senior faculty member at Oxford. And this is precisely what the complete historical record tells us with respect to Friar Nicholas. He was *both* a Franciscan and a Carmelite but at different times in his life.

The essential clue that Ms. Seaver has overlooked is that the friar had completed his overseas mission to the New World by the year 1360. After that time, his disguise as a humble Franciscan was no longer vital. In his absence from England, one other event had occurred that settled for good the issue of his allegiance to the Minorites. Prince John of Gaunt was the Head of the King's Secret Service. He had come to the realization that the Franciscan Order in England was no longer a secure organization for training espionage agents. It was at this time that the Prince transferred the duties of training England's spies to the Carmelite Order at Oxford. That is to say the grant funding for Minorites had run out. It was only natural for Nicholas to follow suit, because the Prince was both his benefactor and his protector. The *Norfolk Biography* of 1829 confirms that Nicholas had belonged to both the Franciscan and the Carmelite Orders.

The Albertin DeVirga Map (1410-1420) has been accepted among historians as an authentic document ever since its discovery in a Croatian antique store in 1911. An Austrian historian, Franz von Wieser, certified that the map was "genuine." And this certification was reported in a little booklet that was published in 1912. He concluded at that time that the continent projecting out of the northwest side of Norway was some sort of mistake that represented the Arctic Island of Greenland. However, he failed to account for fact that DeVirga didn't use the name for Greenland anywhere on the map. Ever since this dismissal, subsequent historians have generally assumed that the map was of little importance to the history of cartography. Several isolationists have echoed Wieser's assessment that the continental mainland with its projecting Florda-like peninsula must have been some sort of imaginary representation for the Arctic Island.

However, not everyone has marched lockstep to the prevailing dogma. The Swiss scholar Arthur Dürst disagreed with the negative attitude that had consigned DeVirga's Map to the so-called "dustbin of history." After reading the author's report that revealed the inclusion of New World continents on the map, Dürst offered to publish an immediate alert in the journal *Cartographica Helvetica*. His article, "The World Map of Albertin de Virga," appeared in the January 1996 edition.

Unfortunately, Dürst's stoic colleagues were both startled and angry. They were shocked that this otherwise esteemed editor of a professional journal would dare to break ranks with the conservative camp of Columbus loyalists. Nevertheless, come "hell or high water," he boldly supported the quest to learn new information about America's past.

Another scholar who actively sought new information was the independent researcher Arlington Mallery. A former U.S. Army Colonel and an iron structural engineer during World War II, Mallery suspected that the certified historians and archeologists were overlooking a lot of evidence in the field. He came to this conclusion after coming across the remains of an ancient iron smelter in the Ohio Valley region. Local historians claimed that there was no evidence of European settlements prior to the arrival of the Pioneers in the 17th century. However, Mallery realized that this assessment was actually caused by a failure on the part of the professionals to actually look for the evidence. Indeed, the remains of the smelter had been found *beneath* the foundations of Colonial houses.

The Colonel spent nearly two decades searching for the remains of America's ancient iron industry. He trekked through the forests of the Ohio River Valley, down the St. Lawrence Valley, and across the hills of Nova Scotia and Newfoundland. This journey through time brought him face-to-face with the haunting images of European immigrants. Once they had lived in hillforts and in villages all along the East Coast. They had farmed, raised cattle, and they had traded with the Indians.

Mallery located dozens of places where the earth was scorched in orange and yellow hues. At all of these promising sites, he dug up the remains of stone chimneys and hearths where the ancient smiths had piled iron ore that they pounded into tools. All around these sites, he found rusted iron tools, melted slag, and hunks of melted iron called "blooms."

Mallery collected over 400 pounds of iron relics in Virginia's Roanoke Valley. He noted that many of the iron artifacts that he found along the East Coast were similar to iron tools that were used by Vikings:

> Easily identified among the items were many Viking-type tools: spikes and rivets, scribers for marking wood, caulking tools used in building Viking ships, chisels and axes, boat spikes and boat rivets. The chisels and axes were formed by welding together thin sheets of iron by cladding. The rivets were duplicates of rivets found in a Viking ship, the *Oseberg*, which was discovered in 1903 under a mound on the shores of Oslo Fjord in Norway.[5]

Hopefully, the Colonel missed finding a few of the ancient smelters and some of the ancient iron relics. And these remain in the undisturbed earth waiting for a future archeologist to uncover. Otherwise, orthodox historians might dispute the existence of America's ancient iron-smelting industry simply by claiming that all the evidence is missing. There are some fears among Mallery's colleagues that the cartloads of artifacts that he sent to museums were simply dumped outside the back doors. At the very least, we have plenty of photographs from the Colonel's collection as well as metallurgical reports on the samples of iron and copper artifacts that he sent to laboratories. Although most orthodox historians have claimed that the Native Peoples had no access to metal tools that had been forged or cast from molten metal, Mallery's tests prove otherwise.

---

[5] Arlington Mallery and Mary Harrison, *The Rediscovery of Lost America*, New York: Dutton, 1979, 31.

At least, the ruins of many of the ancient hillforts along the East Coast are still standing—and they are still waiting for a thorough archeological review. A number of these ruins have been tied to reports made by the early Colonists who claimed that they had encountered "Welsh-speaking" natives. The ruins of "Old Stone Fort" near Chattanooga are particularly striking as they are surrounded by a moat that still holds water.[6]

Consequences for New World Exploration

The secret voyages of the English Franciscans began at a time when the merchant shipping across the Atlantic Ocean was under an embargo. However, that embargo was compromised following the issue of Venetian maps showing that the so-called "Northern Territories" under the Norwegian Crown were actually accessible by sailing west and south of the zone that was patrolled by Nordic cutters. After Haakon's death, Norwegian kings occasionally opened up the ports to unrestricted access—but the vessels from overseas were heavily taxed. Among the many seafarers who traveled by compass bearings, there endured the impression that they must be sailing due north to countries that were situated around the North Pole.

That geographical misconception began to change as a result of the Franciscan expeditions and the circulation of new maps that were based, at least in part, on the new surveys of the Western Isles.

Three maps were of particular importance—and they were all very similar. These were the so-called "Yale Vinland Map" of 1440, the Florentine Planisphere of 1447, and the Genoese Planisphere of 1457. It has been argued that all three of these maps were derived from a Venetian prototype. The key map must have looked a lot like the Albertin DeVirga Map. One feature that they all had in common was the presence of the Peninsulas of Labrador and Nova Scotia, the Gulf of Mexico, and the Peninsula of Florida—all situated directly west of Europe. On the Florentine and Genoese Maps, the northern mainland west of Europe was identified as the forest wilderness of the biblical giants Gog and Magog.

This feature served a particular function in the espionage of the times. God-fearing Christians who actually believed the nonsense about biblical "giants" in the service of Satan were reassured that the best course of action was to stay at home and do nothing. On the other hand, seafarers and merchants who wanted to escape from the limits of medieval thinking realized that the Western Isles offered the hope for a new prosperity beyond the high taxes and the insane social polices of Feudal Europe.

Another feature on these maps was a group of islands in the region of Newfoundland. These were the "Icelandic Isles" or port districts that included "Brest," "Donbere," "Talas," and "Broas." This group of islands first appears on the Modena Compass Map of 135O, the Catalan Map of 1375, and the Zeno Map of 1380. At least one of these port cities was still

---

[6] Joseph Gardner, Ed., *Mysteries of the Ancient Americas*, New York: Readers Digest, 1986, 36.

in existence when French colonists sailed up the St. Lawrence River with Jacques Cartier in 1535. This was the so-called "city" of Brest along the shore of Southern Labrador.

Numerous medieval reports of mariners heading for the "Icelandic Isles" actually refer to voyages that were made in the vicinity of Newfoundland. Many sailors were heading for the Grand Banks fishing grounds off the Newfoundland coast. A map called "the Paris Map" which was produced by an anonymous cartographer in about the year 1490 actually has the Icelandic Isles within a few miles of the precise location of Newfoundland. So there can't be any doubt that some merchants in Europe knew precisely where to find the harbors that featured supplies of dried codfish, native copper nuggets, turkeys, furs, tar, and tobacco.

The so-called "fat birds" that the Spanish Franciscan traveler observed in Great Ireland or Nova Scotia in 1350 were the quintessential North American game birds or "turkeys." As the friar observed in his *Book of Knowledge*, "they were good either boiled or roasted;" and the settlers ate a good plenty of them long before the Pilgrims arrived at Plymouth Rock in 1620 just in time for a Thanksgiving Dinner.

Many of the fat birds were carted across the Atlantic Ocean to be served up at feasts in Europe during the 14th and 15th centuries. The French chef-historian, Magulome Toussant-Somat, observed that Philip of Burgundy had such a feast, complete with *d'indons* or turkeys, in the 14th century. The bird was known in England as the "Welsh hen." The name "turkey" derived from the common European association of the fat birds with Turkish trading vessels that plied the Mediterranean Sea. They also carried in their holds a special kind of birdfeed that was made from dried maize. The feed was often referred to as "turkie corn." This designation of "turkie corn" identified grain that was not regarded as suitable for human consumption. Illustrations of the fat birds were part of the decorations that were used in the 13th century restoration of the Schleswig Cathedral. This church was in a German port city that was frequented by ships from the Hanseatic League. They also traveled overseas to Great Ireland, Wineland, and to a place called "Norumbega."

One of the more odious pastimes in the Western Provinces was tobacco smoking. When the Renaissance explorers reached the Caribbean and the East Coast of the Carolinas, they encountered Native Americans smoking a kind of cigar that consisted of a rolled tobacco leaf. Natives had been smoking the weed for many generations—perhaps more than two thousand years. Periodically, Old World voyagers brought the smoking habit back to Europe. Evidence of tobacco smoking has been found in pipes that were excavated from the ruins of Roman buildings in Old London. John Hawkins reportedly brought a cargo of tobacco to London in 1565; and twenty years later, Walter Raleigh showed up at port with a cargo of America's finest tobacco. Given the uncertain dependency upon New World supplies, the soothing weed wasn't always available.

The same can be said for New World potatoes, maize, beans, tomatoes and pumpkins. All of these plants showed up in various European cities during the Middle Ages without there being much said at the time regarding their origins. Farmers often experimented with planting seeds from these new plants; however few of the New World plants established a foothold in Europe due to climactic variation, humidity, spoilage, and poor handling. Among the plants that were hardy enough to withstand the rigors of planting in foreign soil were "flint maize" and pumpkins. The maize was used for cattle feed; the pumpkins were soon regarded as a "traditional" ingredient of English bread pudding.

In the 14th century, Europeans began to notice that the winters were growing longer and colder. This climactic change became known as "the Little Ice Age." One consequence of this climate change was an increase in the demand for cheap furs from the Western Isles. Unfortunately, some of these imports were infested with fleas; and the transport ships often carried rats. They arrived in the northern ports of Europe at a time when Bubonic Plague was spreading all around the world.

Western scholars assumed long ago that the pandemic of Bubonic Plague that struck Europe in the middle of the 14th century originated in Asia. However, there is growing evidence that Central America was the deadly incubator of this disease. Indeed, plague is still endemic in the mountainous regions of Central America and in the American Southwest. Writing just before his death from the disease in 1349, the Arabic scholar Ibn Al-Wardi mentioned his belief that the disease had come from a place that he called: "the Land of Darkness." Among the ancients, this name referred to the regions of the Arctic where the sun did not shine during three-to-six months of winter. This region was generally believed to be located in the north and the west near "Dusky Norway." Marco Polo mentioned this "Land of Darkness" as being situated far to the northeast of China in the region of Siberia and Alaska.

Infected furs that merchants transported across the North Atlantic brought the disease to Iceland by 1346. This was one year ahead of the first reported cases in England. It was at this time that the trading posts in Nova Scotia, Newfoundland, Labrador, and Greenland became death camps for travelers who sought refuge from the cold. The disease spread rapidly around the world—killing off some 30 million Chinese and perhaps half the population of Europe. Throughout the Americas, native populations shrank suddenly. In some regions of the Eastern Woodlands in the Ohio and Mississippi River Valleys, entire villages were exterminated. The "Moundbuilder Civilization" of the American Southeast fell to this invisible invader from the west.

At archeological sites all along the East Coast, Arlington Mallery found evidence that devastating plagues had sucked the vitality from the ancient European communities. He noted that:

> My detailed examination of a Newfoundland beach for
> remains of Scandinavian settlements has turned up

evidence, though indirect, in support of the theory that settlements there were destroyed by the plague. . . . Proof of Norse occupancy during the period 1250 to 1400 exists in the form of artifacts; but there is no evidence of any settlement for any period subsequent to 1400.[7]

Once more, the faithful clergy of the Mother Church bemoaned the sins of mortals as the cause of this disaster; and they prepared for the "End of the World" to occur at any moment. Those who were wealthy abandoned the cities and took up residence at country estates. Many succeeded in escaping the catastrophe by shutting themselves away from the rest of wretched humanity. Life seemed hopeless to many of those who struggled to survive.

What was needed in these times of doom and gloom was a miracle. And it was about to happen.

source: after 15th-century illustration by Johann Kepler in Tooley (1968, p. 61)

---

[7] Mallery & Harrison, op cit., 1979, 165.

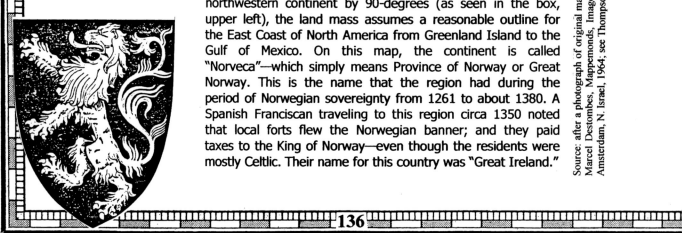

Franciscan Map of Dusky Norway

A Venetian map by Albertin DeVirga shows the North American Continent as a huge land mass that is attached to the northwest coast of Norway. This world map has been variously dated to a period from 1410 to perhaps 1420—with 1414 being the most common in academic writings. If we rotate the northwestern continent by 90-degrees (as seen in the box, upper left), the land mass assumes a reasonable outline for the East Coast of North America from Greenland Island to the Gulf of Mexico. On this map, the continent is called "Norveca"—which simply means Province of Norway or Great Norway. This is the name that the region had during the period of Norwegian sovereignty from 1261 to about 1380. A Spanish Franciscan traveling to this region circa 1350 noted that local forts flew the Norwegian banner; and they paid taxes to the King of Norway—even though the residents were mostly Celtic. Their name for this country was "Great Ireland."

Source: after a photograph of original map in Lucerne, 1932; from Marcel Destombes, Mappemonds, Imago Mundi Supplement IV, Amsterdam, N. Israel, 1964; see Thompson, 1996.

Source: Nordenskiöld, 1889, f. 2.

Norway's Vinland Colony on Maps 1400-1500

One of the conundrums facing orthodox historians is the fact that Columbus sailed north in 1477 looking for a route to the Western Isles. He sailed on a ship that was part of the customary maritime traffic between England, Germany, and the so-called "Icelandic Isles"—that is, Newfoundland and Nova Scotia. Another problem facing historians has been the stubborn insistence that the Norwegian Colony of Vinland (also, Vineland or Wineland) was extinct by the time of Columbus and could not possibly have influenced his notions about isles and mainland in the west.

Lubeck 1475

Augusburg, 1480

However, the location of the Colony (Vinland, Wineland) was shown northwest of Norway on a map called the Rudimentium Novitorium (Lubeck, 1475, 1480). This map was printed in the thousands of copies using the newly-invented Gutenberg Printing Press—and it must have been known to the Genoese mariner. In any case, it was well known to hundreds of German mariners who sailed on trading and fishing ventures to the Western Isles every year. Due to the effects of magnetic declination from True North, sailors who used the magnetic compass mistakenly believed that these isles were due north or even *northeast* of Norway.

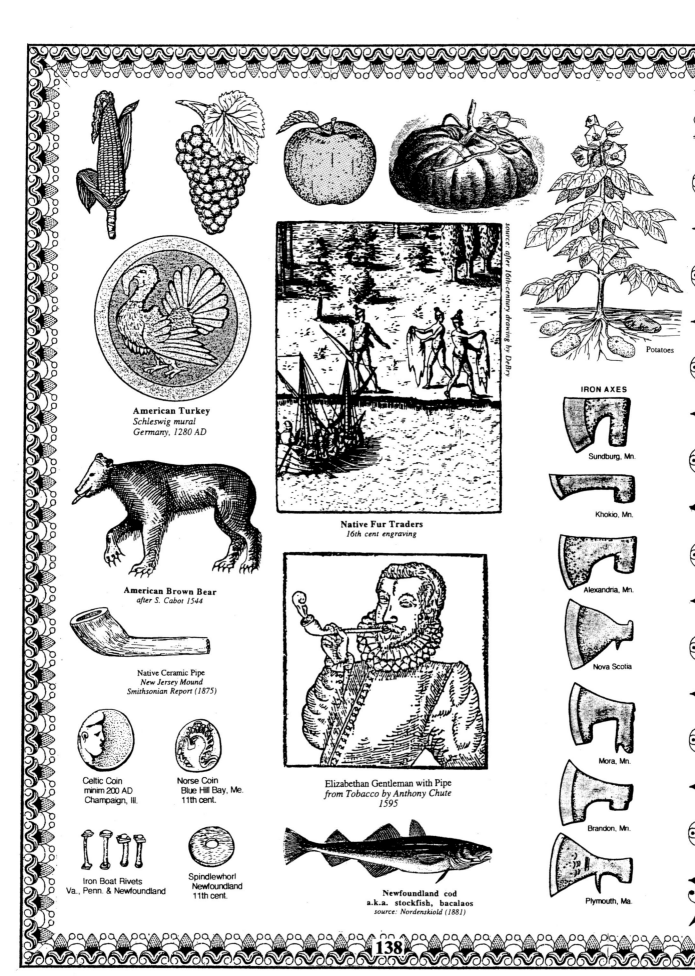

American Turkey
Schleswig mural
Germany, 1280 AD

American Brown Bear
after S. Cabot 1544

Native Ceramic Pipe
New Jersey Mound
Smithsonian Report (1875)

Celtic Coin
minim 200 AD
Champaign, Ill.

Norse Coin
Blue Hill Bay, Me.
11th cent.

Iron Boat Rivets
Va., Penn. & Newfoundland

Spindlewhorl
Newfoundland
11th cent.

source: after 16th-century drawing by DeBry

Native Fur Traders
16th cent engraving

Elizabethan Gentleman with Pipe
from Tobacco by Anthony Chute
1595

Newfoundland cod
a.k.a. stockfish, bacalaos
source: Nordenskiold (1881)

Potatoes

IRON AXES

Sundburg, Mn.

Khokio, Mn.

Alexandria, Mn.

Nova Scotia

Mora, Mn.

Brandon, Mn.

Plymouth, Ma.

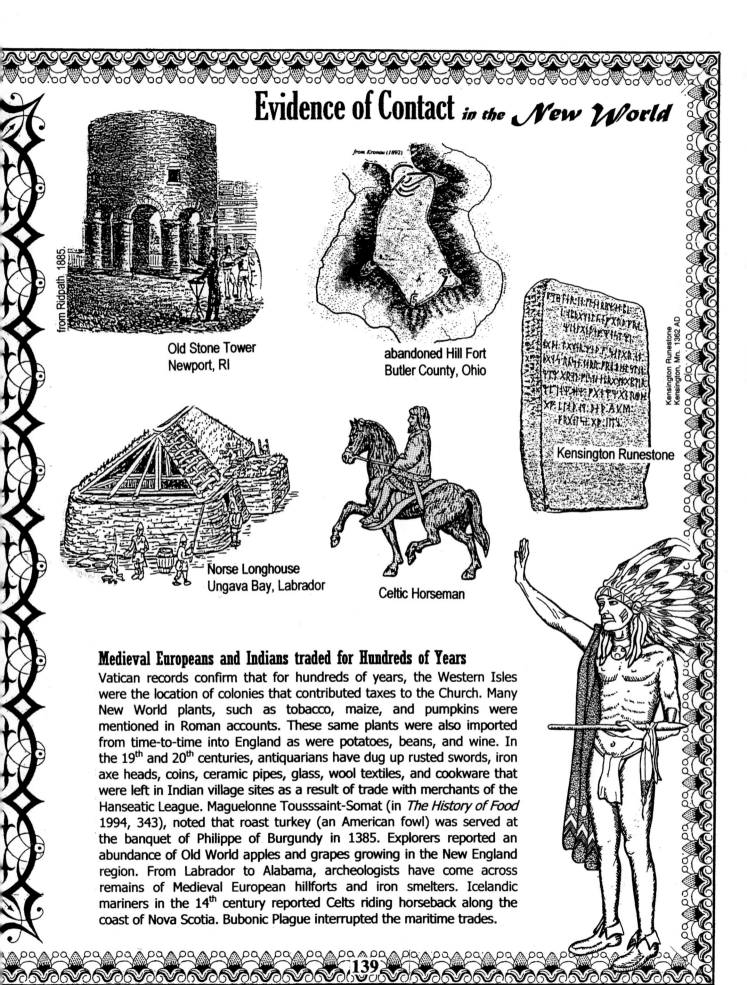

Evidence of Contact *in the New World*

from Ridpath 1885.

Old Stone Tower
Newport, RI

from Kronau (1892)

abandoned Hill Fort
Butler County, Ohio

Kensington Runestone
Kensington, Mn. 1362 AD

Kensington Runestone

Norse Longhouse
Ungava Bay, Labrador

Celtic Horseman

Medieval Europeans and Indians traded for Hundreds of Years

Vatican records confirm that for hundreds of years, the Western Isles were the location of colonies that contributed taxes to the Church. Many New World plants, such as tobacco, maize, and pumpkins were mentioned in Roman accounts. These same plants were also imported from time-to-time into England as were potatoes, beans, and wine. In the 19th and 20th centuries, antiquarians have dug up rusted swords, iron axe heads, coins, ceramic pipes, glass, wool textiles, and cookware that were left in Indian village sites as a result of trade with merchants of the Hanseatic League. Maguelonne Tousssaint-Somat (in *The History of Food* 1994, 343), noted that roast turkey (an American fowl) was served at the banquet of Philippe of Burgundy in 1385. Explorers reported an abundance of Old World apples and grapes growing in the New England region. From Labrador to Alabama, archeologists have come across remains of Medieval European hillforts and iron smelters. Icelandic mariners in the 14th century reported Celts riding horseback along the coast of Nova Scotia. Bubonic Plague interrupted the maritime trades.

139

Puzzles of the Past

When did epidemics cross the oceans?

As reported in the author's encyclopedia, American Discovery—the Real Story, scientists have found evidence of all the world's major epidemic diseases in artifacts and ruins of ancient America. Eurocentric historians once claimed that devastating epidemics among native villages in the 16th century was proof that Columbus was the "first" Old World voyager to reach the Americas. However, it is now clear that worldwide pandemics were involved in the collapse of the Mayan Civilization in the 10th century and in the fall of Indian nations in the Southeastern Woodlands region in the 13th century. Plague is endemic in Central America; and it may have spread along with the fur trade from Nova Scotia to Iceland and the Mediterranean in 1347. That epidemic exterminated many of the Norse-Celtic colonies on the East Coast; and it effectively ended Nordic supremacy in the North Atlantic. Black rats (left) and fur imports were the principal carriers of infected fleas. When Spaniards settled in Hispaniola (Haiti), they encountered swarms of mosquitoes carrying a deadly protozoan parasite. They complained of the "Mal air" or bad air of the swamplands—leading to the naming of a disease—*malaria*—that was also known to the Greeks and Romans. Mexican artists recorded the distinctive red spots of smallpox on illustrations of the Lord of Death in their picture books or codices in the 15th century (bottom row). Epidemics crossed the oceans at least by Roman times. They are an inevitable consequence of commerce.

Puzzles of the Past

Who were the secret sailors?

★ Did they leave behind artifacts?

★ Did they make any maps?

★ What plants did they take home?

★ Are there any ruins or inscriptions?

NOTE THESE CLUES TO SOLVE THE MYSTERY

Norway
Colonial Flag, 1350

Welsh Hen, 1280

Steel Arrow point, 1300

Norse Coin, ME, 1250

Map of Great Ireland, 1413

Iron boat rivets, MA, 1300

Iron chisel, NC mound

Wine Grapes
1250-1600

Fjord Pony statue,
GL, 1300

CHINA—1405 AD Ming astronomers chart the heavens with a telescope at the Nanjing Observatory.

142

Zheng He and the Forbidden Land

A CLOAK OF SECRETS surrounds the efforts of the Ming Chinese Navy to map the World in the 15ᵗʰ century. This enormous undertaking was entrusted to the leadership of a gallant and enigmatic military officer by the name of Zheng He. Although modern historians have recognized the Chinese Admiral as one of the most influential mariners who ever lived, the official chronicles of the Ming Dynasty actually had very little to say about his stunning achievements. Indeed, it was the intention of the Ming Interior Ministry that no one should ever know the true story.

Events leading up to the voyages of Admiral Zheng He provide a theatrical background of court intrigues, assassinations, and political turmoil. The most important element in the social chaos of the times was the abrupt end of the Yuan Dynasty in the middle of the 14ᵗʰ century. It was no coincidence that the Mongol government collapsed on the heels of a global pandemic. The decadent Yuan regime of Sun Ti was unable to cope with widespread famines and rebellions that followed in the wake of the horrendous "Black Death." Climactic changes also altered the landscape of China as the Yangtze River broke out of its banks and found a new way to the sea. Literally, millions of peasants died from disease, starvation, and the failure of the government to provide basic relief.

Historians have estimated that the number of deaths was between 25 and 35 million. However an official government census reported that the population had shrunk by nearly 50 million persons. In addition to the outright fatalities, several million refugees fled the ravages of the plague. Some followed the Old Silk Road and headed east; others sailed off to new homes across the seas.

In the midst of this catastrophe, a peasant named Zhu Yuanzhang led a popular uprising against the alien Mongol rulers and against numerous rival warlords. After thirteen years of struggle, Zhu stood alone as the master of a desolate nation. His principal allies were Buddhist politicians and the Confucian Civil Service. Indeed, the followers of Master K'ung Fu-tzu (that is, Confucius) were exceptionally pleased because they were

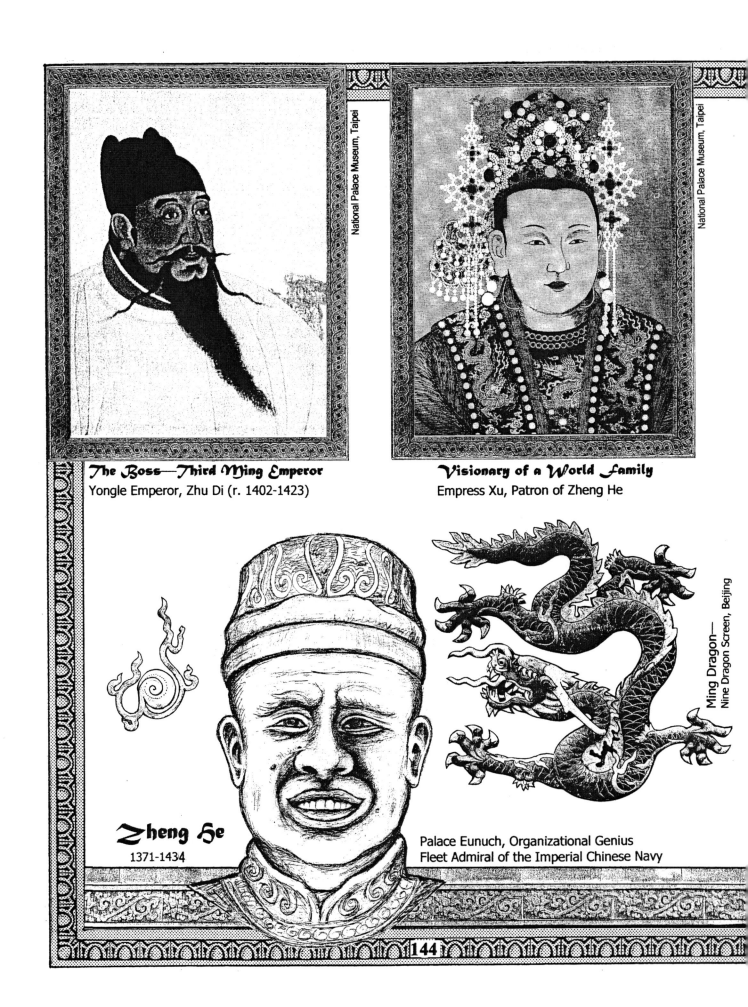

The Boss—Third Ming Emperor
Yongle Emperor, Zhu Di (r. 1402-1423)

Visionary of a World Family
Empress Xu, Patron of Zheng He

National Palace Museum, Taipei

National Palace Museum, Taipei

Ming Dragon—
Nine Dragon Screen, Beijing

Zheng He
1371-1434

Palace Eunuch, Organizational Genius
Fleet Admiral of the Imperial Chinese Navy

able to resume control of the government. Under the alien Mongol regime, the State Bureaucracy had been entrusted to foreigners and incompetent Mongol officers. Meanwhile, the legions of Chinese civil servants who had been trained in the Confucian doctrines of "good government" had been relegated to subordinate positions. They were angry; and they were eager to take back the reins of government power.

With the crowning of Zhu Yuanzhang as the First Ming Emperor, the shrewd, ruthless, and dedicated Confucian ministers were back in control of the new government. Hard times were in store for anyone who threatened their doctrines or their management of the State. Many foreigners and their sympathizers fled for their lives.

Zhu Yuanshang was invested as the "Son of Heaven" in 1368. It was at that time that Zhu took on the title of "Hong-wu"—meaning "Invincible Warrior." This surely was an appropriate title for a man who ruled by the sword. He spent the next thirty years hunting down rivals, fighting in rebellious provinces, and reorganizing the government. In accordance with the wishes of his Confucian ministers, Hong-wu took measures to eliminate the threat of a coup within the palace. His first step was to forbid the education of all women—including wives, concubines, and female attendants. He added court eunuchs to the list of those who were expected to be dumb and obedient; and he barred them from holding positions of influence within the government.

In this manner, Hong-wu's ministers sought to maintain "harmony" within the Emperor's court. As long as the palace women and the eunuchs were ignorant of worldly affairs, they reasoned, no one in the inner circle would complain about the Emperor's edicts. Of course, this enforced ignorance also meant that the Ministers of the Civil Service would also escape the scrutiny and complaints of the Emperor's personal attendants.

However, the Ministers' strategy for Palace Harmony was short lived. When two of Hong-wu's confidants advised him to exercise more compassion towards his people, the Emperor had them arrested and tried for treason. Then he ordered the executions of their families and all their friends. During such fits of royal paranoia, no one was safe.

Eventually, Hong-wu demanded the execution of his most successful military strategist General Lan Yu. This act of madness was driven by the Emperor's fear that the popular general might rally peasants in opposition to the government. While these purges earned for Hong-wu the reputation of "an effective administrator," they sowed the seeds of dissention and rebellion within his own ranks.

The palace women had many accomplices in their schemes to undermine the Emperor's authority. These included numerous intellectuals who belonged to secret societies with such names as "White Lotus Society," "Lotus Blossoms" and "Moon Dragons." They included alchemists, astronomers, Taoists, physicians, and the cadres of royal eunuchs who served the Emperor and his twenty-six sons.

Ships & Shores of the Secret Sailors

where they went & how they got there

Super Junk
c. 1400-1800 AD
200m in length
based on a 18th century painting
of ships near Canton, China

★★★★★ Lands of Eastern Barbarians

Tahan—Alaska, Northwest Coast
Tien Mu—California, Mexico
Tahan-tinsuyu—Peru
Nova Scotia, Florida,
Su Mu—Brazil

Even the Emperor's sons lived in fear of execution or imprisonment. Before Hong-wu's death, when old age had dulled his mind, he was more dependent than ever upon the assistance of his royal ministers. It became obvious to them that the normal order of succession to the throne would not be in their best interests. So, they persuaded Hong-wu to issue an edict naming one of his naïve and incompetent grandsons as the designated heir to the throne. His name was Jianwen.

When the Emperor died in the year 1398, the royal ministers took steps to assure that their control of the government was solidified. Jianwen was enthroned along with two Confucian ministers who were elevated to the status of "Mentors" or "Regents." It was the Confucian Regents who held the real power in the Capital at Nanjing. They controlled the Emperor's royal seal of authority; and they immediately issued orders for the reassignment of all the potentially disloyal military forces. This action effectively stripped the rival princes of the armies that they had personally trained. As soon as this phase of the Confucian plan was implemented, Jianwen's troops were sent out to arrest all those who posed a threat to the regime. Their principal target was Zhu Di—the Prince of Yan. He was the military commander and governor of Dadu (or Beijing).

Forewarned of this treachery by loyal eunuchs, Zhu Di took to the streets of Dadu disguised as a common beggar. He was at that time a popular administrator who was renowned for his wisdom and compassion—thus he had many friends who were willing to give him food and shelter. When the soldiers arrived from Nanjing to take him prisoner, he was nowhere to be found.

Civil war raged in China for the next four years. During this time, the troops who were loyal to the puppet government struggled to put down revolts throughout the country. It didn't help matters for the Regents that the palace eunuchs and concubines actively conspired to undermine their position. They took advantage of their positions within the Palace to inform the rebel princes about the military strategies of the Nanjing forces. In the midst of this chaos, generals who were loyal to Prince Zhu Di managed to fight their way back to Dadu. General Zhu Di then came out of hiding; and he assembled all his loyal forces into a mighty army. They marched on the Capital of Nanjing in 1402; and they managed to penetrate the walls of the city after the concubines and eunuchs smuggled out plans to the Nanjing defenses.

Zhu Di's archers and swordsmen decimated the defenders. However, before they could capture the palace, it was deliberately set on fire from the inside. This desperate act made it seem as though the palace guard had chosen mass suicide instead of surrender. All that the attackers could do was to let the palace burn to the ground. However, Zhu Di was suspicious. When the embers and smoke had died down, he ordered his men to carefully search through the ruins of the palace. In the charred remains, there was no sign of Jianwen's body. Thus, it appeared that the fire was a clever ruse to distract the attacking army while Jianwen slipped away.

Rumors soon spread throughout the land that Jianwen had been smuggled out of Nanjing disguised as a Buddhist priest. Presumably, he had accompanied an innocent-looking train of monks fleeing the carnage. His "escape," whether real or imagined, would continue to influence the government of his successor—because there was an enduring concern that Jianwen might again reappear in the future with an army of loyalists.

In 1402, Zhu Di was crowned the *Yongle* Emperor—meaning the "King of Eternal Happiness." Now, it was time for the Taoist intellectuals, the Palace women, and the Imperial Eunuchs to take their turns as advisors to the new Emperor.

Modern historians have identified the reign of the Yongle Emperor as the era in which the Chinese achieved their greatest florescence as an ancient civilization. It was also at this time that they had their greatest impact upon the rest of the ancient world. This period is remembered for the rebuilding of the Great Wall, the rebuilding of the inland canal system, enormous refinements in the State Bureaucracy, the vast fleets of Ming *baochuan* or "Treasure Ships" that sailed onto the Indian Ocean, and the enormous development of the Indian Ocean maritime marketplace.

The Ming fleets carried enormous supplies of Chinese silks, porcelains, carved ivory, spices, medicines, steel tools, and bronze castings. Many of these goods reached Europe via trade routes linking Hormuz, Constantinople, Venice, and Cairo. There can be no doubt that this influx of Chinese goods into European markets helped to revive the stagnant medieval economy. Interest in *Marco Polo's Travels* blossomed, and merchants as well as commoners began to dream of finding wealth in trade with India, the Spice Islands, and China.

The enormous enterprises of the Ming Government served to achieve Zhu Di's principal goal: the development of a strong sense of National Unity among the Chinese people. For many years, the Nation had been torn apart as a consequence warfare, palace intrigues, plague and famine. Both the new Emperor and his Taoist and business advisors realized that huge public works projects had the potential of building a sense of national pride and loyalty among those who participated in the effort. They further reasoned that support for the National Government would become especially strong among the businesses that stood to gain huge profits from international trade.

The bold idea of sending Treasure Fleets into the Indian Ocean seemed on the surface to offer the best opportunity for the government to stimulate trade and thereby gain the funding in taxes that were needed to pay for the grandiose projects that included restoring the Great Wall, the construction of hundreds of Taoist learning centers and monasteries, and the erection of an enormous Ming Palace at the site of the Forbidden City in Beijing. These projects were intended to become enduring monuments to Chinese National Unity and the greatness of the Ming Dynasty.

Modern historians often characterize Zhu Di as "a megalomaniac ruler." Some writers claim that he ordered the construction of the

Forbidden City and the dispatch of Treasure Fleets overseas just to satisfy his own ego. However, the eventual plan to promote Beijing as the Capital of a New World Order probably had its roots in a synthesis of his Chinese heritage as the "Son of Heaven" and the Taoist desire to build a Universe of Peace and Enlightenment on earth. Certainly, his wife, the Empress Xu was a major inspiration behind the concept of a "World Family."

Taoist intellectuals who influenced the Emperor's decisions realized an unprecedented opportunity to combine their own visions of a New World Order with the overseas trading goals of the business leaders.

At the same time, there were military issues of great concern facing Zhu Di's generals. In 1402, the Mongol ruler of Samarkand had conquered India, Baghdad, and Egypt; and he had his sights set on China as his next acquisition. By sending a fleet into the Indian Ocean, Zhu Di hoped to outflank his Mongol enemies in the west.

Probably, most of the ideas for public works projects, international commerce, and world diplomacy had been argued thoroughly in Zhu Di's camps even before the victory at Nanjing. Even leader for the overseas expeditions had been identified. Among Zhu Di's inner circle was a eunuch named Ma He who had distinguished himself at the battle of Zheng-lunba. On that occasion, the general had renamed his aide with the honorary title of "Zheng He." The lad was also a Muslim who later became known in the traditions of Indian Ocean seafaring as *Ma Sanbao*—or the "Three Jeweled Eunuch." This title has somewhat of a similar meaning to the title "Tres Majesticas" that was at one time very popular in the literature of the Western alchemists. It means roughly: Three Times Magic"—or a "Very Great" man.

As a Muslim who was also regarded as a "Great Man" among his contemporaries, Zheng He was an excellent choice for the position of chief manager or "Viceroy" of a great enterprise. The goal of sending Treasure Fleets abroad was to gain domination of the Muslim commerce in the Indian Ocean. Zheng was a genius at military tactics, an astute diplomat, and a brilliant logistical planner.

Zheng He was also someone who would be carefully watched by the Confucian ministers who still ran the Civil Service. Their Master's Book of Philosophy the *Teaching's of Confucius*, espoused the doctrine that proper government was confined to the borders of the Middle Kingdom.

In order to moderate the philosophical risks that were inherent in the building of huge fleets for overseas trade and military duty, Zhu Di settled upon his plan to underplay both the objectives of the fleets and the full extent of their range of operations. Thus, we see in the chronicles of the Ming History only passing references to the expeditions of Admiral Zheng He. With respect to the secret expeditions that were sent to the New World, there is no mention at all in the official chronicles.

New World Voyages to the Lands of Tien Mu

Fortunately for Zheng He, most of the Confucian bureaucrats were not very enthusiastic about the idea of sailing on the high seas. Nor were they very keen on the idea of hanging out nearby the shipyards and the quays of the port cities. Mostly, they were landlubbers who enjoyed reciting the principles of "proper government" and meticulous accounting. And that sort of occupation required staying on dry ground. The training schools of the Civil Service required rote memory of the Confucian principles and perfection in writing; it demanded conformity to the codes of etiquette and the standards of appropriate attire. Thus, Zheng He had good reasons for believing that the diehard critics in the Civil Service would never learn about the Emperor's greatest secret. Contrary to the dictates of the Confucian Philosophy, he had authorized the mapping of new continents across the Eastern Ocean.

Several factors coalesced to support the novel idea of mapping overseas lands. The Yongle Emperor was obsessed with learning the whereabouts of his archrival—Jianwen. Historians have characterized Zhu Di as being paranoid in this regard; however, he never trusted completely the leaders of the State bureaucracy—and they never trusted him. Since there was no place that Jianwen could hide in the west (because the region was under Mongol control), everybody agreed that the only suitable refuge had to be located someplace in the New Lands. The search for Jianwen would require a systematic mapping and exploration of all the Eastern Provinces until he was found.

Business leaders also wanted a world map so they could pinpoint the locations of overseas markets as well as the best routes for sailing to suitable harbors. Even the Taoists had a motive for the world mapping effort. Indeed, their philosophy of universal peace and the alchemy of the Human Spirit demanded knowing about the entire globe. Those who nurtured the vision that the Ming Dynasty had an important role to play in world destiny also demanded the creation of an accurate world map. They reasoned that China could finally fulfill its Divine Mandate to establish itself as the "Center of the Universe." By making a useful world map and by sending impressive fleets to all the world's major harbors, Zheng He would assure that all the monarchs of civilized nations would look to China for leadership. Finally, an accurate map was essential for guiding the transports that would bring ambassadors from all the civilized nations back to the new capital of Beijing. They would come, quite possibly, from as far away as Mexico, Peru, and Brazil.

It was fortunate for Zhu Di and his Admiral that most of the surveys needed to map the world had already been done. Doubtless, some of the ancient sea captains still had copies of maps from the Yuan Dynasty that featured the Indian Ocean, the East Coast of Africa, Australia, Japan, the East Indies, Alaska, California Island, Toloman (or Mexico) and Peru. The Eastern Isles were also known collectively as Tien Mu (the "Heavenly Land"). Ancient Buddhist missionaries had also mentioned various places in their itineraries such as Fu Sang, Ta Han, and Tien-Tin-Suyu—the "Land of the Forth Quarter." The last of these names derived from either a Babylonian designation for Peru or a Chinese equivalent.

Another motive that the Emperor had for sending huge fleets into the Indian Ocean was to reward and to inspire his Muslim allies. Following Tamerlane's death in 1405, Mongol control of the subcontinent declined. It was an opportune time for the Chinese to play a vital role in the shift of power in the region back to the Muslims. Zheng He's fleets carried as many as 25,000 marines; and they assisted Muslim armies in securing ports along the Malabar Coast (that is, the West Coast) of India.

In most situations, the Chinese marines and cavalry moved against pirate lairs and the isolated garrisons of Tamerlane's troops. In Ceylon (modern-day Sri Lanka southeast of India), Admiral Zheng lured the troops of a Sinhalese tyrant (Alakeswara) into a trap. He outflanked the enemy, captured the tyrant, and then packed him off for trial in Nanjing. Publicity, marketing, and intentional drama were key elements in the operation. Admiral Zheng left the country in the hands of a rival warlord who embraced the idea of joining the Ming Commercial Alliance.

This was the "classic" approach of the Ming military in overseas operations. The goal was not world conquest—but instead the subjugation of hostile governments. A quick infusion of uniforms, Chinese weapons, banners, and commercial experts helped to transform marginal societies and to energize those who wanted to join the Commercial Alliance.

Often times, a Ming version of the "Peace Corps" moved in to rebuild the economic base of newly freed territories. Language experts who were familiar with Arabic and the local dialects set about developing a basic "trade language" that would meet the needs of merchants. Architects organized teams to build factories, while merchants arranged for training programs to develop the skills that were needed to produce suitable export goods. Chinese and Muslim agricultural experts worked with local farmers to establish new crops of dried grains and fruits that could be used to replenish the stores of foreign merchant vessels. Financial experts helped the local merchants establish a standard system of weights and measures as well as a suitable exchange for the regional currency. When all this was accomplished, the Peace Corps members usually packed up their bags and went on to the next assignment—leaving behind tons of Chinese trade goods, occasional colonies of Chinese merchants, numerous mixed-ethnic babies, and lots of good memories.

If news of these military ventures and commercial projects got back to the Confucian bureaucrats in Nanjing, and it always did eventually, the Ming naval authorities could claim that they were merely fighting pirates, outflanking the Mongols, and protecting the interests of the Chinese merchant marine. There would be suspicions on the part of the bureaucrats that the navy had violated the edicts of Confucianism not to meddle in the "external affairs" of foreign governments; however, proving that this was the Emperor's policy would have been nearly impossible. Since the Ming

Peace Corps dismantled its headquarters and moved as soon as the job was done, there was little evidence remaining that they had ever been there.

The beauty of Zhu Di's plan for overseas commercial development was that it seemed to assure future paybacks in the form of import taxes without requiring the establishment of overseas garrisons. Since the vast scale of commercial development in the Indian Ocean guaranteed a flood of useful manufactured products into the region, the quality of life for peasants and business owners improved substantially. Everywhere that Zheng traveled as an ambassador, he made a concerted and very public effort to acknowledge the local deities—often to the extent of making equal contributions to Muslum, Buddhist, and Hindu religious organizations. Thus, he played a role in moderating the religious and ethnic rivalries that often caused regional conflicts.

Zhu Di's Plan for overseas mapping and the search for Jianwen included several phases. First, maps were acquired from Yuan Dynasty archives and from Muslim allies. These maps were used to determine the most likely routes for Jianwen's escape as well as to outline survey zones and search areas for teams of explorers and marines. Second, the teams were sent to the prime coastal locations where the fugitive might have landed and set up camp. And Third, additional fleets would be sent to all those areas that had not yet been adequately charted. In this manner, Zhu Di proposed to map the entire world—with the assistance of his Muslim, Korean, and Japanese allies.

It seems likely that Zhu Di's agents had to inquire among the seafarers for navigational charts that were developed under the previous dynasty—because as was often the case in the Dragon Kingdom—the new regime typically began its own government with a ritualistic purge of the predecessor's documents in public bonfires. The practice was quite similar to the European Christian burnings of so-called "pagan" Roman books at the beginning of the Middle Ages. The message to the public and to loyal bureaucrats was that the new administrators had nothing to gain from their predecessors. Often, the old doctrines and books were deemed a philosophical threat to the undertaking of a new government.

Seafarers, on the other hand, usually kept anything that worked well and that had some practical application. Since the Yuan maps were very accurate, foreign merchants held onto them in spite of the popular anti-Mongol demonstrations and book burnings that had swept across China when the Mings took power. It was probably a simple matter for the Ming Navy to obtain copies of reasonably good navigational charts from Korean and Vietnamese merchants. Indeed, in modern times, antique map collectors have had the greatest success finding copies of the oldest Chinese world maps, the *Tien Xia tu*, *Shanhai Jing* or *Ch'onhado* style maps, from Korean antique stores.

Even before the coronation, Zhu Di ordered elite naval forces to mount an immediate search for the fugitive Jianwen. These forces consisted of flotillas of fast junks or "Galloping Horses" junks. They were dispatched with contingents of marines to search regions of the East Indies and the New Lands across the ocean where Yuan maps had indicated the most suitable harbors and escape routes. We have some idea where these target regions were located because Marco Polo had brought back to Venice maps showing the best harbors and straits located at 74°N, 48°N, and 40°N. These correspond to the Northwest Passage in the Canadian Arctic, Puget Sound, and San Francisco Bay.

There is some evidence that Zheng He and his subordinates searched these targeted areas of the New Land. Indeed, an early Ming map that has been dated to 1418 shows coastal areas of the Pacific Northwest, the Canadian Arctic, and California that are surprisingly similar to these same areas on Marco Polo's maps. This map includes such distinctive features as Mackenzie Bay, Great Bear Lake in northwestern Canada, Puget Sound, and the Gulf of California. As was the case with Marco Polo's maps, the Ming geographers mistakenly assumed that Puget Sound and the Gulf of California were the opposite ends of a continuous sea running from north to south. One delightfully humorous result of this mistake is that all the early Ming maps showed California as an Island.

One very significant feature of this 1418 Ming Map is the placement of a caption naming Ma Sanbao (a.k.a., "the Three-Jeweled Eunuch, or Zheng He) as the leader of expeditions on the Eastern Ocean. This caption is located adjacent to the mistaken "Island California"—suggesting that the Ming Admiral had sailed along the distant shores of the American continents. As far as we can tell, none of the early searches for the fugitive had any endurable impact upon the indigenous peoples; nor did they leave in their wake any remarkable evidence of their passing.

Later Ming expeditions did make an impression on Native societies of the New World. For example, Elders of the Tsimshian Nation of modern-day British Columbia passed on a legend that "the Son of Heaven" had at one time in the distant past visited their villages. This could be a vague legacy from the voyages of Jianwen, Zheng He, or some other Chinese Prince. All along the West Coast, archeologists have dug up Chinese coins and bronze Buddhist religious relics that were traded or given as gifts by passing mariners. In the western region of Zapoteca, Mexican artists manufactured crystal ceremonial objects, as well as stone snuff bottles, and a black-on-red lacquer ware—all of which have characteristics that seem distinctively Chinese. Indeed, the only difference between Mexican snuff bottles and those of the Ming Chinese are the smiles on the dragons. Some Mexican priests wore costumes that were very similar to those of the Chinese Buddhists—both having pointed hats; and in Peru, the Inca rulers wore tunics that were made from Chinese silk.

Zheng He's agricultural experts helped local rulers in Mexico, Peru, and Florida. They established new kinds of orchards, grain stores, and aviaries that could meet the needs of visiting merchant fleets. They are probably responsible for the vast orchards of lemons and pomegranates that the Spaniards found already growing in Peru when they arrived in the

16th century. Both of these plants are Asian domesticates. European colonists and conquerors also mentioned Mexican and Peruvian aviaries that contained chickens; and in many places, the Spaniards found pigs being raised on farms or running wild in the fields. Both the pigs and the chickens appear to have been Asian breeds.

Several lines of evidence converge to identify the Ming Navy as the cause of agricultural innovations in Mexico, Peru, and Florida. First, Admiral Zheng was a logistics genius who planned and then built factories and farms specifically for the support of his international maritime trade network. Second, Asian domesticates that were typically used by the Mings, such as lemons, limes, and almonds, were found by European explorers already growing in Mexico, Peru, and Florida. Third, Spaniards identified the tunics of the Inca rulers as being made from a material that was either "silk," or "like silk." And Finally, the Inca ruler Tupac Yupanqui claimed to have sailed with a fleet across the Pacific Ocean to the East Indies on a roundtrip expedition. This was the sort of long distance voyaging that the Mings were doing in the 15th century. All the Inca leader had to do was to hitch a ride with the Ming fleet.

Further evidence of Ming voyages on the Pacific Ocean is present on a map called the Shanhai Yudi Quantu. This world map was produced sometime between 1425 and 1435. Jesuits found this map during the 16th century; and it was used as an example of the highest attainment of geographical knowledge by the Ming Chinese. The Jesuits hoped thereby to demonstrate the superiority of European maps. To aid in the comparison, the Jesuits added modernized geographical names such as Europe, Asia, Africa, and North and South America. They hoped that a comparison of the "best" Chinese map with the most recent European map would reveal to the Chinese the superiority of European geography. When the Zheng He map was first compiled in the early 15th century, the Chinese were at least a century ahead of the Europeans. By the 17th century, as the Jesuits proved, the European geographers were far in the lead. Mateo Ricci hoped that this revelation would inspire Chinese intellectuals to embrace the Catholic Faith. However, only a few Buddhists made the switch to the European religion.

The important thing is that the Jesuits preserved an accurate copy of the Ming geographical knowledge at the apex of Zheng He's world mapping effort. What we see by comparing the 1418 Map with the Shanhai Yudi Quantu (c. 1430) is that the Ming Navy established the peninsular nature of California; they greatly improved the West Coast outline of South America; and they added such key East Coast features as Labrador, Florida, and the Gulf of Mexico.

Probably more than half of the geographical intelligence that was subsequently incorporated into the Ming mapping effort derived from Muslim sources. Their region of maritime influence in the 15th century included the Indian Ocean, the Mediterranean Sea, the Red Sea, and the eastern Atlantic countries from South Africa to the Iberian Peninsula (that is, Portugal and Spain). They also sent ships across the Atlantic Ocean under the auspices of the Moors.

The chronicles of the Sung Dynasty (dating to the 13th century) reported that the Moors had reached a new mainland after sailing for a hundred days west of Iberia. They called this land "Mu-Lan-Pi." At least, that was how the Arabic name was translated into the Chinese account. It was noted that the Moors returned from this new land carrying a cargo of corncobs that were "three inches long" and also "very large gourds." The Chinese historian Hui-lin Li has identified these corncobs and gourds as "maize" and "pumpkins." Both were indigenous American plants.

We see evidence of the joint Ming-Moor expeditions to the New World in the form of an early map of the Florida Peninsula. In 1436, the Portuguese cartographer Andrea Bianco produced a map of the Atlantic showing a huge island that was situated far west of Spain. He called this the Island of Antillia—meaning basically, the Island Opposite Tile (which was Iceland). Located at the southeastern corner of the Island was a peninsula jutting towards the southeast. This peninsula had an uncanny similarity to the modern-day Peninsula of Florida.

Apparently, Chinese or Muslim surveyors had made a very accurate map of the area prior to 1436. For this purpose, they must have made observations of eclipses; and they employed a method of surveying called "lunar distances." This method requires measuring the angular distances between the moon and certain planets. The result was a reasonably accurate calculation of longitude; while latitude was measured by means of an Arabic astrolabe. All of these measurements were then compiled in the workrooms of Muslim cartographers with a copy of the resulting regional and world maps being sent on to Admiral Zheng.

Taoist priests arranged for the preparation of a world map in 1418 that portrayed the earth as two conjoined hemispheres. This design reflected the knowledge of intellectuals and astronomers who realized that the moon and earth are both round—and that both also revolve around the sun. The priests realized that this awareness of the spherical nature of earth, the moon, the sun, and the planets could be quite terrifying to ordinary people. Instead of trying to explain the nature of the universe, most religious leaders thought it wise to allow the peasants and ordinary bureaucrats to think of their world as simply flat—either in a square shape or a disk— whatever made them comfortable. There was no need, they thought, to burden the simple minds of common folk with concepts that took initiates many months of contemplation to understand.

The world map of conjoined hemispheres would have been regarded among the Confucian ministers as evidence of heresy. Indeed, this document was proof that the Emperor and the Navy were engaged in activities far beyond the realm that required considerable fortunes. They could be seen as a failure of the Emperor to keep his attention on the proper management of government within the nation. Furthermore, such a map was a threat to longstanding traditions of an overseas paradise that was reserved for the "Immortals."

Copies of the Taoist map probably circulated among admirals, foreign dignitaries, and businessmen who were involved in Zhu Di's International Trade Alliance. Such a document would have aided in the planning of transoceanic voyages and the contracting for goods and services between merchants living in distant regions of the globe. However, in the hands of the Confucian ministers, such evidence of global involvement on the part of the Emperor could have led to his assassination, civil war, and the collapse of the government.

Within the borders of China, the Ming World Map remained a secret. The official history barely mentioned Zheng He's involvement in overseas trade. Nevertheless, the Confucian bureaucrats began to groan about the enormous demands that were being placed on the peasants and businesses to supply the enormous fleets. The government continued to print paper money to pay for the overseas commercial ventures, as well as the secret voyages; but the scarcity of goods needed for domestic markets caused inflation; and there were complaints among influential business leaders who were disappointed in the poor returns they were getting on their overseas investments.

Upon Zhu Di's death in 1422, the Confucian ministers succeeded in a palace coup. They replaced the eunuchs as advisors to the new Emperor— Zhu Gaozhi. The new Ming ruler ordered the cessation of overseas expeditions by the Treasure Fleets. Ambassadors were recalled; future expeditions were cancelled; and the *baochuan* (or "Treasure Ships") under construction were to be left unfinished in the shipyards. In subsequent instructions from the new managers of naval affairs, sailing records, navigational charts, and all official documents that might have aided the cause of any future overseas expeditions were confiscated. Later, they were ordered destroyed when a prominent eunuch again suggested the "foolish" idea of promoting international markets. In this manner, the legacy of Zheng He's voyages was nearly erased entirely.

Zhu Gaozhi's reign lasted only nine months. However, the damage with respect to the expansionist visions of Zhu Di was forever beyond the hands of the Court Eunuchs. As a gesture of goodwill towards the venerable Admiral who had won the hearts of Zhu Di's grandchildren, Zhu Zhanji (Xuan De) authorized one final voyage to take the Old Salt on a voyage to Hormuz. From there, Zheng He could fulfill a lifelong yearning as a Muslim to complete the *Hajj*—the pilgrimage to Mecca.

Admiral Zheng sailed off into the sunset, so to speak, never to return. He sailed from Nanjing Harbor in 1432 knowing full well that the politics of China had made a complete reversal and that he had no future with the new government. When the last vessels from his final expedition to Mecca returned to port in 1434, he was not listed among the crews. Did he stay in India or the Persian Gulf? Was he buried at sea? Or did he follow the example of Jianwen and seek refuge in the New Land—as some theorists have imagined?

What do Historians Think?

For the longest time, Western scholars regarded the legendary Ma Sanbao (the "Three-Jeweled Eunuch") as being more of a myth than reality. He was first known to the west as a consequence of the temples that were erected to his honor throughout Southeast Asia. In these shrines dedicated to Ma Sanbao, he was worshipped as a god. He had the image of a giant among men—a magical figure whose "Seven Voyages" were often confused with a popular Muslim fairytale about the "Seven Voyages of Sinbad the Sailor." Even the tales of the huge *baochuan*, or "Treasure Ships," were ridiculed in professional circles.

"Indeed," asked the sarcastic Western scholars, "how could the Chinese build such impossibly giant ships when they only knew how to build small flat-bottomed riverboats?"

It took the dedicated efforts of Chinese archeologists, the Zheng He Society, and the determination of several inquisitive European travel writers to overturn the silly attitudes of Eurocentric scholars.

The first clues that the Chinese Navy might have undertaken some incredible voyages on the Indian Ocean came with the discovery of several stone monuments in Malaya. Written in three languages, Hindi, Arabic, and Chinese, the inscriptions memorialized Ma Sanbao and his praise of the patron gods of the region. These monuments were intended to set an example of respect the various religious beliefs of the inhabitants and to promote the tolerance of ethnic diversity. The testimonials conveyed the wish of Zhu Di for all the world's peoples to regard themselves as equal members of the World Family.

Of course, Zhu Di's vision of a cooperative "World Family" with its Council of Ambassadors located in Beijing was a totally unrealistic dream for the 15th century. Warfare was at that time still regarded as an acceptable means for nations to achieve their ambitions for wealth and glory. In the few scraps of Chinese memorabilia that have survived from the Ming era, scholars have quoted the Yongle (or "Eternal Bliss") Emperor as saying such poetic things as: "All the world's peoples are as One Family;" and "Bring representatives from all the Four Seas to our new Capital." By the "Four Seas," the Chinese meant the entire world.

Ming Chinese authorities knew that Kublai Khan's explorers had visited countries across the Eastern Ocean; and they knew that the world was round. So there was no question that Zhu Di's vision for a World Assembly included representatives from countries and provinces that were in the New Land. It follows that Zheng He's assignment included provisions for bringing representatives back to Beijing from such places as Mexico and Peru. The logistics for that incredible effort would have entailed establishment of diplomatic and commercial relationships, as well as the creation of new factories, warehouses, and farms to supply the transoceanic merchant fleets. Furthermore, maps of the new seas and mainland would have been essential in order to safely convey foreign ambassadors from their own countries to Beijing.

Until quite recently, the idea that the Chinese Navy might have engaged in transoceanic voyaging has not been regarded as a subject worthy of consideration in Western Academia. It is not uncommon to encounter books that Western scholars wrote in the 1960s and 1970s that describe the Chinese as "not being seafarers," as "being too insular in their attitudes to even think about sailing overseas," or as "not having ships that were suitable for ocean sailing." The presumption among the Western historians has long been that the Chinese might have accomplished great things as a maritime power, however the Beijing government decided to shut down its overseas adventurism "just when it was getting started." Western theorists presumed that Zheng He was conveniently stuck in the seas between Africa and Indonesia—where he would not be a threat to the glory of Columbus.

Many Western historians still harbor this Eurocentric ignorance of the amazing achievements of the Chinese Navy. Indeed, until the 1990s, most Western scholars continued to believe that the Chinese failed to develop suitable hulls for oceangoing vessels until they supposedly copied the curved-bottom ships of the Renaissance European traders in the 16th century. However, that belief was purely nonsense. Then came the 1975 discovery of a Yuan Dynasty merchant ship at Quanzhou Bay in Fujian Province. After examining brass coins that were part of the cargo, archeologists determined that the vessel sank in about the year 1273—or just about at the time that Marco Polo arrived in China. The vessel was about 150-feet long; the hull included twelve bulkheads, a keel, and a curved bottom; and the cargo included merchandise from Africa.

Clearly, the Chinese had already achieved a highly sophisticated shipbuilding technology long before the arrival of the Jesuits. In his landmark book, *The Ship* (1961), Bjørn Landström demonstrated that the Chinese were excellent sailors and shipbuilders. They had built huge vessels during the Song and Yuan Dynasties; and they continued to build huge vessels, the so-called "Pechilli" junks, even after the Ming ban on overseas expeditions went into effect.

More recently, in 1983, archeologists excavated a sternpost rudder at the Nanjing Shipyards that was over 12 meters long (or about 36 feet in length). Nautical experts have estimated that this size of rudder would have been suitable for a vessel about 450-feet long. That is about the length that has been estimated for the *baochuan* in Zheng He's fleets.

Historians have determined that the Admiral conducted seven major voyages to ports between Malaya and Africa. The First Expedition to India included as many as twenty *baochuan* with scores of mid-sized vessels and smaller supply ships. Probably, independent merchants took advantage of the protection offered by such a large fleet. On some occasions, the Expeditions may have numbered several hundred vessels.

In order to minimize the scrutiny of the Confucian ministers, the official Ming records (*Ming Shi Lu*) only provide brief and deliberately vague references to Admiral Zheng He and the Treasure Fleets. One entry simply says: "Zheng He led a fleet as emissary to countries of the Western Ocean." Another entry says only: "Zheng He returned." A stone monument that the Navy erected in 1417 near Quanzhou Harbor identifies Zheng He as a "Viceroy Chief of Military" (or Admiral); and it honors his voyages to Hormuz in the Western Ocean. But it makes no mention of expeditions to New Lands in the Extreme East.

The Fujian Monument, which Admiral Zheng ordered in 1431, is a poetic summary of voyages over a distance of *100,000 li*—essentially meaning that his expeditions sailed a distance of about two times around the world. It tells of "waves rising sky-high like mountains;" and it mentions that the fleet sought "to bring a transforming power of virtue to treat distant people with kindness."

Several historical accounts concerning Zheng He's voyages have surfaced in Chinese archives. A Muslim-Chinese journalist, Ma Huan (a.k.a., Muhammad Hasan) accompanied the Admiral on three voyages (third, sixth, and seventh). Ma's book, *Ying Ya Sheng Lan* (or "the Overall Survey of Ocean Shores," 1451) is the principal reference for information concerning Zheng He's expeditions between Nanjing and Hormuz. Additional sources on the Indian Ocean expeditions include Fei Xin who wrote about "Travels of the Astro Vessels" and Gong Zhen who wrote a treatise called "Countries of the Western Ocean." None of these writers mention the New Lands of the Extreme East—probably because they were restricted to travels in the Indian Ocean.

Likewise, the *Wu Bei Zhi* (or Ming Defense Manual) includes chapters on military equipment, troop management, and tactics, as well as a thorough Navigational Chart of the Indian Ocean. The Chart has detailed sailing routes with star charts, compass directions, sailing times, and landmarks. In other words, it has all the essential information that was needed for escorting foreign ambassadors or carrying merchandise to Chinese ports. This document was regarded as a military secret when it was being used as a guide for practical navigation—thus it would have been almost impossible for Confucian bureaucrats to obtain a copy prior to the cancellation of the overseas expeditions.

Muslim maps were also beyond the reach of the Confucian spies; but they were all available to their ally—Zheng He. A map by the Muslim cartographer Al-Idrisi for King Roger of Sicily was produced in 1154. This map identifies a new land in the West as "Far Land." In 1250, another Muslim cartographer, Ibn Said, identified this mainland as "Ansharus;" and it was later called "Antillia" on 15th century Portuguese maps. These Portuguese documents might have been copied from Muslim or Chinese sources. Thus, it seems apparent from the evidence that the

Arabs were sailing overseas on the Atlantic Ocean; and they were engaged in mapping the East Coast. Archeologists have identified a hoard of Islamic coins from the 11th century that were unearthed near Cambridge, Massachusetts. Other Islamic artifacts, including rock inscriptions and trade money, have been found in New York and Tennessee.

Apparently, European geographers were aware that the Chinese and the Arabs were engaged in exploring the Atlantic Ocean. A message that was included on the Fra Mauro World Map of 1459 beside the Cape of South Africa revealed that a *zoncho de India*, that is a Muslim or a Chinese "junk," had been reported rounding the Cape and sailing far out into the Atlantic Ocean.

In 1890, William Sharp summarized the current understanding about ancient Chinese voyages to the New World in his book *The History of New Jersey* (p.12-13) He noted that:

> The Epicerini, a people of Canada, when the Europeans
> first came among them, asserted that very far from them in
> a western direction, there lived a nation who affirmed that
> foreign merchants, without beards, in great ships frequently
> visited their coasts. We are also told that in Quivira, several
> ships have been found whose sterns were adorned with
> silver and gold which was s distinguishing characteristic of
> the Chinese and Japanese ships. ... Some Chinese vessels
> of considerable force were found wrecked in the Mare del
> Nord above Florida.[1]

In modern times, the more conservative Western historians have dismissed the earlier accounts of wrecked junks along the shores of Colonial America as being "wild speculation." Louise Levathes wrote a traditional historical account of Zheng He's celebrated Seven Voyages in her book *When China Ruled the Waves* (1994). However, she didn't speculate about the possibility that Zheng He's mariners might have sailed beyond the Indian Ocean. Such an idea at the time was still regarded as anathema (that is, "forbidden") in Western academia.

It was not until 2003 that British author Gavin Menzies dared to sail beyond the seas where Western historians have feared to tread water. In his book, *1421—the Year China Discovered America*, he broached the idea that the subordinate admirals of Zheng He had effectively circumnavigated and mapped the whole world before Columbus was born.

Prior to this time, Western historians had reserved the title of "First Circumnavigator of the World" for their own hero, Magellan, who served a Spanish king in 1520. So, Menzies' book was not cheerfully welcomed into the Great Library of History. Indeed, few books in recent memory have incited such a vindictive response. One group of vigilante historians even went so far as to petition the Library of Congress in an effort to prevent Menzies from participating in a seminar that was being held to

---

[1] W. Sharp, *The History of New Jersey*, 1890, 12-13.

honor the 600th Anniversary of Zheng He's first expedition. However, the Director of the Asian Division, Dr. Lee, would not be intimidated. He informed the petitioners that it was not his policy of the U.S. Government to restrict freedom of speech.

In any case, Gavin Menzies contribution to filling in the blank pages of history goes far beyond the publication of his landmark book. He has established a Web Site called 1421TV. This Site continues to serve as a dynamic educational forum. Menzies associates have organized study groups in many countries—thereby helping to broaden our cultural horizons and to make learning about the past more fun for everyone.

It was not until 2005 that a Beijing attorney and history enthusiast, Liu Gang, brought forth a map that he had purchased at a Shanghai antique store a few years earlier. Liu Gang was able to read the text on the map that indicated it was drawn by a copyist named Mo Yi-tong in 1763. According to Mo, the original document was a Ming map that had first been compiled in 1418. If this map were genuine, then it represented the only known copy of the land areas that Admiral Zheng He's mariners had charted in the early 15th century. Incredibly, this map showed New World mainland in great detail. Liu Gang brought this map to the attention of Gavin Menzies who then set into motion an exhaustive effort to authenticate the map.

Menzies arranged for a radiocarbon dating of the map by specialists at Waikato University in New Zealand. Meanwhile, Chinese scholars Lam Yee Din and Tai-peng Wang set about the laborious task of tracking down the origins of the terminology that was used on the map. It was my task to verify the authenticity of the geographical information that the map contained in order to determine if the map was an accurate copy of the original document.

Since I had already studied ancient maps of the New World before Columbus, I was aware of several European agents (or spies) who had gone to the Orient with the express intention of obtaining copies of the Chinese geography. Indeed, by the time of the Polo Brothers and the Yuan Dynasty, it was already evident to European leaders that the Chinese were engaged in mapping the world. We even knew the names of some of the European agents: William of Rubruck, John of Plano Carpini, the Polo Brothers, Marco, Niccolò da Conti, and Pero de Covilha. I was also aware that several Venetian, Portuguese, and German charts showed extensive regions of the world that had not yet been explored by Europeans. In other words, these "early" regions on the European maps had to represent the geographical knowledge that had been obtained by spies. Of particular importance were maps by Albert Cantino (1502), Martin Waldseemüller (1507), and Gerhard Kramer, or Mercator—in 1569. Virtually all of the "early" land areas on the European maps duplicated those that were on the 1418 map. This was conclusive proof that Mo Yi-tong had copied the same kind of Ming charts that the European spies had copied during the early years of the Ming Dynasty. (Further details can be found at the author's web site. See the section of this book on "Resources.")

Finally, the results of the radiocarbon dating came back in March of 2006. By this time, Liu Gang, Tai-peng Wang, and Lam Yee Din had completed the investigation of the terminology used on the map. The radiocarbon dating proved that Mo Yi-tong's copy was made on 18th century paper—just as he had reported in the text. All the terminology was proven to have had Yuan or Ming antecedents; so we were certain that the wording on the map was authentic. And my comparison of "Diagnostic Geographical Markers" on the ancient maps had confirmed that the 1418 Ming Map was identical to the charts that were copied by European spies. Therefore, we could reasonably conclude without any doubt that Liu Gang's antique document was an authentic copy of the 1418 Ming Map.

The existence of this map entirely supports Menzie's theory that the navies of Admiral Zheng He sailed on all the oceans of the world; and they charted all the lands prior to the so-called "Great Age of Discovery" that began in Europe under the auspices of Prince Henry the Navigator. The accounts of all the European mariners saying that they already had maps showing them where to go were true. Prince Pedro of Portugal said in 1425 that he had obtained maps from the Venetians. Columbus said that he had a map. Even Magellan said that he had a map showing the location of the strait below South America before he left Spain. In the past, Western historians have rationalized these facts by relying upon the notion that "good luck," "coincidence," or magic could produce such maps before the European champions sailed off to "discover" new lands. However, the close correspondence between the European spy maps and the 1418 Ming geography proves that the maps that were used by the European explorers were actually derived from the Chinese.

Consequences for New World Exploration

One disastrous result of the sudden turnaround in the Chinese government with respect to the influence of the Taoists and the eunuchs was that a number of expeditionary teams were left stranded on foreign shores. Hundreds of Chinese nationals had no hope of ever returning home. Some of these expatriates were probably among the small pockets of Chinese immigrants that European explorers encountered from time-to-time during the Renaissance in the most unlikely places.

In the 1580s, the English explorer Martin Frobisher reported sighting a boat of "Chinese sailors" near Baffin Island while he was searching for the legendary Northwest Passage. He dutifully wrote down what he saw—apparently to no avail. Modern historians typically don't mention that Frobisher identified the mariners as "Chinese," or they simply explain away Frobisher's observation as a simple mistake. According to one popular rationalization in academia, if the natives in a particular area looked a bit more "Asian" than their neighbors, it was simply a consequence of the normal ethnic diversity of the population. Historians made this mistake even though natives sometimes referred to their distinctive contemporaries as "Chinos"—which was the Hispanic word for the Chinese people.

Along the West Coast, the word "Chino" was particularly common. Apparently, that was because there were plenty of ancient Chinese immigrants in the area. In California, divers identified circular, doughnut-shaped anchor stones that had at one time been weights for the anchors that were used on ancient Chinese fishing boats. There was at least one report of beached junks with distinctive woodcarvings that were identified as Chinese; and the missionaries noticed the presence of a diminutive breed of horse that was also called "a chino."

In Mexico, the Spaniards identified one group of people as the "Chams"—which denoted the Vietnamese. Another group of recent immigrants was called the "Tarascans." Mexicans tended to identify the Tarascans as being either Chinese or Japanese. Artists in Colima distinguished an unusual ceramic style (called "Chino pots") as being the product of another immigrant group—the "Chinos." In Peru, Chinese names were as thick as flies on a dead calf. There was the "China River" near Cuzco and the coastal towns of Chan and Chan-Chan. All are references to China or the Chinese people.

One important consequence with respect to European voyages of discovery was that Zheng He's Indian Ocean Supermarket served as a magnet for European exploration. Everybody in Europe, it seems, wanted to find a shortcut to the Spice Islands or to the markets of Cathay. The initial target of Prince Henry the Navigator of Portugal in 1420 was probably Zheng He's Indian Ocean terminus at Sofala, Africa.

The second major consequence was a result of Portuguese intelligence and the ability of their agents, by hook-or-by-crook, to obtain copies of the 1418 Ming World Map. With this map in hand, the Portuguese were able to determine that the best sailing route to the Spice Islands was by way of the eastern approach around the Cape of South Africa. The essential problem facing the Portuguese was this: "How could they possibly keep this vital geographical knowledge away from rival European kingdoms?"

Of course, Prince Henry and King John soon had a grand scheme—or a "Joker"—up their sleeves.

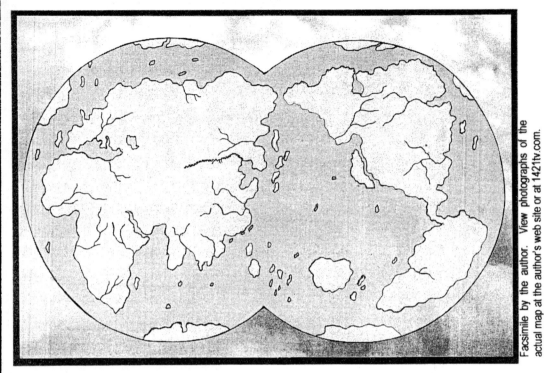

Facsimile by the author. View photographs of the actual map at the author's web site or at 1421tv.com.

1418 Ming Map of the Whole World

This is a simplified rendering of a document that Beijing antiquities scholar Liu Gang discovered at a Shanghai antique store. It shows a remarkably accurate understanding of the world that could only have been achieved by explorers who circumnavigated all the world's inhabited continents. It is conclusive evidence that Zheng He's mariners effectively circumnavigated the earth. Chinese artist Mo Yi-tong diligently copied the original map in 1763 during the Qing Dynasty. It is a composite map that includes details from prior Yuan explorers, early Ming explorers, and Muslim navigators. The "dual-hemispheric" style of the map was part of the contemporaneous method that Taoist artists used to portray simultaneously both sides of the moon (below, right). It was also present in symbolic art in which two superimposed coins represent "both sides" of the world. European geographers probably borrowed the design from the Arabs. See the Arabian map (below) from the Khalili Manuscript.

Khalili Manuscript, Ottoman Turkey, 1756

Chinese Coins showing: The World

Taoist Scroll, Beijing c. 1250-1750

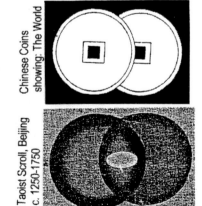

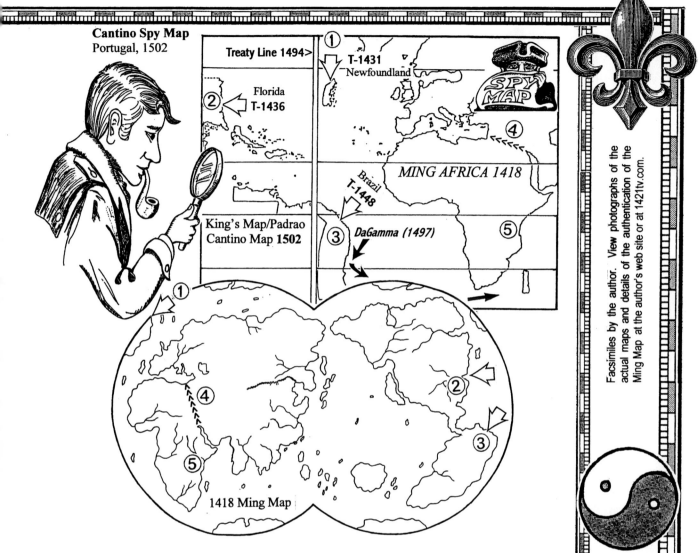

Cantino Spy Map
Portugal, 1502

Treaty Line 1494>

① T-1431
Newfoundland

SPY MAP

Florida
② T-1436

④

MING AFRICA 1418

King's Map/Padrao
Cantino Map **1502**

Brazil
T-1448

③ *DaGamma (1497)*

⑤

Facsimiles by the author. View photographs of the actual maps and details of the authentication of the Ming Map at the author's web site or at 1421tv.com.

① ② ③ ④ ⑤

1418 Ming Map

Time Detectives Look at the Fruits of Espionage

A comparison of the 1418 Ming Map to an Italian "spy map" of 1502 helps to reveal the tremendous geographical advantages that Europeans gained by stealing (or otherwise appropriating) copies of maps from the early Ming discoveries. The so-called "Cantino Map" (1502, above right) is a copy of the super-secret Portuguese "King's Map" or *Padrao*. An Italian spy, Albert Cantino, obtained this map after bribing a royal geographer. The Portuguese map has several errors (or diagnostic geographical "markers"). These errors reveal that the Portuguese map is actually a copy of the earlier Ming Map. For example, Labrador and Newfoundland (1) mistakenly appear as an island east of the continent; North America's East Coast is mistakenly shown with a straight north-south orientation; and the "neck" of Africa at Suez (4) is far too wide. The spy, Niccolo da Conti, obtained Ming geographical knowledge during his trip to India in 1421-1425. This knowledge made it possible for the Portuguese to begin the conquest of Newfoundland in 1431. In 1497, Vasco da Gama sailed beyond sight of land for three months riding the South Atlantic Current to the Cape of South Africa. This incredible feat of navigation was only possible because the Portuguese had prior knowledge of the geography of the South Atlantic. Both maps show an incredibly accurate East Coast of Africa (5)—which was made possible by Zheng He's mariners, astronomers, and Muslim allies in Africa.

Selden Codex
①

Ming Bronze Bowl
②

Ming Bronze disc
③

Buddhist Bronze Scepter
④

Zheng He

Buddhist Bronze Plate
⑤

⑥

⑦

Inca ceramic, Peru
Paul Marcoy 1875 (199)
⑧

166

Evidence of Contact *in the* New World

Petroglyphs in California

Grafitti in Peru

by Edward Curtis, showing Native use of Chinese Coins

Wishram Bride, Oregon, c. 1900

Chinese Trader's Stamp

Artifacts of Ming Overseas Enterprise

Zheng He's overseas expeditions had a considerable impact on New World cultures—leaving behind in their wakes numerous artifacts and testimonials of their passing. Unfortunately, the rapid arrival of Europeans in the 16th century and the European import of Ming ceramics, etc., has left us a murky picture of undated Ming relics in the archeological record.

The 15th century "Selden Codex" (1) from Mixtec Mexico—but found by Mr. Selden in China—is probably a relic from the Ming overseas trade. Two artifacts, a bronze bowl from the Sacramento River Valley in California (2) and a bronze disc from the East Coast (3), have Chinese inscriptions from the period of the 5th Ming Emperor—Zuan Di. Both were found lying in the ground without any meaningful archeological context. A pile of undated Chinese bronze religious artifacts (4, & 5) and some Ming coins have turned up on Indian reservations in the Northwest. There is an archeological context for Inca Peruvian jars with Chinese writing (6, 7, 8). Yin/Yang petroglyphs in southern California and Peruvian graffiti are impossible to date. However, Spaniards reported that the Paramount Inca Ruler, Atahualpa, had silk tunics; and the missionaries found lemons and pomegranates growing in Peruvian orchards—so we know that the Chinese mariners had been there.

Matteo Ricci, c. 1600

The Second Ming Map—Shanhai Yudi Quantu c. 1425

The author presented this map to the Library of Congress Zheng He Symposium in May of 2005. Previously, Western historians had mistakenly concluded that it was simply a map that Jesuits concocted at their Bejing studio in about the year 1600. Actually, the Jesuits had a much more accurate map that was based on the work of the European cartographer Abraham Ortelius. It was the intention of Matteo Ricci who was a Jesuit in Beijing to demonstrate the superiority of European geography (and presumably religion) by comparing Zheng He's last world chart, the Shanhai Yudi Quantu, to the World Map by Ortelius. The author demonstrated that this map is actually based on ancient Chinese traditions extending back to the style and method seen in the ancient Shanhai Jing (Tien Xia Tu). Even though this schematic type of map appears on the surface to look "older" than the 1418 Ming Map, it actually has geographical features (or "markers") that reveal that it was based on more recent explorations. For example, the map includes Peninsular Florida, mainland Labrador, and Peninsular California—all of which were absent on the 1418 Map. Also, there is no southern bulge on the West Coast of South America. This map includes the Antilles and the Gulf of Mexico—also absent on the 1418 Ming Map. Unfortunately, the Ming geographer moved Australia to a position around the South Pole. This placement apparently led to the erroneous idea among European geographers that there was a "Southern Continent" in that location.

after a map by Wang Qi c. 1600/1601
Source: facimile of Shanhai Yudi Quantu by the author
For proofs and further details see author's web site.

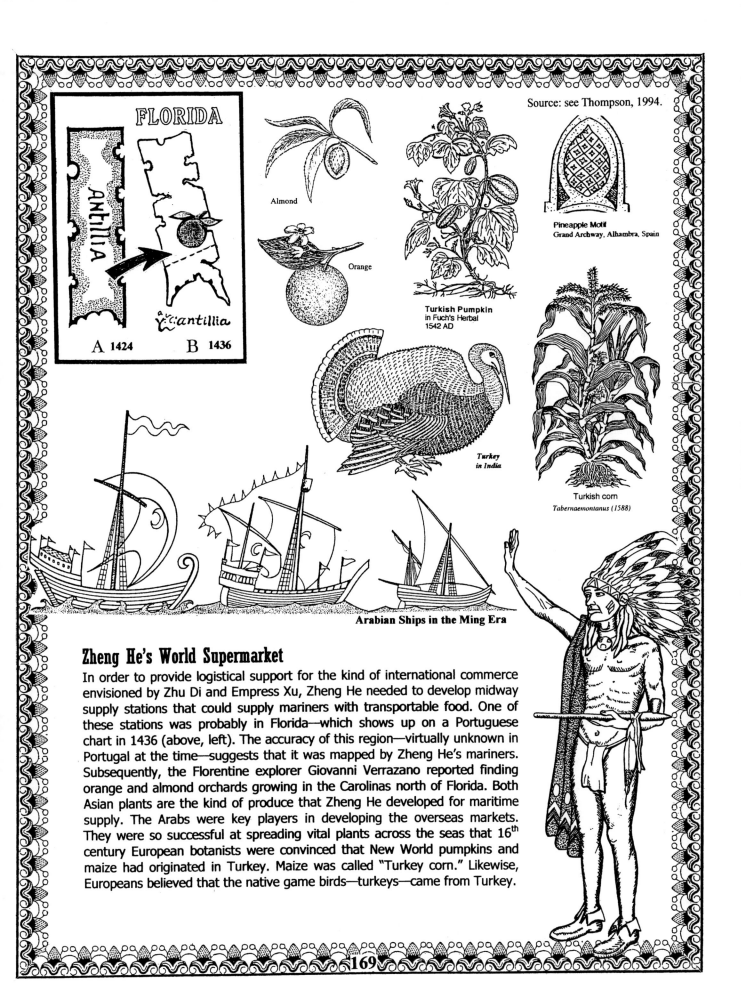

FLORIDA

Antillia

a Cantillia

A 1424   B 1436

Almond

Orange

Source: see Thompson, 1994.

Turkish Pumpkin
in Fuch's Herbal
1542 AD

Pineapple Motif
Grand Archway, Alhambra, Spain

*Turkey
in India*

Turkish corn
Tabernaemontanus (1588)

Arabian Ships in the Ming Era

Zheng He's World Supermarket

In order to provide logistical support for the kind of international commerce envisioned by Zhu Di and Empress Xu, Zheng He needed to develop midway supply stations that could supply mariners with transportable food. One of these stations was probably in Florida—which shows up on a Portuguese chart in 1436 (above, left). The accuracy of this region—virtually unknown in Portugal at the time—suggests that it was mapped by Zheng He's mariners. Subsequently, the Florentine explorer Giovanni Verrazano reported finding orange and almond orchards growing in the Carolinas north of Florida. Both Asian plants are the kind of produce that Zheng He developed for maritime supply. The Arabs were key players in developing the overseas markets. They were so successful at spreading vital plants across the seas that 16th century European botanists were convinced that New World pumpkins and maize had originated in Turkey. Maize was called "Turkey corn." Likewise, Europeans believed that the native game birds—turkeys—came from Turkey.

Field Trip to the Ming Observatory in Beijing—March, 2006

Between meetings with the international press, there was time to explore the Ming Observatory that played a vital role in astronomical observations. Above, Gavin Menzies discusses navigation with the Director of the Observatory. Below, some of the bronze instruments that Ming astronomers used to observe the stars.

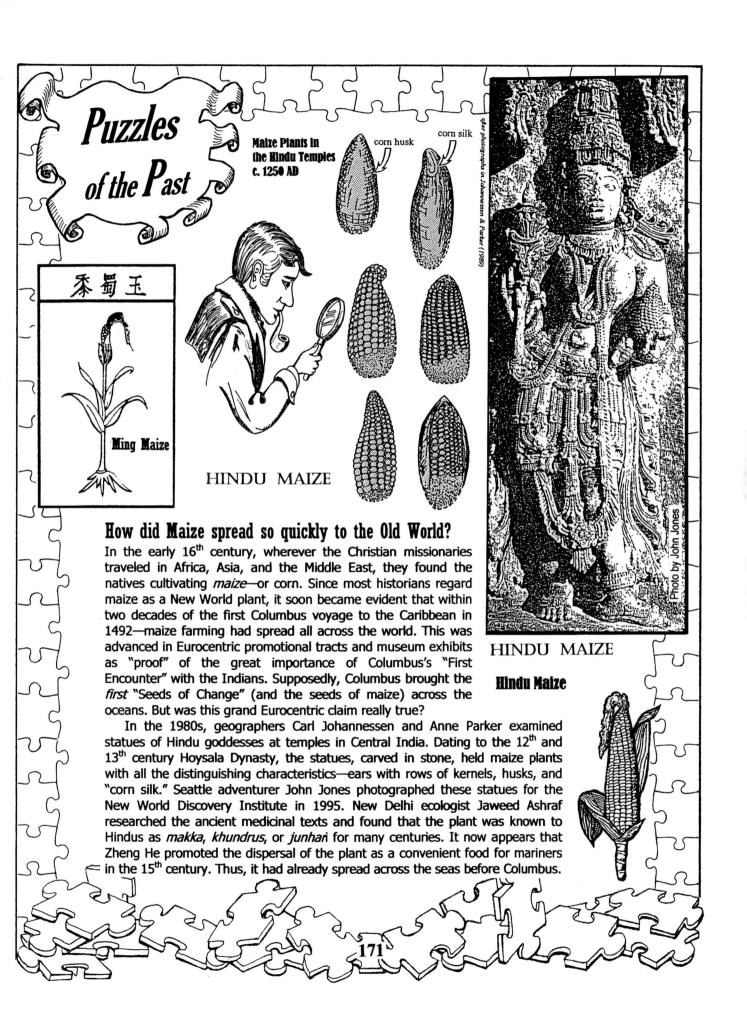

Puzzles of the Past

Maize Plants in the Hindu Temples c. 1250 AD

corn husk

corn silk

after photographs in Johannessen & Parker (1989)

玉蜀黍

Ming Maize

HINDU MAIZE

Photo by John Jones

HINDU MAIZE

How did Maize spread so quickly to the Old World?

In the early 16th century, wherever the Christian missionaries traveled in Africa, Asia, and the Middle East, they found the natives cultivating *maize*—or corn. Since most historians regard maize as a New World plant, it soon became evident that within two decades of the first Columbus voyage to the Caribbean in 1492—maize farming had spread all across the world. This was advanced in Eurocentric promotional tracts and museum exhibits as "proof" of the great importance of Columbus's "First Encounter" with the Indians. Supposedly, Columbus brought the *first* "Seeds of Change" (and the seeds of maize) across the oceans. But was this grand Eurocentric claim really true?

In the 1980s, geographers Carl Johannessen and Anne Parker examined statues of Hindu goddesses at temples in Central India. Dating to the 12th and 13th century Hoysala Dynasty, the statues, carved in stone, held maize plants with all the distinguishing characteristics—ears with rows of kernels, husks, and "corn silk." Seattle adventurer John Jones photographed these statues for the New World Discovery Institute in 1995. New Delhi ecologist Jaweed Ashraf researched the ancient medicinal texts and found that the plant was known to Hindus as *makka, khundrus,* or *junhari* for many centuries. It now appears that Zheng He promoted the dispersal of the plant as a convenient food for mariners in the 15th century. Thus, it had already spread across the seas before Columbus.

Hindu Maize

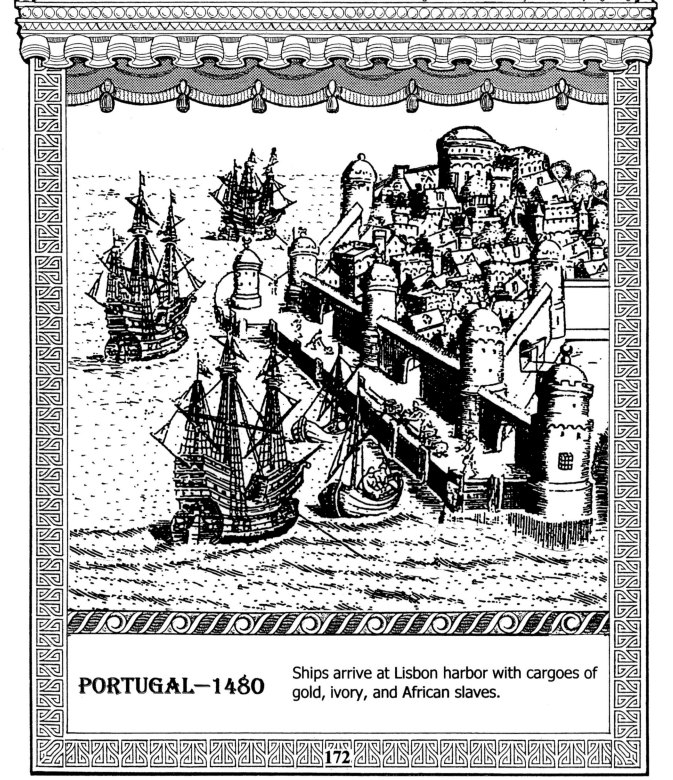

PORTUGAL—1480

Ships arrive at Lisbon harbor with cargoes of gold, ivory, and African slaves.

172

Martin Behaim & Terra Incognita

AT THE VERY DAWN of the Renaissance, a cocoon of intrigue and deception was tightly wrapped around Portuguese voyages to the New World. There was no secret about the fact that the Portuguese were sending expeditions to the far-flung regions of the Atlantic Ocean. Indeed, practically everybody in Europe knew that the Portuguese and the Venetians were engaged in the development of a maritime empire. This venture was launched in 1420 under the auspices of the devout—yet diabolical—Prince Henry the Navigator.

Probably, the two most compelling factors in this maritime initiative were the popularity of Marco Polo's Book of Travels and the success of Zheng He's Indian Ocean Supermarket. Marco Polo's tales about "Isles of Gold" inspired businessmen to dream of getting rich; while the proximity of Zheng He's fleets bringing Oriental goods to the East Coast of Africa seemed to provide quick-and-easy access to the riches of the Orient. This "eastern route" provided a way to obtain Asian imports without having to deal with the unscrupulous Arab merchants in the Middle East. Henry's leadership of the corporation lasted for forty years—from 1420 through 1460. During this time, he sent many expeditions both towards the "Far West," that is, ancient America, and to the Far East by way of the African Continent. However, precisely where his mariners were going and what they found when they got there remained closely guarded secrets.

It was common knowledge throughout Europe that the authorities in Lisbon regarded the new maps of overseas territories as being of the utmost importance to national security. Thus, the punishment for possession of such maps with the intention of selling them to rival kingdoms was execution or life imprisonment. Mariners sailing overseas were issued only those charts that were absolutely essential to the specific missions; thus none of the captains ever had access to maps beyond a very limited region of the earth. Only the king and his closest advisors ever saw a map of the entire world. The Portuguese called the King's secret map the

Royal Cosmographer, Navigator, Spy
Martin Behaim (1459-1506)
German Expatriate; Portuguese Agent

Church Leader of Christian Europe
Pope Nicholas V (p. 1447-1455)
Granted African Sea Route to Portugal—1454

The Mark
Christobol Colon (1459-1506)
Genoese Wool Merchant, Self Promoter

Mastermind of Secret Discovery
& Architect of Deception
King John II of Portugal
Nickname: "The Perfect Prince"
(r. 1480-1495)

Padrao (or "King's Map"). Only this *Padrao* included the latest information that had been assembled from all the overseas expeditions.

Before a new flotilla sailed from Lisbon, the authorities reminded the crews and the officers about the policy regarding maps and geographical secrets. When the vessels returned to port, it was customary for the Secret Police to confiscate all maps and journals that had been produced on the voyage. Official reports in the newspapers of the time did not report the discovery of "New Lands." However, they sometimes mentioned the names of foreigners or traitors who were found in possession of secret maps and the executions that followed. Rumors of such harsh punishments spread to the shanties and taverns of harbors all across Europe. So did the tales of harsh treatment that occurred whenever foreign sailors were captured in "Portuguese waters" along the "Ivory Coast" of Africa. Typically, they were thrown overboard to the sharks.

The assorted maps, chronicles, testimonials, and personal letters that have survived from the 15th century paint a vivid picture of the Portuguese effort to explore and map the Western Atlantic Isles. We know that Goncalo Velho Cabral led an expedition seeking *Antilia* in 1425. Some ancient geographers regarded this "Isle of Antilia" as the remnant of the Lost Island of Atlantis. It was also supposed to have been the refuge for Portuguese Christians who fled the Saracen invasion of the Iberian Peninsula (or southwestern Europe) in the 8th century. Supposedly, there were seven bishops leading this band of Christian refugees; and the established "seven cities" in the New Land. Subsequently, the Portuguese Isle of Antillia was also called; "the Island of Seven Cities." This was probably a general designation for the Eastern Seaboard from Newfoundland to Florida.

There was no report that Cabral found anything on this 1425 expedition; but no "report" should be expected, because that was the nature of secret voyages. On the other hand, Portugal's Ministry of Disinformation sometimes released a bogus report that was intended to confuse rival businesses and the kings of foreign states. If there was a report, you could be certain that the Portuguese had an ulterior motive besides simply trying to make the record clear for modern historians.

What was this Isle of Antilia or the "Seven Cities?" Why, it was nothing less than the isles and mainland of North America. Since the earliest voyages by the Portuguese were only able to sail for a short distance, there was an initial impression that the lands west of Europe were mostly islands. However, the Portuguese soon became aware that there was a new continent that was situated directly west of Europe. Some time before the voyages of Columbus, the Portuguese cosmographers had become convinced that a new mainland stretched all the way from the Arctic to the Antarctic Seas. The northern region was generally called "Antilia," while the southern section was referred to by such names as *Terra Incognita* ("the Unknown Mainland"), the Antipodes, or Brazil.

**Portuguese Caravel
c. 1430 AD—1600**
(from Culver, 1935,91)

Ships & Shores of the Secret Sailors

where they went & how they got there

Portuguese Secret Isles
Corterealis—Labrador
Baccalaos—Newfoundland
Bay'm India—(Bimini) Florida
Paria—Costa Rica
Brazil—Brazil

Goncalo Cabral sailed west again in 1427; and his expedition encountered the Azores. These were a group of vitally important isles in the mid-Atlantic Ocean. There was no official report of this discovery, since the Lisbon authorities did not want other European powers to know what they were doing. Nevertheless, rumors circulated in the mariner's "watering holes" (that is, the pubs and shanties of Europe) that the Portuguese had found new lands to the west.

Diogo de Sevill began the process of establishing colonies on the Azores in 1427. The common belief among the Portuguese colonists was that the continent of Antilia was located only a short distance farther west.

According to Ferdinand Colon (who was the son and biographer of Columbus), a Portuguese ship was driven by storms to the shore of Antilia in 1430. Upon returning to Lisbon, the crew reported that they had found gold in sand that was taken from the island. This was the sort of gossip that was passed along from one drunken sailor to another. Sometimes, these so-called "reports" were overheard by foreigners who engaged in casual conversation with Portuguese officers along the Lisbon quays. Thus mariners gained a vague impression of the locations of overseas isles and mainland that were eventually identified as "North America."

As for the gold, who can say? Ever since Marco Polo's Book of Travels popularized notions about "Isles of Gold" in the South Seas east of China, practically every mariner in Europe dreamed about finding the Isles of Mermaids and the Isles of Gold. Spreading rumors about "gold" on the foreign isles was one way to inspire the enlistment of common sailors on dangerous expeditions across the ocean. It was also a cunning strategy for distracting rivals from the real interests of the Portuguese mariners.

Goncalo Cabral sailed west seeking the Island of Antilia in 1431. The historian Henry Harrisse (1892) noted that Cabral's effort to find Antilia resulted from examining a map that Prince Pedro had obtained from the Venetians in 1428. The source of this map could have been Marco Polo's East Coast voyages with the Venetians or perhaps the expeditions of the English Franciscans to Nova Scotia between 1330 and 1360. The Franciscan charts had by this time been incorporated into the World Commercial Map that the Venetian cartographer Albertin DeVirga had compiled sometime between 1410 and 1420. In any case, the New World mainland was already indicated on a map that the Portuguese had in their possession following Prince Pedro's trip to Venice.

João Fernandes sailed west towards Antilia on numerous occasions. Sometime after 1431, he must have found the mainland and a gulf in the region of Newfoundland, because he was eventually able to lead an English expedition under John Cabot directly to the mouth of the St. Lawrence River in 1498. Vincent Dias led an expedition towards Antilia in 1445; and he was followed by Diego de Tieve in 1454. There followed voyages by Dom Fernão in 1457, João Vogado in 1460, and Jão Vaz Corte-Real in 1464. According to the *History of the Azores* (1717), Jão Vaz had returned to the Azores from an expedition to the "Bacalaos." This was a Portuguese/Basque term that referred to the codfish or "stockfish" of the Newfoundland Banks. Clearly, Jão Vaz had reached the same region of the East Coast near Newfoundland that was already known by virtue of the expeditions of João Fernandes.

We know about these Portuguese voyages to ancient America because the Time Detectives have managed to piece together clues from a multitude of sources. Sometimes, these expeditions were mentioned in personal correspondence that came to light only in the 18th century. Other clues can be derived from contemporaneous reports by foreigners such as Ferdinand Columbus and Sebastian Cabot who conducted their own investigations in order to explain some of the peculiar experiences that we hear about from mariners who were not part of the Portuguese conspiracy. For example, reports that John Cabot's Portuguese pilot, João Fernandez already knew the location of Greenland *before* he sailed with the English in 1497 clearly reveals that he had already been there.

Numerous 15th and 16th century maps confirm that the Portuguese had found and charted mainland along the shores of North America—long before the "official" discovery by Columbus and the other "latecomers" who followed. The Adrea Bainco Map of 1436 clearly shows a southeastern peninsula in the shape of modern-day Florida extending from a huge island west of Portugal that is identified as *Yesla Antilia*—or the Island of Antilia. This mainland, obviously showing Florida and the Carolinas, is situated in the Atlantic Ocean west of the Azores and the Sargasso Sea. An anonymous 1490 world map called "the Paris Map" has a group of islands in the exact location for the Newfoundland Archipelago. Such a map was probably derived from the prior voyages of João Fernandes and Jão Vaz Corte-Real into this region. The exactness of the longitude and latitude for the islands on this Paris Map demands further explanation. Either the Portuguese had succeeded in learning the technique of calculating "lunar distances" by this point in time, or they were utilizing early versions of the portable mechanical clock. It is also possible that they had obtained maps of this region from the Ming Chinese.

In 1534, the Portuguese cartographer Dourado identified the coast of Labrador as having a *Baia de João Vaz*—that is, "the Bay of João Vaz." Such a name indicates that some unidentified Portuguese navigator or geographer believed that that this was the location of a bay that Jão Vaz had utilized on his voyage in 1464.

The Miller Atlas (circa 1519) identified the region of modern-day New England as *Terra Corte-Regalis*—that is, the "Region of Corte-Real." In 1475, the King of Denmark asked the Portuguese for assistance in determining the fate of Christians who had fled the Arctic Island of Greenland. At this time, Greenland had come under Danish control; and the king was reasonably concerned about the fate of his Christian subjects. They had abandoned the Greenland settlements because of the increasing cold weather in the middle of the 14th century. According to an Icelandic bishop, the inhabitants of Greenland had taken refuge among the inhabitants of North America. They had sailed southwest and settled in the temperate region of Old Vineland and Great Ireland.

The joint Danish-Portuguese expedition was under the leadership of a pilot named Johannes Scolvus (or Skolp). He is variously described as a Dane or a Pole who was skilled as a navigator. They sailed in 1476 to a region that is variously identified as *Groetland* (that is, "Great Land") or as *Laboratorus*. This is a Portuguese-Latin title for the Canadian Maritime Province of Labrador. The title derives from the Portuguese word *laborador*—meaning "farmer." It is apparent that the Portuguese-Danish explorers found freehold farmers (that is, Danes, Norwegians, and Germans) living in the region of the Gulf of St. Lawrence. Numerous 16th century maps by Gema Frisius (1537), John Lok (1582), and Cornelius Wyfliet (1597) indicate that Scolvus reached an island or mainland west of Greenland. If we adjust the location of this island for the regional effect of magnetic declination from True North, this Island of Laboratorus then assumes the right location for Labrador. Clearly, there was common agreement among 16th century geographers that the Portuguese-Danish team had traveled to America's East Coast in the region of modern-day Labrador and Newfoundland.

The following year, in 1477, Christobal Colon (later, Columbus) arrived to investigate stories that he had heard about Vineland and a shortcut to Cathay. The Genoese mariner noted in one of his books that:

> I navigated for 100 leagues in the year of 1477, in the month of February, to an island—Ultra Tile. The southern part is 73° and not 63° as some people say. And it is not within the line that includes the West, as Ptolomeo says, but much further west. And to this island, that is as large as England, go the English with merchandise, especially those of Bristol. At the time that I went, the ocean was not frozen, notwithstanding that there were great tides, such that in some parts two times in the day they would rise 25 brazos and descend others the same in height. It is quite true that the Tile of Ptolomeo is where he says; and that it is currently called Frislanda.[1]

As "Tile" was the Norwegian/Danish name for Iceland, this "Ultra Tile" of Columbus would have to refer to the North American coast in the vicinity of Newfoundland or Nova Scotia. This was the region that was known to the English as "the Icelandic Isles," "Great Ireland" or "Wineland"—that is, it was in the same area as the old Nordic colony of farms and hillforts that was sometimes called "Norveca" or "Dusky Norway." This was the same region that the Portuguese called Labrador or Terra Corte-Real. The isle that Columbus called "Frisland" was probably another reference to one of the Icelandic Isles in the Newfoundland

---

[1] Christopher Columbus, circa 1490. From Las Casas, *Historia*, c. 1540. Translation by Yellen, 1992. From a notation in one of the mariner's own books found in the Columbus Library. See Thompson, 1996, 195.

Archipelago. Even at the time of Columbus, this was a customary sailing area for merchant ships from Bristol. Since mariners reached "Frisland" by sailing by compass bearings "due north" of Iceland—there was a common misconception regarding the actual location of this region of European settlements. Many common sailors believed that Frisland was situated near the North Pole. In the seas west of Iceland, the compass has an error of magnetic variation that sometimes exceeds 90°. Mariners who thought that they were sailing north were actually on a course *due west*.

Along the coast of Nova Scotia, near the Bay of Fundy, it is not unusual for the tides to rise and fall by as much as 25-feet (or *brazos*). Clearly, Columbus had sailed to the Maritime Provinces of Canada along with the steady traffic of English merchant ships that plied the northern highway between Scotland, Iceland, and Newfoundland. However, this was a pretty cold territory for a person with Italian blood; so the aspiring discoverer of new worlds, went back home to ponder a more temperate approach for his next voyage to China.

In 1479, Columbus was on the Island of Madeira. Originally, he was sent to this island in the Eastern Atlantic Ocean to obtain a cargo of sugar. However, he wound up courting his future bride, Felipa Moniz Perestrello, who was the daughter of the Governor of Porto Santo. This budding romance might have been part of a scheme by the Genoese mariner to learn the navigational secrets of the Portuguese Navy. In any event, it put him in an excellent position to pump his fiancé for information while romancing the night away with a bottle of Madeira wine. While thus engaged, he was on hand to witness the shipwreck of a vessel under the command of Alonso Sanches DeHuelva. The unfortunate Captain, who Columbus is said to have carried from the pounding surf, was attempting to make port after returning from a voyage to the west. It was probably at this time that Columbus learned valuable information about the distance to the Western Isles as well as the nature of ocean currents and winds.

Two years later, Columbus was in Lisbon. He met with his brother, Bartholomew, and he completed preparations for his meeting with King John II. It was his intention to request royal patronage for his own expedition across the Atlantic Ocean. He called his proposal "the Enterprise of the Indies." This proposal entailed sailing due west of the Canary Islands to the Island of Japan that Marco Polo had identified as being situated 1,500 miles east of China. After establishing diplomatic relations with the Japanese, Columbus intended to sail on west towards a large peninsula of Asia that Marco Polo had identified as the "Zaiton Peninsula" on the East Coast of China. He promised to spread the Christian Faith; and he swore that he would bring back to a considerable fortune in gold, pearls, and spices.

It was at about this time, in 1482, that Columbus met the King's favorite cosmographer. He was a German expatriate named Martin Behaim. Soon, Columbus and Behaim were the best of friends.

New World Voyages to the Antipodes

The arrival of Columbus in Lisbon caused quite a stir in the corridors of the Portuguese Ministry of Secret Intelligence. Ever since the glorious days of Prince Henry the Navigator, the heads of the Secret Service had anticipated that foreign captains and foreign agents would try to take advantage of the Portuguese leadership in world exploration. Usually, those who enlisted in the ranks as officers in the Navy were simply tested and watched in order to determine their loyalties and their intentions. If it was suspected that they were spies, they were simply dumped overboard while away on some cruise; and if needs be, they were reported as "lost at sea." However, the Portuguese authorities regarded the Genoese mariner as a particularly grave security risk because he was intelligent; he was a skilled mariner; and he was unusually handsome.

By compromising the daughter of a Portuguese Governor, Columbus had already shown his ability to use his masculine charms to gain access to secret information. In Porto Santo, they hailed Columbus as "a hero" for carrying a dying captain from the surf. But in the dying words that he heard from the captain's lips, the Genoese hero had learned vital secrets of the Portuguese Navy. Since Columbus was a veteran of the Genoese merchant marine, his intentions were of grave concern because the Genoese were allies with the Spaniards; and the Spaniards were the principal commercial rivals of the Portuguese.

You can be certain that there were plenty of "cloak-and-dagger" intrigues involved with the arrival of Columbus in Lisbon. However, when the man who is the target of your own security agents is also popular among the young damsels who are the daughters of influential businessmen, then more "cloak" than "dagger" is required. Simply put: the Portuguese authorities did not trust Columbus; but they at least had to make it appear as though they were treating him fairly.

It was therefore decided to hook up the Genoese mariner with another foreigner who had already proven his loyalty to the King. The foreigner's name was Martin Behaim. A German expatriate, Behaim had come to Lisbon in about the year 1480 as an enterprising cosmographer. That is to say: he was a mapmaker and geographer by training. His hometown of Nuremberg was one of the most prominent Cities in Europe. It was a cosmopolitan center of philosophy, technological development, and astronomy. Indeed, Martin had studied the latest Arabian methods of determining longitude by a method that was known as "lunar distances." And he had studied under the famous German mathematician Regiomontanus. This German scholar was renowned for making the most reliable astrolabes and mechanical clocks. By calibrating his clocks down to minutes, he was able to increase the accuracy in estimating longitude from several degrees to only a few minutes of arc. This improvement in calculating time resulted in the enormous improvement that we begin to see in Portuguese maps towards the end of the 15th century.

King John's advisors appointed Martin to a position in the India House (or Ministry of Geography) where he presumably had access to the *Padrao*—the super-secret world map.

This appointment gave Martin the kind of status in the government that made his friendship seem of great potential benefit to the Genoese mariner—Columbus. The two individuals saw each other often in social and business activities. Perhaps they first met in the offices of Bartholomew Colon who was the Chief of the Colon Map Company in Lisbon. At the time, Bartholomew was commissioned to copy navigational charts for the supply ships heading to Africa. In any event, their friendship blossomed to the point that Columbus trusted Behaim implicitly. In later years, he even wrote a letter to the Sovereigns of Spain praising Behaim as a thoroughly reliable cosmographer.

At some point in their budding friendship, Columbus may have asked Behaim to use his influence with the authorities to get him a commission on a naval vessel; or the German cartographer might have advanced such an offer. In any case, Columbus was sent as an observer or navigator on a supply ship heading for the "Ivory Coast"—which was the location of Portuguese colonies along the coast of West Africa. During this expedition, Columbus was able to compare his own observations and precise navigational measurements that he made with what he saw on the Portuguese charts of Africa. It was clear to him that the charts were incredibly accurate. It was also apparent that the Portuguese were "grooming" him for some future voyage of great importance. Otherwise, why would they have gone to all the bother to let him see the secret maps and to let him learn the techniques of mapping with the astrolabe and astronomical observation. He was therefore led to believe that if he proved trustworthy, King John would approve his request to lead an expedition west across the Atlantic Ocean to Cathay and the Indies.

While King John mulled over his proposal, the Genoese mariner learned all that he could about the Portuguese expeditions from Martin Behaim. It was at this time that Portuguese authorities, perhaps even Martin himself, showed Columbus a letter from the Florentine cosmographer Paolo Toscanelli. According to this letter that Paolo had sent to a Lisbon scholar (Fernao Martins) in 1474, it was possible to reach Marco Polo's Cathay by making a voyage of only 3,000 miles to the west of Portugal. Since Japan was a mere 1,500 miles to the west, according to Toscanelli's map, there was a convenient stopping point midway across the ocean. Indeed, Japan was so close, and so huge, that it couldn't possibly be missed. Thus, the proposed voyage west seemed like an easy trip for a Portuguese caravel.

We might reasonably pause to wonder why the Portuguese hadn't already decided to make the trip themselves—if it was so incredibly easy as their maps indicated. If Columbus was able to see the advantage of this route so clearly, then why not the Portuguese? A few years later, a

Nuremberg official even proposed that the Portuguese should send Martin Behaim by this route—since he already knew it so well.

Anyway, Martin Behaim concurred with the accuracy of Toscanelli's geography and his estimate for the sailing time to China by the western route across the Atlantic Ocean. He confirmed that the expeditions of King Afonso V's mariners and those of John II had indeed reached mainland only 3,000 miles to the west. He informed his trusting friend, Columbus, that the Portuguese explorers had already begun mapping a large peninsula that extended down from the Asian mainland in a southeastwards direction towards the Tropic of Cancer. (This was, by the way, Florida.) Martin indicated that they presumed this peninsula was the so-called "Zaiton Peninsula" that Marco Polo had identified along the coast of China.

Columbus must have inquired why it was that the Portuguese had failed to establish a colony along the China coast and why it was that they had neglected their obligation to spread the Christian faith among the Chinese people. Martin Behaim's response made it clear that the Portuguese were no longer interested in Marco Polo's Cathay. The Portuguese, he said, had been so busy with their colonies in Africa, and that they had made so much profit from the "Ivory Coast," the "Gold Coast," and the "Slave Coast," that there simply were insufficient resources to follow through with the establishment of a Christian colony in China. That rationale seemed to make sense to the Genoese mariner who had seen through firsthand experience the valuable cargoes of gold, ebony, ivory, salt, and slaves that the Portuguese continually brought north from their African colonies.

By late 1484, King John's Special Committee of Royal Cosmographers finally reached a decision with respect to the feasibility of the Columbus Proposal. They said it was an absurd proposal primarily because the Genoese navigator had based much of his reasoning on the absurd notions of Marco Polo. Here's what they had to say:

> Christavão Colom read a great deal in Marco Polo who spoke persuasively of Oriental matters, of the Kingdom of Cathay and of the Great Island Cypango (*that is, Japan*). He formed the idea that one could sail over the Western Ocean Sea to this Island Cypango and to other unknown lands. With these fancies . . . he came to ask the King Dom João to give him ships to discover the island of Cypango across the Western Ocean. ... The King, seeing that this Christavão Colom was full of words, boastful of his achievements, and that he spoke of the Island Cypango out of imagination and fancy rather than from certain knowledge, gave him little credit. ... They (*the King's advisors, Oritz, Rodrigo, and Vizinho*) all decided that the arguments of Christavão Colom were worthless as they

were based on the imagination or on rumors like that of Marco Polo's Island of Cypango.[2]

Columbus was devastated by the Conclusion that had been reached by the King's advisors. It was a final decision. The immediate consequence was that Columbus was dismissed as a potential Captain on a Portuguese expedition of Chinese discovery.

This decision must have struck Columbus as a farce, because he had for several years kept the company of Martin Behaim who had confirmed that the Portuguese cosmographers regarded Marco Polo's maps and travelogue as a valid representation of world geography. Immediately, Columbus suspected that he was being targeted for an assassination; and he was convinced that the Portuguese fully intended to steal his proposal—his "Enterprise of the Indies." He therefore expected that the deceitful Portuguese would launch their own expeditions to link up with China and Japan. He abruptly fled Lisbon on a boat heading for the border with Spain. At this point in his declining fortunes (he was deeply indebted to private financers in Lisbon), he still believed that his Franciscan friends in Spain would provide him with sanctuary.

Barely a year had passed before Columbus received a note from friends in Lisbon informing him that King John intended to steal the idea of establishing a colony in China. Indeed, he had assigned Martin to accompany an expedition sailing west to Japan, Cathay, and the Indies. Columbus was incensed by this duplicity on the part of King John; yet he was grateful that his friendship with the King's cosmographer gave him inside information regarding Portuguese plans in the Atlantic Ocean. He was now more convinced than ever before that the island the Portuguese were calling *Cypango* (or "Japan") was actually the location of King Solomon's Gold Mines of Ophir. He therefore vowed to seek patronage from the Sovereigns of Spain in his effort to win the race to Cathay and the Golden Island by sailing west.

Behaim sailed as a cosmographer in a small expedition that was under the command of Captain Affonso de Estreito in 1486. A personal agent of the King, Jacobus Carnus, was assigned to supervise the venture. There were three objectives for this expedition. First, they were to establish the accurate longitude of the isles that the Corte-Reals had explored in the region of Newfoundland. This region was a source of vital supplies (such as lumber, tar, masts, and copper). The products of Newfoundland were needed to support the vast shipbuilding programs that were under way in Lisbon in order to build up the fleets that were needed for Da Gama and

---

[2] João de Barros, Da Asia (Lisbon), 1552, I, iii, 2. See J. H. Parry, *The Discovery of South America*, New York: Gaplinger, 1979, 50. Words in italics are added for clarification. The duplicity of Portuguese espionage diplomacy, and propaganda is apparent from the fact that they simultaneously promoted Marco Polo's book—even to the point of issuing their own publication of the book and calling it an important resource for mariners sailing to the Far East. They also promoted Martin Behaim's globe which was propagandized as the latest geography of the whole world; and half of that globe was advertised as having been derived from Marco Polo's Travelogue and maps.

the expeditions *east* to India. Second, they were expected to evaluate the best seaway approach to the southern continent—that is, to the Antipodes. And Third, the Royal Cosmographer (Behaim) was specifically charged with mapping the region that was known as "Brazil."

Ever since the 12th century, rogue mariners sailing along the Atlantic corridors of Europe had been bringing in cargoes of a valuable dyewood called "brasil" or "brasilwood." These cargoes were imported from someplace along the distant shores of the Atlantic Ocean. The Irish were the most notorious importers of this cargo that was of great importance to the wool merchants of London and Florence, as well as the bankers of Venice. Of course, the Irish mariners wanted to keep the location of the brasilwood forests a secret from rival merchants—because it was a valuable source of income. When the Portuguese royalty became allied with Venice in the early 15th century, they were expected to follow through with efforts to locate the forests of dyewood. The next step in the plan was to establish a suitable maritime transport network so that wool merchants in England could rely on a regular supply.

Finding the brasilwood forests raised other concerns. The most important issue was one of religious doctrine. Prince Henry's father, John of Gaunt, had been involved in the early espionage efforts of the Oxford Franciscans who were mapping Norwegian territories in the Newfoundland region. This survey suggested that there was a huge mainland reaching out to the northwest. The Franciscan map, as we noted on a copy of the map by Albertin DeVirga, created the impression that the mainland of "Norveca" was attached to the coast of Norway by an isthmus of land or ice. However, after the Portuguese obtained copies of Ming Chinese Maps, they had no choice but consider the possibility that there was an entirely new continent in the west. Subsequently, they sent explorers to Newfoundland and Brazil who confirmed that there was new mainland that was not part of China. The Portuguese agent, Pero de Covilha sent back reports to Lisbon from the Indies between 1487 and 1493 confirming that the entire East Coast of Asia had been charted; and there were no new lands like those that the Portuguese had found across the Atlantic Ocean. Clearly, the so-called "Western Isles" were actually part of a whole new continent.

This discovery of a new continent raised serious issues regarding the accuracy of the Bible and Church doctrine. However, the Portuguese King was not about to issue a decree stating that the biblical geographers were "all wet." Indeed, the Portuguese people were devout Catholics; although they were not fanatics. After all, they had welcomed the Jewish refugees who had fled from persecution in Spain. Nevertheless, the Portuguese had gained the support of several popes, particularly Nicholas V—who had given them special rights to African territories in exchange for spreading the Christian Faith. Thus, the contingencies of economic diplomacy made it essential for Portuguese geographers to uphold the fiction that mainland across the Atlantic Ocean was part of China.

Portuguese and Venetian explorers charted the eastern coastline of both North and South America by 1447—and they did so with reasonable accuracy. Venetian cosmographers issued a standard map of this New World coastline including Labrador, the Icelandic Isles (or Newfoundland), the Florida Peninsula, the Gulf of Mexico, and the southern continent. Subsequent copies were issued in Florence (as the "Florentine Portolan" of 1447) and in Genoa as the so-called "Genoese Map" of 1457. In order not to offend Church authorities, the New World coastline was indicated on the Venetian Map as though it were the coast of Asia. It was a magical game of geographic deception. Thus, some of the terminology used on the maps, such as Gog & Magog, Tartary, and Cathay, were intended to appease Church authorities. And there were only three continents—in accordance with biblical geography. Meanwhile, the maps depicted the entire northern region as a vast forested wilderness that was wide open to European settlement and trade. The proximity of the Icelandic Isles to this wilderness made it obvious to sailors that these were the lands of early European colonies that could be reached by sailing "north" by compass beyond Iceland.

Thus, cartographers refrained from offending the Church; mariners had a useful tool for planning their voyages across the North Atlantic; and the rival kingdoms of Venice had no idea that a totally new land was situated across the ocean.

Captain Estreito, Fernão Dulmo, and Martin Behaim sailed west with a small flotilla of caravels in 1486. The caravel was a new kind of naval vessel that Prince Henry's designers had developed expressly for the purpose of long-distance sailing. The vessels included several features that had been borrowed from the Chinese—including multiple masts, sternpost rudders, welded iron anchors, brass cannons, and square-shaped sterns. These ships were rigged for either square or lateen (that is, triangular) sails. The optional shape of sails improved the ability of the vessels to sail either down wind (using a square rig) or towards the wind using the "lateen" rig and triangular sails.

The Estreito Expedition spent two or three years sailing along the New World shoreline. From time-to-time, the vessels anchored in a suitable estuary where the cosmographer and astronomers set up an observatory. It was in these locations that Martin Behaim utilized his skills as a mathematician. By plotting the sun's shadow, he was able to determine the exact geographic coordinates—that is, North, South, East, and West. By comparing this result to the direction of the magnetic compass needle, he was able to calculate the amount of magnetic error in compass measurements that were used by surveying crews to plot the land. By taking the altitude of the sun with an astrolabe and by measuring the hours of daylight, Behaim was able to calculate the accurate latitude. At night, he used a nocturnal to measure time. The nocturnal is another Chinese invention that uses the alignment of constellations around Polaris as a kind of clock.

We also know from a mural that was painted in Brussels in about 1450 that secretive European clockmakers had by this point in time developed a portable mechanical clock that was the size of a small suitcase. It was driven by a wind-up steel mainspring. Although its accuracy is debatable, such a device greatly improved the calculation of longitude by the middle of the 15th century. Behaim's training with the German clockmaker Regiomontanus suggests that the student probably had access to such mechanical devices for determining longitude. Probably, the accuracy was within a few minutes or about 100 miles.

Martin also used a telescope to measure the angular distances between two planets (Mars and Venus) and the moon. This technique, called "lunar distances" enabled the calculation of longitude. Another method, which depended upon measuring the local time of lunar eclipses, was also used to estimate longitude. From this massive amount of field measurements, Behaim was able to construct a reasonably accurate coastline on a map between the Carolinas and Brazil. A copy of that coastline was included in the King's Map that an Italian spy, Albert Cantino, obtained from a Portuguese agent in 1502.

Shortly after his return to Lisbon in 1490, Martin was again called upon to undertake a mission for the Portuguese Secret Service. King John II and his advisors were well aware that a number of Italian navigators were parading through the palaces of European kings seeking patrons for their proposed expeditions to new lands across the seas. It seemed that practically everybody was anxious to find Marco Polo's Golden Isle, Japan, Cathay, and the Spice Islands. It was also clear that sooner or later, these rivals would build fleets that could challenge the temporary monopoly that Portugal had obtained from the pope over trade with the African colonies. Both Portugal and Venice stood to lose a considerable fortune. The Venetian bankers had a stake in the outcome because of the huge loans they had given to Lisbon merchants. These financial arrangements involved economic advantages that come from trade treaties and the sharing of confidential information about overseas markets.

King John's advisors proposed a daring scheme to alleviate the threat of competition from European rivals. What they had in mind was to create a state of total geographical confusion throughout Europe. Martin Behaim was chosen as the lead agent because of his stellar reputation as a "Favorite Son" of Nuremberg an as the favorite cosmographer of John II.

The plan was really quite simple. Martin would offer to design a huge globe of the earth revealing for the first time all the latest geographical discoveries of the Portuguese explorers. This globe would be produced in Nuremberg where it could be seen on display at the Town Hall. Since Nuremberg was a prominent center for trade and learning in Europe, the project was guaranteed an immediate audience of the most influential merchants as well as many university students who were on tour. Also, everybody knew that it was the Portuguese and Marco Polo who had acquired the latest geographical information of the world spanning the entire globe from East to West: so there would be no doubt that Martin Behaim's globe would show the world the way that it truly was.

Two years were allotted for the project—1490 to 1492. This was also the time that the Spanish champion, Columbus, was preparing for his so-called "junket" to China. It was therefore not at all coincidental that Martin's project was intended to convey the idea that the Columbus voyage was not such a "big deal"—since he was only sailing to lands that had already been described by Marco Polo and the Portuguese geographers. Furthermore, the reports that Columbus was certain to make—that he had encountered mainland and isles just where it was indicated on Portuguese maps—would have the effect of confirming the veracity of the grand Portuguese deception.

Martin Behaim spent the next two years in Nuremberg. Some days he sat at drawing tables; other days he supervised the artist who crafted the hollow sphere or the painters and cartographers who were charged with filling in all the text that was needed for this thoroughly scientific map of the world. Most of his time, however, was spent in the salons of aristocratic ladies or in the offices and homes of influential business leaders. They were all either "charmed" or "delighted" to entertain such a prestigious guest. By the time that the globe was finished in 1492, all of Europe had heard about his masterpiece; and many scholars had come to Nuremberg at great expense just to see the latest Image of the World.

This globe that Martin called the *Erdapfl* or ("Earth Apple") showed the world as consisting of three continents: Europe, Africa, and Asia. It was in every respect a traditional globe that reflected biblical notions regarding geography. There was a notation for the location of Prester John who had promised to recapture the Holy Lands; and there was a notation regarding the location of the apocalyptic monsters "Gog and Magog." Several notations indicated that the regions of China across the Atlantic Ocean and the Arctic Regions were all portrayed in accordance with Marco Polo's Travelogue. The entire world, said Behaim, was only 18,000 miles in circumference (versus the actual 24,690 miles).

It was clearly evident from this globe that the shortest route to China was by sailing *west* from Spain or Lisbon and heading along the Tropic of Cancer. Right smack in the middle of the Atlantic Ocean was Japan. It was so large that it couldn't possibly be missed. It was loaded down with gold, pearls, and spices—just as Marco Polo had said. So anybody who bothered to sail in this direction for a modest three weeks was bound to become extremely wealthy. Anyone who didn't sail in this direction in order to reach China and the Spice Islands had to be absolutely stupid.

Of course, this version of world geography was totally inaccurate; nor did it have anything at all to do with the kinds of isles and mainland that Portuguese explorers actually found across the Atlantic Ocean; nor did it in fact have any similarity to the real world geography that was charted on the King's secret *Padrao*. In hindsight, it seems incredible that anybody would believe this Grand Deception. However, Behaim's reputation was extraordinary; the reputation of his family in Germany was beyond reproach; he was a "good" Christian who wouldn't dare tell a lie—particularly not one so big; and the name "Marco Polo" carried the whole scheme into outer space. People were convinced that anything attached to his name had to be "the wave of the future." Boy were they in for a ride!

The Portuguese were overjoyed in the spring of 1493 when the Spanish Captain Cristobal Colon arrived in Lisbon. He was kneeling in prayer amidst the wreckage of his storm-driven ship, the *Nina*. Nevertheless, his ego was still going strong. He demanded to see King John—not as a commoner might be received but as a "Prince." Now that he had completed his mission for the Spanish Sovereigns, that is proving that China was west of Europe, he was entitled to be given the courtesies that were due an Admiral and a Viceroy of Spain.

Columbus also intended to shame King John for failing to take advantage of the great opportunity that had been lost by Portugal's failure to back the Enterprise of the Indies. He announced, in he King's presence, that he had followed the maps and spheres that he had seen in Lisbon; and these maps had led him directly to Japan, China, and the Gold Mines of King Solomon. Thus, Spain would reap the rewards that could have gone to the King of Portugal.

The Royal Chronicler, Rue de Piña, wrote that the Spanish Captain boasted about reaching the isles of Marco Polo and King Solomon. However, de Piña gave his own observation that the vain Spanish Captain was mistaken in this assessment. According to the Chronicler, the Genoese mariner had only reached the traditional Portuguese isles of Antilia. This region of earlier Portuguese exploration in the Caribbean Sea is still known by the designation of the "Greater and Lesser Antilles Islands." In an amusing demonstration of his superior geographical knowledge, King John informed Columbus that there was a new continent situated directly south of the Antilles. This continent was not shown on any published Portuguese map. That's because it was still regarded as a geographical secret. Nevertheless, King John felt compelled to put this ignorant Spanish Viceroy in his place. Indeed, by this point in time, Martin Behaim had confirmed that mainland of Brazil or the Antipodes was south of Cuba.

At this point, with Columbus completely at the mercy of the Portuguese, he could have been arrested for piracy. Indeed, there was plenty of evidence that he had sailed into Portuguese possessions in the West; and he had not only stolen from the inhabitants, he had kidnapped some of the residents. Columbus and his crew could have been thrown to the sharks as was the customary punishment for such misdeeds. However, King John realized that Columbus was worth much more alive than he was dead. The Spanish Captain was therefore accorded every diplomatic courtesy; his injured sailors were nursed back to health; and supplies were provided for the repair of his caravel and the trip back to Spain.

Within a few weeks, after paying his respects to the assorted saints and shrines in Portugal, Columbus sailed on to Palos, Spain. Apparently, he was none the wiser following his confrontation with King John. He rationalized that de Piña's insistence that his expedition had only reached Antilia was just a ruse that was designed to conceal the fact that he had indeed found King Solomon's Isle of Gold. One apocryphal claim was that the King of Portugal had struck his chest and exclaimed his grief at failing to back the original Columbus Enterprise. If true, it was only a case of excessive "theatrics" on the part of the bemused Portuguese monarch.

The parade that Columbus led from Palos to Barcelona had the makings of legend. It was bold: that is, it had a band. It was glamorous—with jugglers and mimes. It was a full-scale media circus that was designed to inspire, delude, and seduce. And it was a great success!

Columbus styled himself as the Spanish "underdog," the Champion of Queen Isabel, who beat the haughty Portuguese intellectual, King John II. It was commonly known that John's subjects often referred to him as "The Perfect Prince;" and this was out of consideration for his deceptive qualities. Indeed, his ruthless management style seemed to be tailored after a character called "the Prince" in a book by Machiavelli.

So, Columbus believed that he had beaten the Portuguese Master of Deception. He gave his formal report to the King and Queen of Spain claiming that he had reached China, Japan, and the Spice Islands. As proof of these achievements, he presented the Sovereigns with several Indian captives, some native plants, and a small amount of gold. Since the ship's log and a map by Columbus matched fairly closely the maps that Columbus had brought from Lisbon, it seemed apparent that he had indeed found the land that Marco Polo called Cathay on those maps.

At the time, it seems that nobody in Spain had the slightest inkling that the names on the maps were wrong or that the maps had been altered deliberately in order to mislead trusting Christian mariners. Nor did it seem to occur to anybody that the public display of the latest Portuguese geography was entirely a contradiction to the official Portuguese policy of keeping secret geographical discoveries overseas. Thus, the fanfare surrounding the success of the Columbus voyage and the public euphoria was unstoppable. The Spanish Sovereigns promptly dispatched an embassy to Pope Alexander VI requesting (if not demanding) that he issue a monopoly over the newly discovered shortcut *west* to China.

Pope Alexander did indeed issue a Bull of 1493 giving Spain a monopoly over the western seaway to China. This act would prove to be one of the most embarrassing moments in Church history. It effectively barred all Christian nations from interfering with the Portuguese effort to reach the Spice Islands by sailing around the Cape of South Africa. And it helped to launch the public confrontation between Church authorities and scientists in the 18th century that was known as "the Enlightenment."

What do Historians Think?

Martin Behaim seems a lot like a very rusty nail sticking up from the oaken planks of traditional history. As a German expatriate who served a Portuguese King and the Secret Service of a foreign nation, he has the questionable record of someone who was disloyal to his own country. As a spy, he knew too much. However, he left behind insufficient documentation for historians to have a clue about what he was really doing. In other words, the historical record pertaining to this devious character presents historians with an enigma that they would generally rather ignore. There is simply too much risk for stoic academics to mess with. If the truth about Martin Behaim were ever known, it would upset too many apple carts of traditional history.

The historical record is by no means barren; but it is quite disconcerting—to say the least. There is a passage in Hartmaan Shedel's *Nuremberg Chronicle* of 1493 expressly stating that: "Martin Behaim had sailed across the ocean south of the equator to the *alter orbis* (or "Other World") that was previously unknown to Europeans." The so-called "Other World" was the same title that the Romans, Marco Polo, and Columbus all used in reference to the southern continent or South America. A voyage with Estrito in 1486 would have placed the German cosmographer smack dab in the middle of South America almost ten years before it was "officially discovered" by Columbus.

This passage in the *Chronicle* inspired a number of German historians to conclude that it was Martin Behaim, and not Columbus, who first "discovered" America. At a memorial celebration in 1682, the German Professor J.C. Wagenseil called Martin "a divine hero" in recognition of his New World expedition and maps that led Columbus and Magellan across the ocean. Even the Colonial statesman, Benjamin Franklin, praised Martin Behaim as the "true" discoverer of America. All he had to do was to examine some of the copies of maps that Germans still had from Martin's expeditions in order to confirm the awful truth: Behaim had mapped the coast of Newfoundland, the Carolinas, and Florida ahead of the Spanish hero. This style of early map is essentially the same version of the Eastern Seaboard that showed up in a map by Martin Waldseemüller in 1507. There were other versions still extant when Franklin toured Europe.

However, by the 19th century, most European historians had joined ranks behind the doctrinaire hero—Columbus. In this era of academic elitism and proud Eurocentrism, the notion that anyone might have preceded Columbus was regarded as unacceptable scholarship if not downright heresy. The popular scholar E.G. Ravenstein condemned Professor Wagenseil as being "an unprincipled historian." Supposedly, his supporters were "ignorant" and his evidence was "worthless."[3]

It didn't help the German cosmographer's reputation that he was above all a spy who was loyal to King John II. Unlike Columbus, he was

---

[3] Ravenstein, *Martin Behaim—His Life and Globe*, London: George Phillip & Sons, 1908, 39.

never inspired to concoct the propaganda that he had discovered a shortcut to China; nor did he hire a parade to announce what he had found across the seas. Even his famous globe, which still survives in a Nuremberg museum, had a precarious existence. Within a few years of its creation, it became evident to the City Fathers of Nuremberg that the globe was quite defective with respect to its portrayal of earth's geography. By 1505, the Spanish agent Amerigo Vespucci had revealed the existence of a new southern continent that he called the *Mundus Novus* (or "New World"). Of course, there was no such continent on Behaim's globe. At least, there was no southern continent directly south of the Caribbean Sea where it should have been. Behaim did feature a huge southern extension of Asia on his globe; and the distinguished Mexican historian Gustavo Vargas Martínez has argued that this was an early version of South America.[4]

Regardless of whether or not there is a southern continent on the Nuremberg globe, the City Fathers soon became aware that Martin had deliberately misled them and practically everybody else in Europe regarding what the Portuguese mariners actually knew about the nature of overseas lands. Furthermore, Gerhard Mercator made an inventory of the locations of islands that were mentioned in Marco Polo's Travelogue; and he found only a very limited relationship between the geography of the Travelogue and what was portrayed on Behaim's globe. Thus, during most of the 16th century, Behaim was regarded by his own family and by the City Fathers of Nuremberg—not as a "Favorite Son"—but as a scoundrel.

Consequences for New World Exploration

When the couriers arrived in Lisbon with news about the Papal Bull giving Spain a monopoly over all the new territories in the West, King John II was furious. He summoned his advisors to the palace; he placed the Navy on alert for war; and he dispatched a messenger to Barcelona. If it was war that Ferdinand and Isabel wanted, then war they would have.

It was about at this time that Columbus embarked for the Caribbean with a fleet of fifteen vessels and over a thousand volunteers who were destined to establish the first Spanish colony in the New World. In his absence, and for the next eight months, the ambassadors of Spain and Portugal labored over the details of a Treaty that was designed to settle the territorial dispute and preserve the tenuous peace between the rival nations. In the end, the Treaty of Tordesillas (1494) split the entire world between the two maritime powers of the Iberian Peninsula. Spain was to have access to all the lands beginning at the Line of Demarcation that was placed 170 leagues west of the Canary Islands. The sphere of Portuguese influence included all the Atlantic isles that might be found east of the Line as well as the African coast and the Indian Ocean. In other words, all of Portugal's rivals in the great race to Cathay were effectively shut out

---

[4] Gustavo Martínez, *America en un mapa de 1489*, Universidad Nacional Autonoma de México, 1995.

from the only practical route. Only Portugal was authorized to send ships round the Cape of South Africa to the Indian Ocean.

It was not a coincidence that this Treaty gave Portugal sole access to the valuable dyewood forests of Brazil. Although modern historians have argued vehemently that this good fortune was merely a "stroke of luck," the evidence clearly shows that the Lisbon authorities were aware of the location and the value of this vital natural resource that meant so much to their Venetian allies and bankers. Not only does the coast of Brazil show up on Andrea Bianco's Atlantic Map of 1448, the English spy Robert Thorne was able to uncover the truth regarding the secret expeditions of the Portuguese to the southern continent. According to a letter that Thorne sent to King Henry VIII in 1527:

> The King of Portugal had already discovered certain islands that lie against Cape Verde, and also a certain part of the mainland, towards the south, and he called it the land of Brazil.[5]

Of course, King John was able to advise Columbus regarding the location of the southern continent when he visited Lisbon in 1493. This was not simply a lucky guess or a vague reference to the "mythical Antipodes of the Romans" as some isolationist historians have suggested. It seems most likely that Martin Behaim's navigational charts must have provided the evidence that was needed to prove that Portuguese mariners had by 1486 explored and mapped the coast of Brazil. And it is probably for this reason, the discovery of new lands in the Indies, that King John knighted his lowly cosmographer into the austere "Order of Christ."

Although historians have resoundingly castigated Martin Behaim for the geographical inaccuracies of his globe and his theatrical approach to the business of espionage, King John regarded the German expatriate as one of his most important assets. The King once said of his loyal servant that of all his mariners, "none had traveled farther than Martin Behaim."

His great Nuremberg World Globe changed the course of history. By misleading the rivals of Portugal into believing that Marco Polo's Cathay and the Spice Islands were located directly west of Europe, Portugal was able to build on the original Plan of Prince Henry without undue interference from rival navies. Thus Columbus, Cabot, Vespucci, and Verrazano all sought to find the Spice Islands across the Atlantic Ocean. It was not until Vasco Da Gama returned from India with the first shipment of cloves, ginger, and pepper in 1499 that European kings began to realize that they had all been bamboozled by Martin Behaim's marvelous globe. Never before did a lowly cartographer have such an enormous influence on the course of world events.

---

[5] Robert Thorne, letter to King Henry VIII; in Jack Beeching, Ed., *Richard Hakluyt—Voyages & Discoveries*, London: Penguin, 1972, 50.

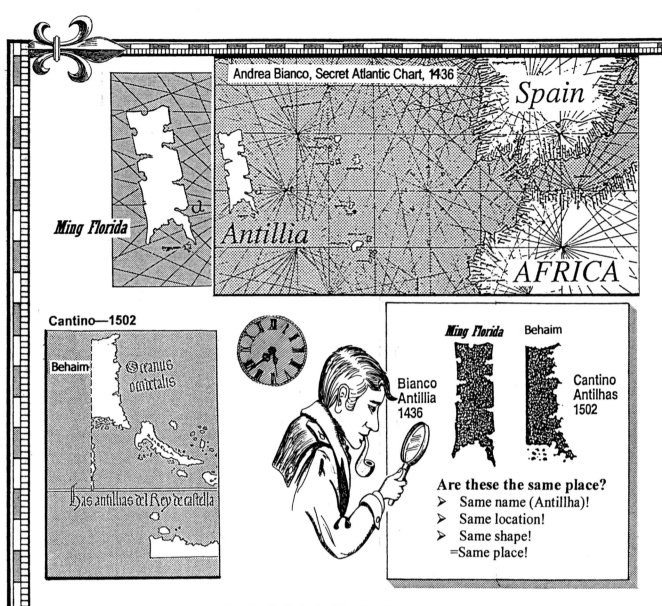

Ming Florida

Andrea Bianco, Secret Atlantic Chart, 1436

Spain

Antillia

AFRICA

Cantino—1502

Behaim

Oceanus orientalis

has antillas del Rey de castella

Ming Florida   Behaim

Bianco
Antillia
1436

Cantino
Antilhas
1502

Are these the same place?
➤ Same name (Antillha)!
➤ Same location!
➤ Same shape!
=Same place!

Martin Behaim's Florida Map

Andrea Bianco's Atlantic Chart (top) included an excellent survey of the Florida Peninsula that was probably derived from Ming maps that Niccolò da Conti brought back from India in 1425. Behaim accompanied an expedition with Fernão Dulmo and João Affonso do Estreito to the East Coast in 1486. It was at this time that he completed a new survey map of the Florida Peninsula. A copy of Behaim's East Coast was included in the Cantino Spy Map of 1502 (above, left). Benjamin Franklin examined copies of Behaim's maps while touring Europe. He concluded that Behaim was "the true discoverer of America."

Q. *"What can you tell from Ben's endorsement?"*
Q. *"Why did Martin make the West Coast so straight?"*

Source: Thompson, 1994, 1996, 2000

Andrea Bianco—1448

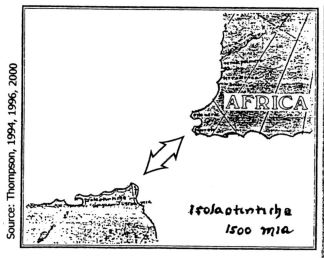

AFRICA

Isolaotintiche
1500 mia

Johann Schoner's Globe 1515 A D

Early Portuguese Knowledge of South America & Brazil

When Columbus stopped at Lisbon in 1493, the King of Portugal—John II—informed him that his voyage had only taken him to "the Antilhas." Portuguese geographers were already aware of these isles that were shown on Portuguese maps due west of Europe. They are the same isles that are today known as "the Antilles"—Cuba, Haiti, Jamaica, etc. The Portuguese did not lay claim to these isles—probably because there was a current interest on the part of Venetian authorities and bankers who were the principal lenders to the Portuguese government. John II also informed Columbus that there was "mainland" directly south of the Antilles—which indicates that the Portuguese were familiar with the region. This should not come as a surprise since the Portuguese had charted mainland along the coast of Brazil—which appears on Andrea Bianco's chart of 1448 (above left). Probably, the Portuguese investigated this coast after gaining access to Ming maps. The Portuguese spy, Pero de Covilha sent back reports from India between 1487 and 1493. A report in Shedele's Chronicle of 1493 stated that "Martin Behaim had crossed the Equator and reached the 'Other World'" in the company of Jacob Canus." The "Other World" is the name that the Romans, Marco Polo, and Columbus all used for South America. The regions that Behaim surveyed before Columbus are indicated on the map by Johann Schöner (1515, above, right). Behaim probably used a mechanical clock and a technique called "lunar distances" to calculate longitude. Precise mapping of the Brazilian coast was a prerequisite for Da Gama's 1497 voyage. Of course, all of this information was regarded as extremely secret; and it was therefore withheld from Columbus and the European geographers.

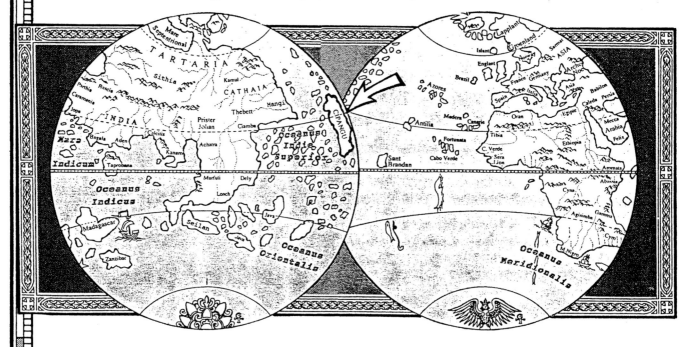

Martin Behaim's Globe and the Defective World Geography

Most historians who write about the Great Age of World Exploration concede that the geographical ideas of Columbus mirror those of the Royal Portuguese Cartographer, Martin Behaim. They also maintain that Behaim's Globe, which was made in Nuremberg between 1490 and 1492, shows the world the way that Europeans believed it to be on the eve of American discovery. However, the evidence actually shows that Behaim and the Portuguese published defective maps in hopes of misleading Columbus and the rest of their European rivals. The principal defect that fooled Columbus—and practically everybody else—is the placement of the coast of China only 3,000 miles west of Europe. Right smack in the middle is Cipangu, or Japan, which offers the deceptive promise of a "Land of Gold, & Spices" as well as a convenient way station along the route to Cathay. This is a very effective "Spy Map"—which serves as a testimonial of the incredible geographical ignorance of Europeans as well as the cupidity of the Catholic Sovereigns of Spain who believed in their hero and his map.

So, what did the Portuguese really know about the New World, and when did they know it?

Flemish Compass
after Anne Colllinder, Marine Navigation, 1954, 46.

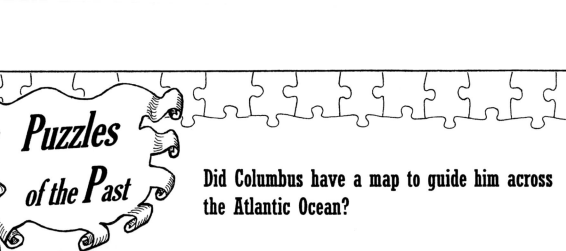

Puzzles of the Past

Did Columbus have a map to guide him across the Atlantic Ocean?

Illustrations from early 20ᵗʰ century American textbooks

Traditional historians praise Columbus for boldly sailing across what they call "the unknown Sea of Darkness"—that is, the Atlantic Ocean in 1492. Yet, most history textbooks picture the Spanish Captain holding maps.

So, what's the story? Did he have a map showing his intended destination—or not?

Columbus went to Lisbon, Portugal, in about the year 1482. His intention was to gain the patronage of King John II; or at least, he hoped to learn the secrets of Portuguese geography. He at least got his hands on maps by the Florentine cosmographer Paolo Toscanelli or the Royal Portuguese Cartographer—Martin Behaim. Historians note that the geographical misconceptions of Columbus were identical to those of Behaim—who showed mainland China only 3,000 miles west of Europe. On the voyage in 1492, the Columbus flotilla came upon islands of the Caribbean precisely where Columbus expected to find the Indies. So, he definitely had a map. But was the placement of land on his map purely coincidental?

GULF OF MEXICO
—1497 AD

Riding high seas, a Spanish espionage mission approaches the Yucatan Peninsula.

Amerigo Vespucci's Mundus Novus

KING FERDINAND OF SPAIN was always a little suspicious about his Machiaviallian neighbor—the King of Portugal. And he was never quite at ease with his wife's Champion of Far Eastern Exploration, her devout courtier from Genoa—Christobol Colon. The only time that he really felt pretty confidant was when the vainglorious mariner was far, far away on one of his expeditions to "the Indies."

Ferdinand breathed a sigh of relief when the Fleet of the Indies departed from Cádiz on September 25th, 1493. Columbus was in command of the Fleet; and he was safely ensconced in the elegant cabin of his flagship the *Marie-Gallant*. No longer a mere captain, the humble Genoese explorer was now endowed with suitable titles that reflected his self-image as a world-class Crusader. His crew addressed him as "Viceroy of the Indies" and as "Admiral of the Ocean Sea." Under directions from Pope Alexander VI, he was to proceed to the Indies where he was expected to begin the process of converting the native population of naked, promiscuous, and heathen Indians into "Civilized Christians."

King Ferdinand was happy to see him go. Presumably, in his colonies far from Spain, he could do no harm to King Ferdinand's peace of mind; nor would he do further damage to the Queen's reputation, or the upstanding glory of the Catholic Nation.

In retrospect, it would appear that King Ferdinand had completely miscalculated the damage that a well-intentioned, opportunistic Genoese mariner could do to the politics of the Kingdom. Soon, his wife was suspected of having an affair with the handsome Viceroy. Rumors circulated that she had offered her own jewels to underwrite the first expedition. Probably, there was never an illicit affair; nevertheless, she undoubtedly let it be known that she enjoyed the mariner's company.

Such rumors were bound to subside after Columbus sailed back to the colonies; however, there was no stopping the flood of bad news that spread from the seaside taverns every time a supply ship returned from overseas.

King Ferdinand of Spain
Patron of Crusaders, r. 1474-1516

Queen Isabel of Spain & Castile
Principal Patron of Columbus, r. 1474-1504

From Jacques Reich's illustration of Grazzini's statue in Florence (1898)

Alberico ("Amerigo") Vespucci
Florentine Agent of the Medici Merchant Company
Travel Journalist, Secret Agent for King of Spain (d. 1512)

Admiral of the Ocean Seas, Viceroy of the Indies
Christopher Columbus, Mariner, Self Promoter
Champion of Queen Isabel (1451-1506)

200

Sailors lamented that the Indians had "run amok" killing innocent Spaniards. They claimed that the Viceroy had punished the wrong people and that the government was in disarray. So many Spaniards were dying of malaria and spoiled food that many of the "volunteers" who had sailed to the Indies with hopes of getting rich wanted to go home. They began calling Columbus "the Viceroy of Mosquitoes" behind his back.

In a desperate measure to scrape some kind of income from the islands, Columbus issued an edict requiring each Indian to produce a "hawk's bell" full of gold—or face stern punishment. When the time came to collect the loot, one senseless administrator decided to make an example of the natives who failed to produce the gold. He did this by cutting off their hands. It was not long before the natives were in open rebellion. Many were maimed or killed when Columbus sent out troops to quell the unrest. That response further upset both the Spaniards and the Indians. Next, Columbus ordered his men to round up hostile natives who were then loaded up in the empty supply ships heading back to Spain. His intention was to sell them as slaves—as he had witnessed the Portuguese do with Africans. However, many died on the arduous trip across the Atlantic; and the Queen promptly turned the ships back—declaring that it was the mission of her champion to save the souls of the Chinese—not to burden the Nation with shiploads of heathen savages. Amidst all the suffering in the colonies and the rumors that spread back to Spain, the reputations of the Viceroy and the Catholic Sovereigns who had employed him sank like a cannonball.

Over the course of the next ten years, King Ferdinand took measures to restore his control over the government at home and the chaos that was taking place in the Indies. In 1495, an Inspector-General, Juan Aguado, was assigned the mission of making an evaluation of Columbus and his mismanagement of the Colonies. The responsibility for arranging Aguado's transportation and supplies for a three-year excursion fell to the Seville Branch of the Medici Family financial empire. The Medici Company held the principal contract for keeping the colonies supplied with the essential grain stores and military equipment from Spain.

It was at this point that the seemingly inconsequential appointment of a supply agent began to have an incredible impact upon the course of world events. It so happened that the Medici Family had in its employment at the Seville Branch a young manager who was also a very competent cosmographer. He was a Florentine who had studied in the schools of Toscanelli and Leonardo DaVinci. His name was Amerigo Vespucci.

By 1496, Vespucci's portfolio had reached the hands of the King's highest advisors and his Secret Service. News from the Colonies had continued to cause foreboding in the royal household. Not only was the Colonial Governor being mocked by his own soldiers, he had failed to send back the cargoes of gold and pearls that had been promised.

Ships & Shores of the Secret Sailors

Portuguese Caravel c. 1480-1550

where they went & how they got there

☆☆☆☆☆

Secret Expedition
1) Paria—Costa Rica in 1497; Yucatan & Florida

Reported Expeditions
2) Venezuela in 1499; 3) Brazil in 1502;
   4) Rio de Janeiro 1503-04.

This obvious discrepancy between the huge shipments of gold that had been promised and what actually came back in the ships returning from the colonies led to the inevitable concerns that Columbus was collecting the loot and then hiding it for his own future use. In the eyes of government officials, theft of money counted as a more egregious error than mismanagement.

It was also clear from intelligence reports that the Portuguese had succeeded in reaching the Cape of South Africa; and they were on the verge of sending an expedition under Da Gama straight to the Spice Trade in India. Thus, King Ferdinand was in a quandary regarding how to best proceed with his foreign policy.

Was Columbus truly sailing along the coast of China as he had claimed? Or was he someplace else entirely—perhaps far, far away from the Spice Islands and Marco Polo's Isle of Gold? Ferdinand could only hope that the Medici cosmographer could resolve the bewildering geographical conundrums of the western Atlantic Ocean.

Amerigo's Voyages to the New World

In May of 1497, a large caravel sailed from Cádiz Harbor carrying supplies for the Spanish Colony of Hispaniola. There was nothing at all extraordinary about this vessel or its cargo and equipment—aside from the fact that the Seville Agent of the Medici Warehouse customarily remained behind after making an inventory of the cargo. This time, however, he chose to accompany the voyage. His presence must have puzzled the captain as well it should have.

The vessel, carrying nearly twenty tons of cargo, stopped briefly at the Canary Islands before heading due west on the Mid-Atlantic Current. Over the course of the two-month voyage that it took to reach the Caribbean Sea, the captain had numerous opportunities to discuss trivialities, the lore of the sea, and the latest scuttlebutt regarding the travails of the Spanish Colonies. Doubtless, his curiosity regarding Amerigo Vespucci must have led to some inquiries that were brushed aside or that went unanswered to the captain's satisfaction. Nevertheless, as an employee of the Medici Family, he was duty bound to transport all those who were engaged in Company business or who had paid the usual fare. If the passenger was somewhat evasive, it mattered little—as he would doubtless be left behind in the colonies.

When the vessel arrived at Hispaniola, all the passengers went ashore—except the Company Agent. At this point in time, the captain was no longer merely curious about the Florentine Gentleman; he was downright suspicious. He asked more questions of the traveler in his midst; but he got fewer answers. Finally, the time came to depart; yet Amerigo Vespucci and his cumbersome trunk were still onboard his ship. As they passed by the entrance to the harbor, bound for Spain, the captain's patience had reached the limit. He was, after all, the master of his own ship; and by his command, the Florentine would have to provide some suitable explanations or risk being thrown overboard.

Perhaps, it was at the very last moment that Amerigo handed to the captain a sealed envelope. Inside, he found a letter from the Company Director instructing him to relinquish navigational control of the vessel to this passenger who was also acting under instructions from the "Highest Authority." Probably, care was taken not to divulge much more information regarding the nature of the mission or who was the "Highest Authority;" but indeed, it was none other than the King of Spain.

After clearing the harbor and leaving behind all the Spanish ships and mariners who might have noticed their passing, Vespucci instructed the captain to sail almost due west. It was his intention at this point in time to steer the ship towards the coast of Asia. According to the maps of Martin Behaim and Henricus Martellus Germanus, the vessel should have been very close to the coast of Thailand. They should have made landfall within a few days; but they sailed on-and-on towards the west. All the while, the captain and crew wondered about their destination and the purpose of this unprecedented voyage.

Nearly two weeks passed before the lookout, using a spyglass, finally sighted the sandy beach of the Yucatan Peninsula. All along the shore, there were parties of natives, fires, and buildings. There were also many canoes along the coast—some of which were propelled by sails; while others had up to twenty natives who paddled furiously. The captain ordered his marines to keep a lookout; and he kept the supply ship at a safe distance. Clearly, the region was heavily occupied—and quite likely, there were unfriendly troops of armed warriors on land who might easily overwhelm a single vessel. Wisely, they refrained from landing until reaching an area that seemed more desolate and uninhabited.

Occasionally, Vespucci ordered the captain to lower the anchors and remain on guard while he took a landing party ashore. From dawn-to-dusk, he monitored the passage of the sun; and he took readings with his astrolabe. The landing party stood guard, hunted, or filled the freshwater barrels. Sometimes, Vespucci took measurements with his nocturnal and astrolabe during the night. By measuring the angular distance between the planets—Mars and Venus—and the moon, he hoped to be able to calculate the approximate longitude of the coastline. Unfortunately, he would not be very certain of their location until he was able to consult maps and astronomical tables in Barcelona. However, he was already beginning to suspect that they were nowhere near the coast of Asia.

They headed southwards for several weeks along the East Coast of modern-day Honduras, Belize, Costa Rica and Panama. Vespucci was hoping that they would come across a strait leading to the west; but they found none. Suspecting that they had reached a region of the Antipodes (or the southern continent), Vespucci identified this area as "Parias." That is an old Latin term meaning "woodcutters." He believed that it was in this area, or near this area, that Phoenician and later Roman merchants had brought teams of *parias* (or "woodcutters") to harvest the valuable brasilwood.

When the coastline began to turn steadily towards the southeast, Vespucci ordered the captain to reverse their direction of sailing and head back up north. They again passed by the Yucatan Peninsula; and they followed the shores of the Gulf of Mexico along the coast of modern-day Mexico, Texas, Louisiana, and Alabama. Finally, they came to the distinctive West Coast of Florida that extends towards the southeast. From the abundance of flowers, fruit trees, and birds—and from the pleasant climate—Vespucci identified this region as the homeland of the Roman goddess—Florida (the goddess of eternal Spring). He didn't actually name the Peninsula "Florida." That name had been given to the region eons in the past.

They cruised on, sailing around the Florida Keys, and into the Atlantic Ocean north of Cuba. It was now apparent to Vespucci that the so-called "Peninsula of China" where Columbus claimed that he had first landed in 1493 was actually an island. He observed that there were none of the "Golden Pagodas" that Marco Polo had mentioned in his Travelogue, nor were there thousands of Chinese junks that Marco had said were encountered off the coast of Asia. Therefore, Vespucci concluded that either Marco Polo was lying (which was a distinct possibility) or else this region was the Portuguese Antilles—just as King John II had claimed.

In any case, Vespucci decided that he needed more information before he could issue a suitable report to the King. After 18 months at sea, Vespucci finally reached Cádiz. He had spent a year-and-a-half away from home; and about all that he could say with any certainty was that all the maps that the Portuguese had made public, including the exalted Nuremberg Globe, were practically worthless. Indeed, a new map of the Atlantic shores would have to be made; and he proposed to do just that.

Vespucci spent several months conferring with the King's astronomers in Barcelona before getting his next assignment. In 1499, he sailed with Alonso de Hojeda who was ordered to chart the Venezuelan coast that Columbus had explored the previous year. Columbus had gone to the Southern Continent in 1498 in order to learn what King John II had meant when he said that "there was mainland south of Hispaniola." Upon reaching the coast, Columbus speculated that he had come across the Earthly Paradise (or the Garden of Eden). He certainly knew that it was "a new continent"—but he was rather tardy in making that assessment.

Since the Church Fathers had always maintained that it was heresy for living Christians to seek out this most holy of places on earth, there were immediately serious issues at stake with respect to Church dogma. Columbus explained that he believed his self-appointed mission as Christoferens—that is, "the Christ Bearer"—entitled him to visit Paradise while he was still alive. In any case, this landfall immediately gained the attention of Church authorities who were called upon to explain how it was that Columbus had succeeded in sailing up the Orinoco—supposedly one of the Four Eternal Rivers of Paradise—without having Jehovah smite him with a thunderbolt.

Columbus had also mentioned, that while he was sick and near death, his crews had brought onboard samples of the brasilwood and pearls that were abundant in this region that he called "Paria." This was the second area of South America to be called "Paria"—which again probably refers to the ancient "wood cutters" from Rome. According to the Ship's Log, Columbus used this name in reference only to the gulf where his ships were anchored in 1498—because, he said, this was the name that natives had used for the gulf. Subsequently, Spanish geographers applied the name to the northeastern coast of South America where brasilwood was found growing in abundance. This name "Paria," derived as it was from ancient Roman sources, would haunt and confuse historians for many years to come.

Incidentally, the oldest known usage of the name "Paria" appears on a 1st century Roman map by the geographer Pomponius Mela. He used the name in reference to a region of the Antipodes (that is, for South America). Marco Polo identified a country in this region as "Vita-peria"—which is yet another reference to the ancient woodcutters.

Naturally, King Ferdinand was anxious to learn the extent of the brasilwood forests in this region as well as the extent of the pearl fisheries. In response to those concerns, de Hojeda ordered his crews to fill the holds of several vessels with a harvest of brasilwood; and they loaded trunks full of the beautiful white pearls. Meanwhile, Juan de la Cosa and Amerigo Vespucci proceeded to make a very accurate navigational chart of the area. While the crews toiled in the forests, they established astronomical observatories on the beaches and hills where they measured the heights of stars with their astrolabes. The accurate chart that they produced would make it easy for merchants to reach this valuable coast in the coming decades. Vespucci was elated by this expedition because he added nearly 600 leagues (or about 2,000 miles) of coastline to his growing map of the New World.

Officials of the Spanish Government were stunned to learn about Vasco Da Gama's return to Lisbon in 1499 with a cargo of spices from India. The Spanish grew anxious to learn if there might be a shortcut to the same trading center directly south of Venezuela. (Of course, Venezuela was thousands of miles away from India; however the Spanish officials were still operating virtually totally in the dark with respect to the actual geography of the world.) Two secret expeditions under the commands of Vicente Pinzon and Diego Lepe were sent to explore the coastline in this area. There is no question that they penetrated deep into the region of Brazil that was within the Portuguese sphere of Influence under the stipulations of the Treaty of Tordesillas.

Portuguese spies operating within the hierarchy of the Spanish government alerted Portugal's King Manuel of this treachery. This realization that the Spanish were prepared to violate the Treaty was one of the reasons why the Lisbon authorities sent Pedro Cabral to "accidentally discover" Brazil the following year. In another cunning move to distract and intimidate their Spanish rivals, the Portuguese actually requested the services of Amerigo Vespucci to chart the coastline of Brazil. In other words, Vespucci's role in mapping the Spanish territories was being monitored by King Manuel's espionage agents. They knew precisely what he was doing; and they wanted to make sure that he learned everything that they wanted him to know.

By this point in time, King Manuel had already announced the successful return of Da Gama with a valuable cargo from India—so it was practically evident to everyone that they had won the race to the Indies. It was no longer imperative to keep the nature of the New World continents a secret. Instead, it was their intention to make the regents who were their rivals realize that they were stuck with a continental barrier, a wilderness barrier, right smack between them and the treasures of the Orient.

Amerigo accompanied a flotilla of three vessels that sailed from Lisbon in May of 1501. The Portuguese commander was Nuño Manoel. They headed down the African coast as far as Cape Verde; and then they headed west using the Equatorial Current as a conveyor belt carrying them directly to the Brazilian coast. Once more, Vespucci used his astrolabe and nocturnal to measure lunar distances; and from these calculations, he was able to estimate the longitudes and latitudes along the shore. These measurements enabled the creation of a reasonably accurate map that was useful for practical navigation. The expedition lasted for 17 months; and it extended to the south beyond the mouth of the Rio de Janeiro.

During this expedition, Vespucci not only charted the coastline, he also recorded in his journal details about native costumes, weapons, rituals and exotic sexual practices. He wrote down details of breathtaking landscapes and dense jungles. He observed flocks of parrots in stunning plumage; and he saw animals that were unknown to Europeans—such as ocelots, anteaters, condors, ground sloths, and anacondas. It was on the basis of witnessing this vast land of incredible biodiversity that he began to think about the southern continent as a totally "new" world—what he called the *Mundus Novus*. He even wrote a letter to his patron in the Medici Family in 1502 describing the vastness, the richness, and the beauty of the New World. This letter was published in 1505.

As a consequence of his voyaging beyond the traditional physical and intellectual borders of Christian Europe, Amerigo Vespucci had undergone a spiritual transformation. He no longer thought or acted like a normal clerk or cosmographer; it would have been difficult by thispoint in time to even regard him as an ordinary Christian. He lived with the natives; he joined in their erotic games; he became one of them in spirit.

Most of his neighbors back in Seville had grown accustomed to the revival of the fundamentalist religious view of the world—one that accepted the burnings of Jews and heretics by the Inquisition as "normal" behavior that was necessary to prepare for the Apocalypse. However, what

Vespucci had witnessed in his voyages overseas caused him to see the world in a totally different light. Intellectually, he broke away from the past; and he became very much like the mystics and the idealists whom Roger Bacon had led across the boarder of orthodox thinking into the twilight of the Renaissance. He could no longer imagine a world of a single religion nor could he accept the ignorant notion of a world that was on the precipice of Doomsday.

Thus, his *Mundus Novus Letter* was a testimonial not just of the existence of a New Continent—it was also a manifesto for the creation of a Whole New World of the heart, the mind, and the Spirit. The vast resources of the new continent, he stressed, were limitless: thus, the potential for human knowledge, growth, and imagination should be equally boundless. It was a manifesto for Utopia—for a New Jerusalem.

Back in Europe, there was a spiritual and cultural revolution. It was nurtured in part by the writings of Marco Polo; and it was sustained in part by the flood of Oriental goods and by the technological innovations that emerged from the cauldrons of the scientists and inventors. But it was the *Mundus Novus Letter* that truly opened the doors to the prisons of orthodoxy and dogma. So powerful were the words and the maps that Vespucci brought back from his journeys that all the priests in all the cathedrals could not hold back the rush to transform and to modernize European Civilization. Oh they tried; but the reformers and the Reformation was at their doorstep—in one case nailing down the proclamation of a new religion.

Vespucci retired to a comfortable position as the Chief Pilot of the India House in Barcelona. From this intellectual sanctuary, he supervised the training of captains and pilots who were destined to help build up the colonies. All around him, kings, professors, bishops, and confessors scrambled to get their bearings—because, quite literally, Amerigo Vespucci had blown the foundation of orthodoxy right out from underneath their feet.

What do Historians Think?

Orthodox historians have never liked Amerigo Vespucci. To begin with, as a lower-echelon warehouse manager, he never had the kind of credentials that Columbus had as a luminary of important events. Thus, the so-called "serious scholars" have typically regarded him as being unworthy of much attention. He was "just a clerk"—not even a university graduate. It is not unusual for him to be ignored entirely in history textbooks; or if he is mentioned at all, it is simply to explain that Vespucci is one of those unfortunate characters who mucked up a good story by stealing the glory that rightfully belonged to the hero that the historians have chosen as their favorite guy.[1].

The prestigious scholar Samuel Eliot Morison summarized the contributions of Vespucci by quoting from the fairytale that Washington Irving wrote in the 18th century. The early American poet dismissed the Medici Agent as "a pickle dealer from Seville who may never have even sailed across the sea." By "never having sailed," Irving was referring to the favorite pastime of scholars of nitpicking to death the scanty documentation regarding the four voyages that he made with Spanish and Portuguese expeditions to the New World.

Regardless of this fistfight over the evidence, Vespucci's participation in the Second Expedition (in 1499) was documented in the testimony that Alonso de Hojeda gave in a court deposition on December 7th, 1512. Hojeda testified that he took along Juan de la Cosa and Morigo Vespuche as pilots on that expedition.[2] Nor was there any dispute raised by any of his associates at the India House regarding his claims to New World travels. That he went as a spy on the First Expedition might be questioned—as the evidence is tenuous. Nevertheless, his appointment as Chief Pilot of the India House clearly demonstrates that King Ferdinand placed considerable reliance on the Florentine cosmographer; and the King never showed the slightest dissatisfaction with his performance.

Historians have never been happy that a German mapmaker named Martin Waldseemüller chose to honor Amerigo Vespucci by christening the southern continent in his honor. Many believed that the continents should have been named "Colulmbia." That Amerigo was chosen for the honor reflected the thinking at the time that it was the Florentine and not Columbus who realized that the place where the Renaissance explorers were sailing was not China (as Columbus believed) but was instead a new continent that was separate from Asia. It was this conceptual breakthrough that had such a great impact upon European Civilization. Indeed, the East Coast of North America had been visited often for hundreds of years without there being the kind of change in the thinking of Europeans that followed the publication of the *Mundus Novus Letter* and the new World Map that Waldseemüller issued in 1507.

It is true that Waldseemüller's 1518 map did not use the title "America" for the southern continent. And this elimination of Vespucci's name from the map has been propagandized as proof that the German mapmaker had decided to repudiate the honor that he had previously given to the Florentine cosmographer. However, there was never any indication on the part of the German that this was his intention; nor did he bother to rename the southern continent in honor of Columbus. Indeed, he simply left it blank. And this lack of any title survives as the silent protest by a

---

[1] Arthur Newton, The Great Age of Discovery, Freeport: Books for Libraries Press, 1932, 119, says that the fame of Vespucci entirely eclipsed that of Columbus. Peter Martyr, a Spanish historian, noted that Vespucci had assisted the Portuguese in preparing a map (p. 124).

[2] Newton, *op cit*, 1932, 121.

Christian subject whom the Inquisition ordered to remove the offensive name of Amerigo Vespucci. Indeed, the Florentine had been declared *persona non grata* (that is, unacceptable) following his witty declaration that there wasn't sufficient room in Noah's Ark to hold all the different kinds of animals that were found in South America.

Vespucci had denounced the story of the Deluge as a "fairytale;" so the bishops renounced him as a heretic. However, as the King's personal minister in the India House, he was untouchable.

Most historians are content to expunge the record of Vespucci's first voyage to Costa Rica in 1497. By invalidating this feat, the claim is then advanced that it was Columbus who in 1498 was the "first" European to discover South America. This is an academic charade that has as its only objective the creation of an excuse to glorify Columbus as "the first" European to reach mainland—and "the first" to realize that it was a continent. However, even if we ignore the clandestine voyages of Amerigo Vespucci, there are still the testimonials of Rue de Piña and Robert Thorne, as well as the map by Andrea Bianco (1448), confirming that the Portuguese had already been to Brazil long before Columbus ever entered the theater.[3]

Consequences for New World Exploration

It was really Amerigo Vespucci who initiated the concept of making geographical information freely available to the public. Following his return to Barcelona, he set up a method for measuring the circumference of the earth—in a manner quite similar to what Eratosthenes had done almost two thousand years earlier. He determined the distance between two cities in Spain; then he measured the angle of solar light at noon. Simple trigonometry yielded a distance of 24,700 miles—which was remarkably close to the actual distance. Up until this demonstration by Spain's Chief Pilot, most geographers had assumed that the circumference was only 18,000 miles. Vespucci's larger earth enabled a much more accurate portrayal of the distribution of continents on the earth's surface.

Vespucci made a copy of his Atlantic Ocean Map available to the German mapmaker Martin Waldseemüller. His composite World Map of 1507 included Vespucci's portrayal of the new continent within the new space on the surface of the globe that had been opened up by the recent calculation of the earth's circumference. It was this revelation of the existence of a New World—and the provision of a place to put it on the glob—that motivated the naming of the southern continent in Vespucci's honor. Meanwhile, Columbus had died; and with him died the notion that China was located directly west of Europe.

---

[3] Alfred Newton, *The Great Age of Discovery*, New York: Freeport, 1932, 120. Historians have also insisted that the 1497 voyage was impossible because supposedly the insularity of Cuba was unknown until Ocampo's voyage around the island in 1508. Nevertheless, Florida is clearly shown on the Roman map by Macrobius 440 and on the Cantino Map of 1502.

Considering the severity of Church opposition to the name "America" that honored an avowed heretic, the survival of the name on European maps was at best a tenuous affair. Many mapmakers chose instead to use such titles as "Mundus Novus," "Brazil," or "India Nova." However, everything changed with publication of Gerhard Mercator's Map of 1541. Mercator was also a "heretic" who was arrested and tortured because of his Protestant religious beliefs. He was therefore determined to promote the legacy of Amerigo Vespucci as an example of the importance of geographic truth over dogmatic ignorance. His popularity as a mapmaker meant that the name "America" eventually prevailed as the choice for two continents in the Western Hemisphere.

Drawing by Theodore de Bry, 16ᵗʰ Century

Measuring the New World Skies

Amerigo Vespucci uses an astrolabe to observe the Southern Cross along the shore of Brazil. In the Year 1502, he accompanied a Portuguese expedition to this region of the New World.

Amerigo Vespucci's "New World"

On a map dated 1507, the German scientist and map printer, Martin Waldseemüller, announces to Europeans the End to the Era of Ignorance that historians call "The Dark Ages." In his atlas of world maps, he presented the first published portrayal of the Mundus Novus—or "New World" that had recently been reported by the Medici Company secret agent—Amerigo Vespucci. Based on this incredible revelation, which the Church authorities had tried for centuries to prevent, Waldseemüller proposed the naming of a newly-found continent in honor of its discoverer—Vespucci. Indeed, it was the Medici agent who had provided copies of the map featuring the remarkable Southern Continent (shown above). This was the first publicly available image (based on scientific surveys) showing mainland that had been rumored to exist since Roman Times. It was known to the ancients as the "Fourth Part of the World," as "the Antipodes," or simply as "the Southern Continent." This mainland was once presumed to fill up most of the Southern Hemisphere. Waldseemüller didn't know at the time that Vespucci's map was actually copied almost entirely from Portuguese charts; nor did he know that the Portuguese had relied upon earlier charts that spies had obtained from Ming Chinese sources. Almost immediately, Church authorities advised him that Vespucci was a heretic and that he jeopardized his own life by honoring the Medici agent. Thus, in subsequent years, the German printer, reverted to the customary practice of calling the Southern Continent simply "the New World."

Shanhai Yudi Quantu

山海輿地全圖

內一圖地球小天
地亙州區塊墨圓以

外三圖天球定天
鹿書茂長短蛇陝

圖中橫豎三千六
方每方中各三十度

地球橫豎經緯界
線別方隅稀度數

Shanhai
Yudi
Quantu

Wang Qi
c. 1601
Zheng He/Ming

Shanhai Yudi Quantu, c. 1425
Jesuit copy of Ming map in 1601—facsimile by Thompson, 2005, as presented to the Library of Congress Zheng He Symposium in May of 2005.

Zheng He

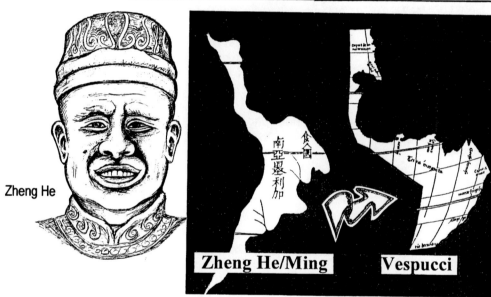

南亞墨利加

Zheng He/Ming   Vespucci

Shanhai Yudi Quantu—the Portuguese Source Map

The Portuguese source for the incredible New World geography that was revealed on Waldseemüller's map was based on modified Chinese sources. By comparing the Southern Continent as it is shown on a Jesuit copy of Zheng He's c. 1425 World Map to the map that Waldseemüller obtained from Vespucci, we see a strikingly close similarity. By this point in time, the Portuguese had completed (under Behaim's direction) their own survey of the East Coast from Florida to Argentina. Thus, we see distinct improvement in this part of the New World map. However, the Portuguese still relied entirely upon the Chinese version of the West Coast—a coast that was unknown to any European navigator.

Puzzles of the Past

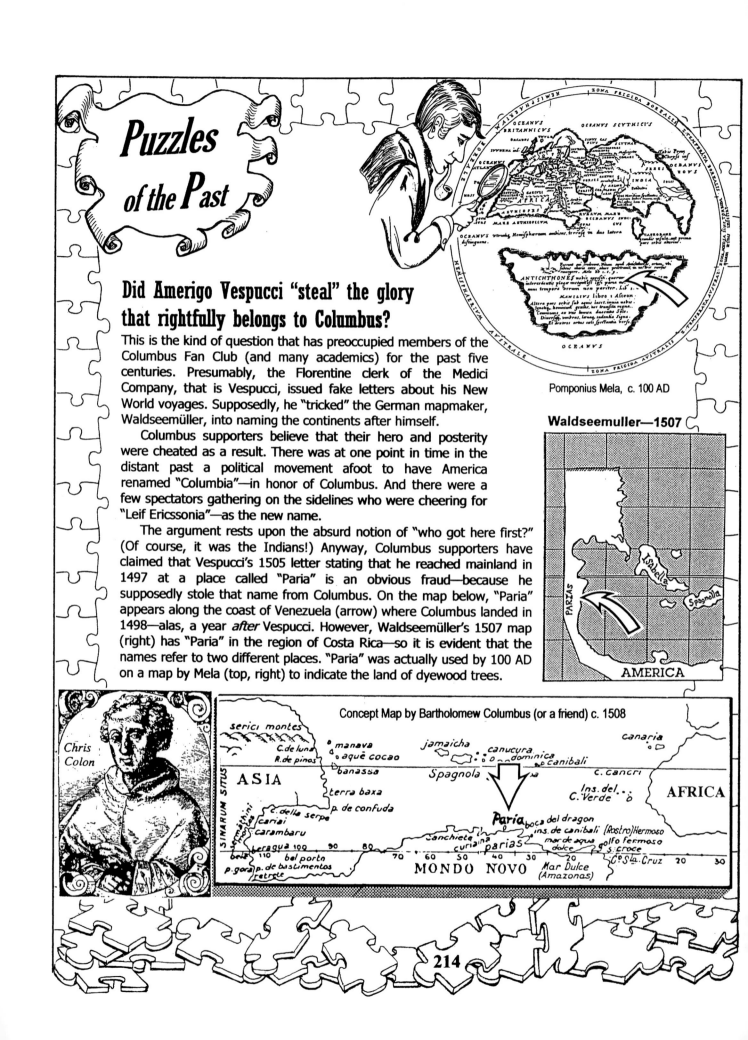

Pomponius Mela, c. 100 AD

Did Amerigo Vespucci "steal" the glory that rightfully belongs to Columbus?

This is the kind of question that has preoccupied members of the Columbus Fan Club (and many academics) for the past five centuries. Presumably, the Florentine clerk of the Medici Company, that is Vespucci, issued fake letters about his New World voyages. Supposedly, he "tricked" the German mapmaker, Waldseemüller, into naming the continents after himself.

Columbus supporters believe that their hero and posterity were cheated as a result. There was at one point in time in the distant past a political movement afoot to have America renamed "Columbia"—in honor of Columbus. And there were a few spectators gathering on the sidelines who were cheering for "Leif Ericssonia"—as the new name.

The argument rests upon the absurd notion of "who got here first?" (Of course, it was the Indians!) Anyway, Columbus supporters have claimed that Vespucci's 1505 letter stating that he reached mainland in 1497 at a place called "Paria" is an obvious fraud—because he supposedly stole that name from Columbus. On the map below, "Paria" appears along the coast of Venezuela (arrow) where Columbus landed in 1498—alas, a year *after* Vespucci. However, Waldseemüller's 1507 map (right) has "Paria" in the region of Costa Rica—so it is evident that the names refer to two different places. "Paria" was actually used by 100 AD on a map by Mela (top, right) to indicate the land of dyewood trees.

Waldseemuller—1507

AMERICA

Chris Colon

Concept Map by Bartholomew Columbus (or a friend) c. 1508

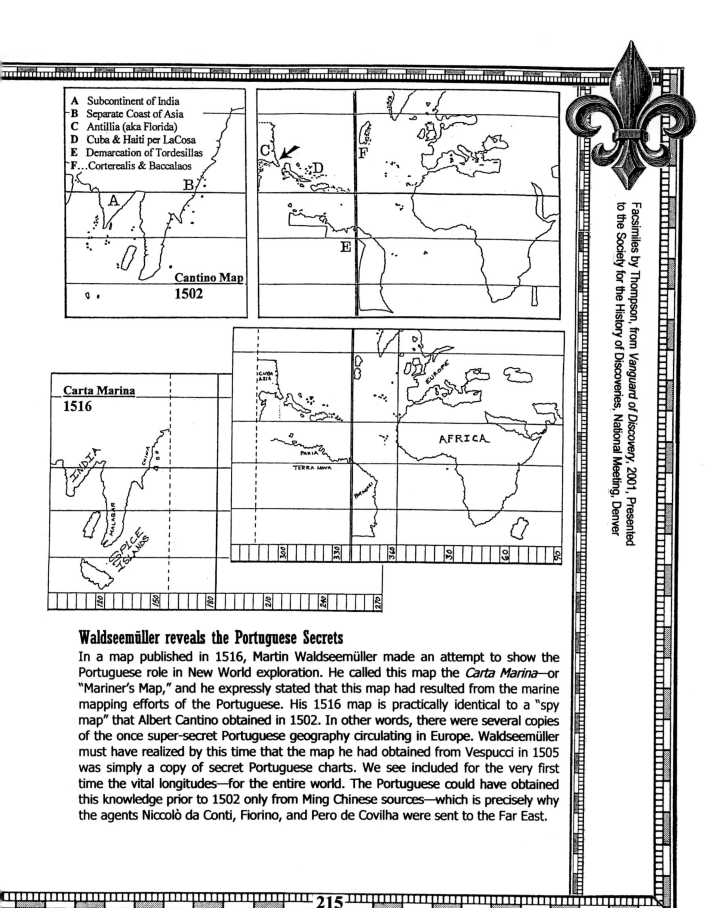

A Subcontinent of India
B Separate Coast of Asia
C Antillia (aka Florida)
D Cuba & Haiti per LaCosa
E Demarcation of Tordesillas
F...Corterealis & Baccalaos

Cantino Map
1502

Carta Marina
1516

Facsimiles by Thompson, from *Vanguard of Discovery*, 2001, Presented to the Society for the History of Discoveries, National Meeting, Denver

Waldseemüller reveals the Portuguese Secrets

In a map published in 1516, Martin Waldseemüller made an attempt to show the Portuguese role in New World exploration. He called this map the *Carta Marina*—or "Mariner's Map," and he expressly stated that this map had resulted from the marine mapping efforts of the Portuguese. His 1516 map is practically identical to a "spy map" that Albert Cantino obtained in 1502. In other words, there were several copies of the once super-secret Portuguese geography circulating in Europe. Waldseemüller must have realized by this time that the map he had obtained from Vespucci in 1505 was simply a copy of secret Portuguese charts. We see included for the very first time the vital longitudes—for the entire world. The Portuguese could have obtained this knowledge prior to 1502 only from Ming Chinese sources—which is precisely why the agents Niccolò da Conti, Fiorino, and Pero de Covilha were sent to the Far East.

Empire of the Virgin Queen

THE THRILL OF GEOGRAPHICAL DISCOVERY captivated the attention of Europeans throughout the 16th century. It began with the daring expeditions of Da Gama, Columbus, John Cabot, Amerigo Vespucci, and Giovanni Verrazano. These were the navigators who served as the official "Champions" of Portugal, Spain, England, and France. The inhabitants of coastal towns grew accustomed to the spectacle of royal appearances and festivals as the gallant mariners departed from the quays on their daring voyages of New World discovery. Then, there followed an exasperating waiting period that sometimes extended for more than a year as anxious citizens awaited news of their heroes. Did they find gold across the Ocean? Did they meet up with the Grand Khan of China and learn the secrets of Marco Polo? Or had they foundered on the High Seas—or perhaps become trapped in the icy desolation of the Northwest Passage?

All of the pomp, publicity, hoopla, and intrigue made for Grand Public Theater. The monarchs of Europe didn't miss the point that world discovery was vital entertainment for the common folk—even if the principal players in the overseas expeditions didn't always know where they were going. Part of the thrill was in the suspense. The Ending wasn't really known until the survivors sailed back into port; or they didn't—as the case may be.

With the proliferation of the Gutenberg Printing Press, there emerged a new genre of public entertainment: "travel journalism." Owners of the earliest newspapers exploited the public hunger for excitement in their lives by reporting the latest information and speculations regarding the overseas voyagers. These sensationalistic and often inaccurate reports were liberally frosted with rumor, propaganda, and outright fantasy. They were published in assorted "rag sheets" or tabloids in all the large cities of Europe. It was the Age of Shakespeare, the Age of the Spanish Armada, the Age of the Reformation, and the Elizabethan Age. It was a glorious time of pretense, intrigue, and drama—a time when the idea of overseas colonies began to blossom among the competing maritime powers.

John Cabot's North America Map, c. 1500

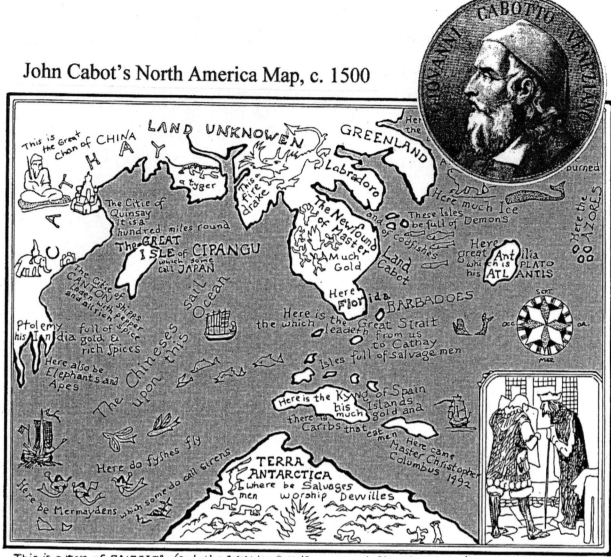

This is a map of AMERICA (and the Way to CHINA as Men believed it to be) which an old PILOT shewed to King HENRY VII in the year 1500

John Cabot solves the riddle of "lost" Cathay

The Genoese expatriate John Cabot sailed as a captain and navigator for Bristol merchants as early as 1490. By this point in time, his patrons had been sending out expeditions to hunt for "Brazil and the Isle of Seven Cities" for over a decade. The merchants insisted that they hadn't found what they were seeking; however one ship was at sea on the Atlantic Ocean for 9 months—and that's plenty of time to pick up a cargo and sneak it into a port in Ireland in order to avoid paying tax. After Columbus failed to find China, Cabot thought he knew the answer: the Spanish Captain just wasn't sailing far enough north and west. This route took him around Florida—a peninsula that he called "Floresta." However, what he thought was the China Sea was actually the Gulf of Mexico. This map has been attributed to John Cabot in 1500; but historians generally don't like the idea that he beat Ponce de Leon who supposedly "discovered" Florida in 1513. It's another secret of the Past.

Europeans lived in a dichotomous yet dynamic world. On the one hand, there was the security of the Mother Church, tradition, and orthodox beliefs in Heaven and Hell. On the other hand, there was the Reformation that demanded innovations in religion and science; and there was the "free enterprise" movement in business that encouraged the exploitation of foreign markets. Often times, the common people were forced to choose sides in the political, economic, and military conflicts that ensued. And it was in this arena that the tabloid journalists played into the hands of the propaganda masters. They were "faceless" information managers and secret agents who manipulated the apparent "realities" of the human stage from behind the scenes.

The battle lines between opposing nations and religious organizations were not always clearly distinguishable. For example, the Protestants rallied against the Catholic domination of New World territories, the mistreatment of the Indians, and the cruelty of the Inquisition. But the legions of Luther and Calvin were also stuck in the quagmire of medieval thinking. They had their own religious tribunals that punished heretics, witches, and Jews. Both sides in this conflict Protestant versus Catholic conflict assumed that "God was on their side;" both sides assumed that divine favoritism justified killing their enemies; and both sides assumed that their enemies were "all going to hell." Because religious fanaticism was a potent force in manipulating public opinion and mob action, self-serving politicians and Church leaders often exploited the religious loyalties of the ignorant masses. In this strife-torn era, espionage was an essential and a lucrative business.

During the reign of King Henry VII, English interests in the New World were advanced with the expeditions of John and Sebastian Cabot between 1490 and 1512. Johan Cabotto, as the Elder Cabot was known in Genoa, was one of many young mariners who became enchanted with the exploits of Marco Polo. In order to gain access to Marco Polo's secret navigational charts, as well as to gain the support of influential patrons in the woolen industry, John decided to obtain citizenship in the rival State of Venice. This change in his official nationality was possible; but it required ten years of service in the Venetian maritime service.

Apparently, John was sent on a trading and mapping venture to the Icelandic Isles—the same region of the Far West that Columbus had visited in 1477. His son, Sebastian, noted that his father had visited the New Found Land in 1494; and there is some speculation that it was his mapping of the Icelandic Isles that portrayed the Newfoundland Archipelago in the correct location on the Paris Map of 1490.

John Cabot reached England in about 1494, and he was soon offered the position of overseas pilot in King Henry VII's Navy. His first "official" expedition for the English took place in 1497—at which time he began work on a map of the East Coast in the region of the Gulf of St. Lawrence. At the time, this was presumed to be the location of Marco Polo's "Strait of Anian." This was the name of a seaway across Northern

Canada that many cosmographers believed would be a shortcut to Marco Polo's Cathay. Over time, this "shortcut" to the Orient would come to be called "the Northwest Passage."

During a voyage that took place in 1498, John Cabot continued mapping the East Coast as far as the Florida Keys. The reports that he sent back to London and Bristol were very misleading. Either he was the victim of unbridled optimism; or, like Columbus, he was totally confused by the cunning deceptions of Portuguese geography. Anyway, John Cabot led his financial backers in England to believe that the gulf that he discovered in this region (that is, the Gulf of Mexico) was Marco Polo's "South Sea." Actually, he was about 10,000 miles away from this objective. Cabot promised that this sea would lead directly to Cathay; and he assured investors that they would soon profit from huge cargoes of brasilwood and spices. He also produced a map illustrating this concept of his that China was directly west of Florida.

On Cabot's map, the so-called "Oxford Map of 1500," he drew the picture of a Chinese junk in the middle of the Gulf of Mexico. The Grand Khan, Japan, mermaids and the land of spices and gold were not far away. It was an excellent example of how maps could be misused to promote fanciful journeys to the Far East. Cabot's promises of cargoes from the Orient and his fanciful map raised great expectations among his patrons. However, when Cabot failed to produce the fortunes that he had promised, his patrons accused him of deception and negligence. Historians have bemoaned the lack of documents that have survived from John Cabot's voyages and those of his son, Sebastian. On the other hand, those scraps of information that have survived give the distinct impression that most people who were involved in these costly expeditions to China simply wanted to forget the unfortunate outcomes.

The English effort to develop commerce in the West was dependent upon private business investments. Those investments were curtailed as soon as it became apparent by 1507 (thanks to Amerigo Vespucci) that a new wilderness continent and not Marco Polo's Cathay was situated west of England. Meanwhile, the Portuguese Navy sailed into the seas surrounding Newfoundland—and they came with a papal blessing. They harvested stockfish, lumber, gold, and a human crop of pagan farmers that they found living in the Old Norwegian Colonies. These wretched captives were the descendants of Irish, German, and Norwegian pioneers. They were carried off as slaves to Lisbon.

When the Portuguese vacated the Newfoundland region in the 1520s, the French were already making plans to colonize the Gulf of St. Lawrence—or the "Grand Gulf" as it was known in those days. Giovanni Verrazano charted the area in 1521; and Jacques Cartier followed with the first colonists in 1535. The general impression among Europeans at the time was that Spain was taking the real wealth from the New World. Galleons returned from the "Spanish Main," that is Mexico and New India carrying the enormous gold hoards of the former Aztec and Inca Empires.

Meanwhile, the French and English were stuck in the Northwest Region—the "dregs" of New World real estate. It was a forested wilderness that offered good fishing off the Newfoundland Grand Banks; but Europeans had their hearts set on gold and spices.

Henry the VIII was crowned King of England in 1509. Wars in France sapped his energy and the resources of his Kingdom. He had an insatiable appetite for wine and women; and he was often preoccupied with starting or ending amorous affairs. The endings proved to be particularly burdensome to the King, as they tended to require the approval of the local bishop and the Roman Church in his efforts to secure a convenient divorce. Occasionally, his romantic dealings ended on a rather sour note—as the executioner's axe fell upon the neck of an unfortunate wife who had fallen from grace or who had failed in her duty to bear him a son. Failure to please the King was regarded as "Treason;" and the amorous sovereign set his eyes on the next victim. Henry managed only to resolve the issue of his own independence from papal authority by declaring himself the Head of a new Church of England in 1534.

The hiatus in foreign religious domination led to a brief resurgence in the interest of investors in colonial enterprises across the seas. However, the respite from Roman Church authority was of a very short duration. Henry's daughter Mary, a devout Catholic, grabbed the throne in 1553. Her coronation followed a bloodbath of her Protestant opponents that included the execution of Lady Jane Gray. One year later, she married Prince Philip who was a staunch Catholic and also the heir to the Spanish throne. Amidst this social and political turmoil, she had her sister, Princess Elizabeth, imprisoned in the Tower of London under suspicion of high treason. Although Elizabeth claimed loyalty to the Church, her sympathies towards the new Protestant Movement and her father's separate Church of England were well known.

During Queen Mary's reign, the torture and burning of Protestants became something of a sport—as the deranged monarch, dubbed "Bloody Mary" by her subjects, sought to prepare England for the Apocalypse.

Once more, the specter of the biblical Doomsday appeared on the horizon of Western Europe. More than six hundred Protestant intellectuals were roasted alive at Queen Mary's barbecue of wayward souls. Since the Queen was a devout Catholic and the wife of a Spanish prince, she had no intention of allowing any colonial ventures in the Western Isles. There would be no American colonies simply because such ventures would have been in conflict with the Papal Bull of 1493 and the provisions of the Treaty of Tordesillas. Meanwhile, English investors who wanted to develop overseas commerce were limited to the charter of the Muscovy Company. This charter allowed for exploration of a sea route towards the east via the North Sea, Norway, and northern Russia. It was called the "Northeast Passage."

Illustration from a painting in the Royal Archives, artist unknown; date—about 1575.

Madame of Mysteries, Mastermind of Destiny
Architect of the British Empire

Queen Elizabeth kept everybody guessing. She juggled, balanced, and cajoled—while unnerving courtiers and upending her opponents. Her espionage toolbox included romance, surprise attacks, denial, unfulfilled promises, changes of heart, disinformation and charm.
Her Majesty—born 1533, ruled 1558-1603.

The destiny of England and the world underwent a dramatic transformation in the weeks and months following Queen Mary's illness and death in 1558. From the very outset of her reign, the young Queen Elizabeth announced her intention to promote religious tolerance and commercial investment abroad. She had no desire to engage in costly foreign wars; nor did she want her business supporters to become entangled in military alliances with foreign nations that might prevent lucrative investments abroad. In other words, she understood the plain reality that England was dependent upon vital supplies from overseas.

In order to maintain the appearance of neutrality in foreign affairs, she conducted her personal life in a manner that either seduced or confused English rivals. She encouraged the courtship of foreign princes—including loyal Catholics. But it appears that she never had any real intention of making herself subordinate to any of them as a royal wife. She always kept them "guessing" what her next move might be. Thus, neither she nor her Country was forced into wars simply as a consequence of some screwy, ill-conceived royal marriage to a foreign prince.

Her small cadre of immediate advisors included some of the most intelligent and the most unscrupulous men in all of Europe. Francis Walsingham was her commander of intelligence and the Captain of his own secret police. Anyone who crossed his path or who threatened his Queen was not long for this world. He was a Machiavellian sort of master spy who might charm his adversaries with whit and praise—then quickly shove them out the window of a Renaissance high-rise apartment building.

Elizabeth's "Treasurer" was the stern but adorable Lord Burghley (who was also known as William Cecil). He was the sort of chap who was an excellent manager of finances and a thoroughly trustworthy administrator. In other words, he was the perfect individual to fill the post of the National Money Manager. The only problem with Burghley was his ethical principles. He was a true follower of the Christian code, and as such, he was totally against any kind of piracy on the high seas or intrigues on foreign soil. In other words, he was against any plan or scheme that was remotely immoral.

Burghley's presence on the management team was absolutely essential. His competence, his loyalty, and his exceptional relations with the manor lords and the business community brought to the government a measure of credibility and efficiency. However, if the time ever came when the Queen needed the services of someone whose reputation was a bit on the dark side, as she sometimes needed to do, then keeping Burghley's attention elsewhere could be a real challenge.

Of all her most trusted male attendants, none were more close to her heart or her mind than the esteemed Doctor John Dee. He was one of her favorite tutors when she was only a young princess who walked in the shadows of King Henry VIII. He taught her the fundamentals of such subjects as English history and world geography. Among her fondest memories were the chapters that he read to her from Marco Polo's *Book of*

Sir Francis Drake
Queen's Champion
Pirate, Navigator; 1540-1596

Sir Francis Walsingham
Member of Queen's Star Chamber
Chief of Intelligence, Head of Security & Secret Police

Sir Thomas Cavendish
Sea Captain
Followed Drake round the world.

Sir Humphrey Gilbert
Sea Captain
Sent to Newfoundland.

Travels or from Ranulf Higden's *Polychronicon*—(that is, the 14th century text of World Geography). John Dee stood by her when she was taken to the Tower of London. At that moment, practically everyone expected her immediate execution for "High Treason" by order of her sister, Queen Mary. The Doctor, however, argued for a more optimistic view of the future. His crystal ball didn't reveal that a Spanish prince would intervene on her behalf; but his suggestion that "the future is *not* written in stone" carried the day.

Doctor Dee was an avid collector of books on almost every subject—particularly those subjects that were referred to as the "arcane" or secret arts. He was a chemist and an experimenter in the traditions of the Oxford scientist Roger Bacon. He was a master in the art of cryptography—that is, in the developing and the breaking of secret codes. And he was a close personal friend of the world's leading geographical talent of the time—Gerhard Mercator of Holland.

Modern historians have credited John Dee with inventing the concept of the "British Empire." This conclusion rests solely upon the one piece of evidence that has turned up so far in English archives—a letter that the honorable Doctor sent to one of his friends. What is really surprising about this single piece of evidence is that the concept of building a British Empire was the central theme of Queen Elizabeth's reign. Yet, it was also the most closely-guarded secret of the realm.

In one sense, it might truly be said that the idea of planting overseas colonies originated with the farsighted King Arthur of the Early Middle Ages. Historians tend not to think so far back in time—that is, back to the 6th century—because there is so little documentary evidence. Nevertheless, the cultural inheritance of the Past that actually guides our decisions in the Present and the Future has its roots far back in Time.

To some degree, Elizabeth chose to infuse her own effort to build national pride on a revival of Arthurian romance. Of equal importance, there was the contemporary example of the successes that Spain, Portugal, and France had achieved in their efforts to establish colonies in the New World. Many English businessmen were anxious to follow that example, but they were all dependent upon a favorable national policy and the protection of the Royal Navy in order to achieve their dreams. Ultimately, the decision to go forward with the plan to build the British Empire was solely in the hands of Queen Elizabeth. And it is evident from her actions that this secret scheme for developing overseas colonies was at the very heart of her vision for England.

In the planning phase of her Empire Strategy, Queen Elizabeth invited proponents of various commercial development programs to present their arguments before the Privy Council. These seminars discussed such vital subjects as the most suitable places for colonies, the best routes to reach the colonies, how to fund the enormous preparations and supplies that were needed, and how to meet the requirements of a new navy. All of this had to be accomplished without taking money from the Royal Treasury.

Ships & Shores of the Secret Sailors

Drake's Flagship
Golden Hind
Racing Galleon, c. 1577

where they went & how they got there

Secret Destinations in Ancient America

Secret Circumnavigation 1577-1580

Rio de Janeiro, Magellan's Passage, Chile, Peru, Mexico, Baja California, Bay of Isles (Puget Sound), Alaska—while searching for NW Passage, Marco Polo's Quivira (Oregon, San Francisco Bay), cruised by Hawaii (on Spanish charts), on to Spice Isl.

The Privy Council decided by consensus to build up the Royal Navy using the model of "the Citizen Fleet." Lord Burghley argued against even attempting to match the kinds of huge ships and huge navies that were present in Spain and Portugal. While the Great Carracks and Great Galleons of the Iberian superpowers were spectacular under full sail and with banners flying from all the masts, they were just too damned expensive for a little Island Nation. Furthermore, while they looked impregnable with their tiers of huge brass cannon, they were notoriously difficult to control in heavy seas. Instead of building such expensive behemoths, Burghley and the naval advisors argued for a research and development program to improve the accuracy of long-range cannon and the speed of standard merchant vessels. This was sort of a "hit-and-run" approach to naval defense.

The most promising English vessels for naval service were called "racing galleons." These merchant vessels featured sleek hulls that were the Renaissance equivalent of modern racing yachts. The theory was that merchant ships should be able to outrun pirates or foreign warships; and they could be organized into regular naval flotillas in the event of a foreign invasion. In this manner, it would be the responsibility of the individual ship owners to maintain their vessels—thus relieving Lord Burghley of many restless nights worrying about the prohibitive costs of building a regular navy.

Raising money for government projects, public services, and the perennial costs of maintaining the royal households was a major concern of Elizabeth's council. By some estimates, as much as half of the English population was unemployed due in part to the dependence on the woolen industry for income. However, the major problem was the inflation that resulted from the enormous flood of gold and silver that reached Barcelona and Lisbon from their colonies in Mexico and Peru. Most English bankers believed that the solution to England's economic woes depended upon expanding overseas markets. In this regard, practically everyone believed that the commercial success of the Nation depended upon two conditions: first, the establishment of colonies in the Americas; and second, finding a practical route to the Indies—that is, a route that circumvented the powerful Portuguese and Spanish Navies.

Spain was anxious to help the English out of their economic dilemma by advertising the existence of Marco Polo's secret "shortcut" to the Indies—that is, "the Northwest Passage." One of Her Majesty's favorite courtiers, Sir Humphrey Gilbert, happened to be lodging at the manor of Henry Sidney in 1568 when a Spanish priest named Andreas Urdaneta stopped by for tea. According to the priest, a merchant named Salvaerra had sailed along a passage in the north of Canada between Labrador and China. At about this time, there appeared in the London tabloids further arguments in support of an English expedition to the South Seas by way of the "Northwest Passage." These arguments in the press had three sources: 1) Spanish spies who wanted to mislead the English; 2) Propagandists working in secret for the Queen or her business patrons; and 3) Creative journalists, or fiction writers, who hoped to spice up the tabloids and increase the interest of the reading public. To paraphrase Longfellow: "Things aren't what they seem in the English tabloids."

It was at this point that Elizabeth's financial backers and her gallant courtiers made their way across the world stage. Martin Frobisher led an expedition west across the Atlantic Ocean towards Greenland in 1576. His "official" objective was to reach China by sailing along the Northwest Passage; but his sealed orders had another objective in mind altogether. He was expected to scout the shores of Newfoundland for a suitable base. It was the first step in a scheme to gain control of the valuable lumber, fur, and fishing resources of the region. There were arguments in the tabloids that identified Newfoundland as the "Gateway to the Northwest Passage." However, John Dee was of the opinion that the Northwest Passage was situated farther north. His associate, Gerhard Mercator, had also advised him that the so-called "Passage" was usually impassable due to the extreme cold of the Arctic Regions.

Francis Drake, the Queen's favorite buccaneer, was instructed to lead a "scientific mission" to the Mediterranean Sea in 1577. However, his real destination was on the other side of the world.

Captain Drake's Secret Voyage Across the Oceans of Time

A veil of deception surrounded the English merchant vessel *Pelican* as she sailed from Portsmouth on November 15th, in 1577. The tabloids reported that the destination was Morocco. The ship's owner and captain, Francis Drake, was being sent to purchase a cargo of currants. At least, that was the "official" explanation. Since Drake was also a notorious privateer, or "pirate," practically everyone imagined that something else was going to happen. It was a perfect lead story for the tabloid journalists.

Two weeks later, the rumors stopped. The *Pelican* was back in port after having sustained considerable damage in a storm. The sailors went ashore; they boasted and sang songs as sailors do; and the rumors of a Mediterranean destination were revived. It would be a short trip, they said; everyone would be home for Christmas. Someone using a spyglass spotted Captain Drake pacing on the quarterdeck—so the speculation was revived that something ominous was brewing in the Queen's Chambers.

Sometime later, it would be revealed that Lord Burghley was also suspicious of this particular vessel and its captain. He had his own spy on board a companion vessel; and the spy had instructions to disrupt the mission if the captain got involved in any sort illicit activity.

On a foggy December 7th, the townspeople of Plymouth awoke to another mystery. In the twilight hours, the *Pelican* had cast off her moorings along with four other ships, and they were all heading out to sea—destination unknown. The London gossip mill was chirping away; and in the Privy Council Chamber, Lord Burghley exchanged glances with his enchanting Queen. She smiled, knowing that the mission she had launched would forever change the course of English history. Lord Burghley smiled in his own Cheshire-cat fashion. He had faith that whatever plot Her Majesty was conspiring to commit behind his back was destined to fail, because he had his own man on the scene to block her immoral intentions.

When the *Pelican* reached the coast of Morocco, after one week of brisk sailing, Captain Drake announced that he would be leading the flotilla on a raid of Spanish shipping in the Pacific Ocean. No mention was ever made regarding the Queen's involvement in this privately funded enterprise. Indeed, Her Majesty had expressly forbidden any such raids against the Spanish. The prohibition was a matter of Official English Policy. On the other hand, Queen Elizabeth had grown accustomed to saying one thing in public, while secretly encouraging just the opposite from her loyal captains. All that it took was one wink from the beguiling redhead (that is, from Her Majesty), and the rascals in her service knew precisely what she wanted them to do.

Captain Drake understood the strategy of the Star Chamber implicitly. Or at least, he believed that he understood what they wanted him to do. His flotilla was one of three separate expeditionary forces that was being sent to the New Land. These included flotillas headed by Drake, Martin Frobisher, and Humphrey Gilbert.

Sir Humphrey was ordered to establish a garrison in the Newfoundland Archipelago. Frobisher's expedition along the Northwest Passage north of Labrador was intended to follow-up on the earlier voyages of Sebastian Cabot who had sailed as far west as Hudson Bay in 1513. John Dee was skeptical that this approach would succeed because of the trend of cooler temperatures in the Arctic Regions. Nevertheless, Walsingham stressed his desire to make the Spaniards believe that they had taken the bait from Urandeta's deceptive report. That is, the English wanted to make it seem as though they believed in the existence of a viable Northwest Passage. The English deception overseas and the tales that the sailors told in the taverns had the effect of exposing the Spanish spy network in England. This strategic maneuver enabled Walsingham's agents to penetrate the Spanish Secret Service where they were able to monitor the activities of spies as well as the plans of military strategists.

Meanwhile, Drake was expected to slip around to the backside of the Spanish Main where he would be least expected—that is, along the West Coast of Mexico and Peru. (Incidentally, this region was known as the "Golden Hind" of the Spaniards.) Precisely what he did when he got there was a matter of improvisation. Officially, he was on his own to determine the best way to implement English foreign policy—although someone in authority might have mentioned that the Spaniards might be less inclined to promote the assassination of Queen Elizabeth or to consider an invasion of England—if they received a good hard kick "in the backside."

It was Walsingham's style to add a touch of humor to his espionage game. Marco Polo had invented Isles of Gold; Jacque Cartier had claimed that he found "diamonds" in the St. Lawrence Gulf; and the Spaniards had claimed such wonders for the Northwest Passage. It was all a sort of "carrot-and-stick" approach to espionage and recruitment. Historians tend to dismiss the foolishness of the leaders who issued the false reports. However, the important factor is that many of the common sailors believed such fables at the time; and these beliefs impacted foreign policy. Thus, Captain Frobisher was instructed to return from his outing to the Northwest Passage with tales that he had found "gold mines." When his ship reached London, his crews unloaded barrels of "gold;" and they proceeded to boast of their good fortune in the dockside taverns. Of course, the cargo was actually "fools gold;" but the splash that rippled across the Spanish spy network exposed foreign agents to Walsingham's crafty associates.

Christopher Hatton (the Queen's Captain of the Guard) had advised Drake before his departure that there were four objectives for his expedition. First, he was to make a precise navigational chart of America's West Coast. Second, he was to investigate two promising bays that Marco Polo had reported at 40°N and at 48°N as possible locations for English colonies. Third, he was to explore the western entrance to Marco Polo's Arctic Passage that was supposedly situated at 74°N. And Fourth, he was to reconnoiter the so-called "Continent of Australis" that European geographers believed extended from Terra del Fuego (south of Chile) all the way to Southeast Asia. In other words, Drake was expected to conduct a considerable amount of geographical exploration. His charts of these previously unknown regions would guide English colonial activities in the Americas and the Pacific Ocean for the next two hundred years.

Drake's flotilla headed south along the African coast as far as Cape Verde. In their first naval engagement, they surprised and captured a Portuguese merchant ship. Aside from a welcome supply of "free" wine, the most valuable assets from this engagement were the capture of a veteran pilot and his satchel of Atlantic navigational charts. The maps and pilot were vital to the successful crossing of the ocean; however, the crews spent all of February and March beating their way against headwinds and doldrums before they managed to raise the coast of Brazil. By April 14th they had coasted to the Estuary of the Río de la Plata—where Drake organized hunting parties to replenish the dwindling supply of fresh meat and fruits. The captain's insistence that his sailors have regular rations of fresh and dried fruits protected his men from the deadly mariners' disease of scurvy. Subsequently, Drake obtained supplies of fresh fruit from several plantations that may have ties to the Ming Chinese and Zheng He.

By June 20th the flotilla had reached a safe harbor just north of Magellan's Strait. It was Drake's desire to fill the freshwater barrels, hunt for fresh game, and give the mariners shore leave for some recreation and entertainment. The Captain believed that this time of rest was essential for morale before running the gauntlet of the harrowing passage between the Atlantic and Pacific Oceans. After spending more than half-a-year at sea, the crews were getting pretty grumpy; and many felt uncertain about the risks that they would have to face in the dreaded Magellan Strait.

One afternoon, Drake foolishly engaged in an archery match with some supposedly "friendly" Patagonian Indians. At one point in the match, the natives had all the arrows; and they decided to kill—and probably eat—the English sailors. Two of Drake's men died in the first volley of arrows before the Captain managed to fire off a shot with his matchlock gun. The natives never suspect that Drake had such an awesome weapon. Upon seeing their leader literally torn in half with birdshot, the natives ran for their lives. The English sailors fled to their rowboats, as there was no doubting the swift arrival of hundreds of armed and angry warriors.

After reaching the safety of the *Pelican*, Captain Drake had his physician treat the wounded crewmen. It was at this moment that several officers informed Drake that many of their company wanted to give up the expedition and return to England. After all, none of them had expected to be away from home for so long; and this wasn't strictly speaking an official military operation. Also, the rumors that Drake intended to raid Spanish ports were distressing because such raids were of questionable legality. Some suspected that the Captain was after personal revenge against the Spaniards or that he was mentally unfit for command.

The Queen's favorite buccaneer had no choice but to face this challenge of his leadership head-on. Privately, he interviewed the officers and crew so that he could understand their concerns. He also wanted to determine if his suspicions were correct—that Lord Burghley had planted a spy in his midst. It did not take very long to establish that a subordinate captain, Thomas Doughty, had been undermining Drake's authority. He had solicited the favor of crews in other ships; and he had encouraged the sailors to dwell on their fears and to criticize the Commander.

In later years, Drake justified his actions saying that: "The Queen had given him full authority to act as Her Agent." Thus, a threat to his leadership was deemed a threat to the Queen—that is, it was regarded as a treasonable offense. Doughty was brought before a jury of seamen, tried, and convicted of being a spy. As was his customary style, Drake treated the condemned man to a sumptuous feast while being serenaded by the ship's violin quartet. Then a guard marched the proud spy to the block where his head was severed from his neck. Drake raised Doughty's decapitated head into the air and declared to the assembled crews: "Thus be the end for traitors!"

Several days later, after the officers and sailors had mulled over their fates and the recent events, Captain Drake gave them a pep talk about England's destiny as a world power. This was a moment of decision, he said, for the Nation. It was also a time of commitment for everyone who respected freedom of religion and who wanted a future of unlimited prosperity. From this moment forward, he declared, there would be no differences in status or wages of the crew. They would all pull together as a team—gentleman and sailor working side-by-side. All would share equally in the booty that they would relieve from the Spaniards; and he stressed that by raiding the colonies of the gold that was taken from the mines of Peru, they would spare the backs of the Indians who would otherwise have to carry the loot across Panama to the Spanish galleons waiting along the shores of the Atlantic. Then, he concluded by offering them all a choice: any man who wanted to quit the team was free to go home. He drew a line in the sand; but no one dared to step across.

The time had come to brave the contrary winds, currents, and the deadly cliffs of Magellan's Strait. This so-called "strait" was actually an intricate maze of channels and bays along the shores of Chile to the north and Terra del Fuego (or the Cold Land) in the south. This was hardly a place for a "pelican" to survive; so Drake decided to rename his vessel the "Golden Hind" (that is, a Golden Deer). Some said that this mascot was chosen in honor of Sir Christopher Hatton—whose emblem was the Golden Hind. However, it was also a pun on the exposed Spanish rear.

For two weeks, Drake's three ships and crews battled against ferocious gales and monstrous waves. They finally managed to break out onto the Pacific Ocean on September 6th during a lull in the storms. But their ordeal was no yet over. The desperate seamen daily risked their lives pulling at the ropes holding the sails, climbing the ratlines while the icy seas raged around them, and clinging for dear life as monstrous waves engulfed the decks of their ships. Two months of stormy weather battered the vessels in what the Captain called "an intolerable tempest."

By the time that a break came in the weather, they had been swept far south of Terra del Fuego; one ship had foundered with all hands; and another vessel had given up the fight and headed back toward England. Lookouts strained their eyes scanning the horizon with telescopes until they finally spotted the tops of mountains towards the east. After finding sanctuary in a small harbor and dropping anchor for the first time in nearly two months, the Captain ordered his longboat lowered over the side of the *Hind* and he went ashore.

It was at this point that Captain Drake began his serious work as the Queen's appointed field geographer. The assignment was vital to the interests of the Nation—because there were no accurate charts available of this unexplored region of the globe. Everyone in the Queen's Privy Council understood that it would be virtually impossible to undertake a program of establishing and supplying colonies without first obtaining accurate navigational charts.

Drake took a reading of the sun's height with an astrolabe. He had to rely upon the sun, because at this time of year in the Antarctic Region, the sun was above the horizon for twenty-two hours; and there were no stars visible. He determined that the small island where they had landed was situated at 56°S. It was as desolate a place as anyone could have imagined. It was barren of trees and only had a few penguins for inhabitants. As far as the eye could see to the south, the east, and the west—there were only open seas. The Captain found this severe isolation to be somewhat surprising, because his world map indicated that there should be a huge mainland in this region. On the map, it was called "Terra Australis." But there was absolutely nothing in this part of the globe besides the relentless westerly gales blowing across the waves. This awareness of the open seas below South America was Drake's first vital geographical discovery; and like all the others that he made on this incredible voyage, it was destined for filing away in the Admiralty chest of top secrets.

The weather continued to moderate for several days—with partly cloudy skies and steady warm westerly winds. After a few days of rest on dry land and fresh fowl for dinner, the spirits of the crew soared. Drake hastened to sail north before their luck changed. With a northerly heading, he steered the *Golden Hind* towards Chile. They kept to this northerly heading for several days—far beyond the point where the Captain was sure there must be mainland. However, there was no land to be seen in any direction. Once more, Drake checked his map. It was the latest version by the Dutch cartel of Mercator, Ortelius, and Judaeus. Clearly, their map showed the coast of Chile right where he was sailing. In fact, by this point in their travels, they should have crashed upon the shore several days before. Drake had his men check the depth of the bottom with their lead lines—but there was "no bottom" in this region of the ocean.

After several days sailing on an easterly heading, the lookouts finally spotted the tops of mountains along the horizon. It was Chile!

They cruised along the coast riding the Humboldt Current until they came upon a suitable harbor. The crew dropped the anchors; and Captain Drake went ashore accompanied by a boatload of heavily armed marines. Once more, the Captain set up his astronomical equipment. He chose a suitable hilltop where he could take sightings of the altitude of the sun at dawn, noon, and sunset. Meanwhile, the marines spread out to forage and to keep a lookout for hostile natives—as the Captain was wary of native hospitality ever since the incident with the Patagonian archers.

It was at this point that Captain Drake made his second vital geographical discovery. He used the sundial on his astronomical compendium to determine the time of high noon. Then he checked the time on his spring-driven mechanical clock. This device, which he had kept secret from all but a few of his most-trusted officers, enabled him to keep track of "London Time." That is, the clock had been set to "noon" when they left Plymouth; and Drake had faithfully wound the device every day. The clock still indicated London Time. Actually, it would be more accurate to say that it showed London Time *plus* the mechanical error that had accumulated during the whole year that they had already been at sea. By subtracting the time that was indicted by his sundial (that is, local time) from the time that was shown on the mechanical clock, Captain Drake was able to estimate the difference in time—or longitude—between their present location and London. This calculation made it possible for him to accurately chart his location on the globe.

Drake was stunned. The Dutch map indicated the presence of a huge western bulge along the Chilean coast; but there was no such bulge in this region. He must have wondered if this so-called "map" was any more accurate with respect to the western coast farther north. If his previous experience was any guide, he might just as well sail blind with a blank sheet of paper.

Unfortunately, there wasn't much time to ponder this geographical anomaly—as the shouting and screaming of his marines and gunshots announced the arrival of trouble. Hundreds of warriors armed with bows and arrows rushed in upon them. In the melee that followed their retreat to the boats, two marines were killed. Nine were wounded, including the Captain who endured an arrow that lodged in his face just below his right eye. English gunfire decimated the attackers; while cannon fired from the *Hind* finally sent the natives back into the bushes.

As soon as the shore party had been hauled on board, the *Hind* put out to sea—far ahead of the native canoes. For more than a week, they hugged the coast sailing north. Finally, they reached the Spanish outpost at Valparaíso. By this point, Drake had recovered substantially from his wound; and he was anxious to implement his plan to singe the "hind-side" of the Spanish Main. Drake loaded his marines in the ship's boats; and they quietly rowed ashore. After a short hike on the beach, they pounced on the unsuspecting garrison catching the Spaniards totally by surprise. Nobody had ever dreamed that English pirates would emerge from the darkness in this peaceful outpost of the Spanish Empire. Screams of terror filled the air as soldiers, priests, and native laborers all fled the town. In their haste to escape the Devil of Darkness, they left behind a great store of wine, silver, gold, emeralds, and provisions. These were all loaded into the holds of Drake's vessel while the astonished and terror-struck Spanish officers gazed at them in bewilderment and anger from the hills.

After stripping the town bare of valuables, the English sailed on north to a convenient harbor along the Chilean coast. They completely unloaded the *Hind*; and then they beached the gallant lady on the sand. This was first tedious episode of Captain Drake's ship maintenance program. The crew scraped the hull clean of barnacles and seaweed; they applied a fresh coating of grease and lime; and they replaced all the worn rigging. The vessel was re-floated at high tide. Finally, the crew reloaded the *Hind* with the Spanish treasure serving as part of the ballast. Once more, the galleon was trim and ready for battle.

As they continued their voyage northwards, the English paused from time-to-time to intercept a Spanish trading vessel; or they landed marines in order to confiscate the loot that was being transported on a mule train. On February 13th, 1579, they reached Callao Harbor near the Peruvian capital of Lima. It was Drake's intention to rob the Spanish Treasury—which at that time had an enormous store of gold ingots. However, the element of surprise was lost; and Drake had to settle for terrorizing the town and humiliating the Spanish authorities by cutting the anchor cables of all the merchant ships that were sitting in the harbor. The English managed to scour up another 1,500 bars of silver that had been abandoned in the confusion; and more ballast had to be thrown overboard from the *Hind* in order to keep the ship in good trim.

The *Hind* continued sailing north with a squadron of sluggish Spanish warships nipping at her heals for several days. Then the Spanish captains were forced to give up the chase because they had failed to bring along sufficient food to feed their crews. Probably, the sailors on the galleons were not too eager to catch up to the privateer, anyway. Indeed, the governor had identified the raider of Callao as the notorious English pirate—"Francis Drake." The governor even sent couriers riding north to spread the alarm; but invariably they arrived too late.

On March 1st, Drake's lookouts spotted the topsails of the Spanish treasure galleon *Cacafuego*. The *Hind* followed from a distance so as not to alarm the Spaniards. It seems most likely that the crew of the *Cacafuego* were not even keeping a careful watch for pirates. Indeed, they had no reason to believe that anybody would dare to confront such a powerful warship. As evening closed in about the galleon—so did Francis Drake and his team of midnight raiders.

The Spaniards felt a dull thud as the Hind drew up along side; grappling hooks were tossed over the gunwales; and Drake called out for his opponent, Captain San Juan de Anton, to surrender. It all happened so fast that the Spaniard had no time to think. He responded by ordering his marines on deck; but that was a senseless command as they were cut down by steady gunfire from Drake's harquebussers. Already, Drake's marines were rushing the Captain on the quarterdeck; and he promptly surrendered when the pistols and cutlasses all around him made it plain who was in command of this naval engagement.

Captain de Anton was quickly escorted onboard the *Hind*. He remained locked in Drake's cabin while the treasures of gold and silver on his ship were transferred to the holds of the English vessel. The ordinary seamen on board the Spanish galleon proved to be a very cooperative lot once they realized that they had been captured by the infamous "Dragon." While the Spanish crew carried the innumerable chests of gold coins, silver, and jewels onto one side of the *Golden Hind*, Drake's crew dumped ballast over the other side. The transfer of loot took several days to complete. Meanwhile, Francis Drake preserved his reputation as the "gentleman bandit" by wining and dining Captain de Anton in his cabin. De Anton was entertained by a violin ensemble while he enjoyed a feast that included wines from his former cellar. Meanwhile, Drake treated the crew and passengers on the *Cacafuego* with kindness.

Almost a month later, the *Hind* caught up with another Spanish treasure ship, the *Espírito Santo*, sailing along the coast of Mexico. Once more, Drake's crew struck the unsuspecting Spaniards by moonlight. They caught their adversary completely by surprise. Upon such extraordinary good luck and precision attacks would the reputation of England's swashbuckling hero ascend to mythical heights.

As incredible as it may seem, Captain Drake was still not content with the Spanish treasures that he had loaded aboard the *Hind*. There still remained several tons worth of stone ballast that he yearned to replace with Spanish gold. In hopes of intercepting the "Manila Galleon" that sailed annually from the Philippines loaded with treasure, he directed his vessel far out into the Pacific Ocean. They sailed west for several days before turning once again to a northerly course. In this manner, the *Hind* managed to avoid the contrary winds and currents that flowed along the coast in a southerly direction.

Historians have been completely bowled over by this expert maneuvering by Captain Drake because it gives the impression that he had some kind of devilish forehand knowledge of the ocean currents along the Pacific Coast of the Americas. Probably, this course around the coastal currents was not simply a coincidence. Indeed, there is some evidence that Drake carried with him Marco Polo's chart of the North American coast. This chart, which was given to him by John Dee, identified the principal harbors of Nootka (or Vancouver Island) and Quivira (or San Francisco Bay).

Drake estimated his latitude while standing on the rolling quarterdeck of the *Hind*. When they had reached 48°N opposite the modern-day Strait of Juan de Fuca and Puget Sound, he directed the helm towards the east. At this point along the Northwest Coast, the seas are treacherous, the currents are swift, and the bottom is an obstacle course of shoals, rocks, and sandbars. The crew onboard the *Hind* were very cautious in these waters—particularly when the fogs grew thick and cold. Drake's chaplain, Francis Fletcher would later remember his complaints about the "thick and vile fogs" of the Pacific Northwest Coast.

Probably, they headed north from this latitude, bracing against constant headwinds and gales. Since the Captain was under orders to look for the western entrance to the Northwest Passage, he felt compelled to scour the coastline for such an entrance that was supposed to be several hundred miles wide. Against blistering cold and hail, they continued northwards until the rigging was sagging under the weight of icicles.

Once more, Captain Drake consulted the maps that were available before his departure; and he found them to be totally useless. A map by map that George Best had used to promote the Northwest Passage Venture Company indicated that the West Coast turned sharply eastwards at 50N. However, the real coast that Drake recorded on his own navigational chart actually turned in the opposite direction—towards the northwest. It was patently obvious to the Captain that the charts that the Admiralty had used to plan its New World expeditions in this region were woefully inaccurate.

They sailed as far north as 58°N before Drake ordered the helmsman to reverse course. To the relief of the crew, they were soon back in the more temperate costal waters near Nootka Island. Probably, they stopped at a native village on Nootka Sound where they traded the glass beads and copper nails that were later found by archeologists in this region.

As they sailed southwards hugging the coast, they put into small bays where they could forage for fresh game, fill their water barrels, and make the astronomical measurements that were needed for the Captain's map of the West Coast. It was along the scenic shores between the Olympic Mountains of Washington and the towering redwood forests of California that Francis Drake made his fourth vital geographical discovery.

Because he was able to daily use his wind-up clock as a reliable measure of longitude, Captain Drake soon determined that the real coastline was nearly two thousand miles farther *east* than it was shown on Mercator's map. This discovery proved that the Continent of North America was only three thousand miles across instead of the five thousand miles that was shown on the maps by the Dutch Masters. Such a discovery was of vital importance to colonial planners; but it would never be known beyond the confines of the Queen's Star Chamber.

When they reached the latitude of 40°N along the California coast, the lookouts began searching the shores for signs of a bay that was marked on Marco Polo's map as the Bay of Quivira. But there was no sign of such a bay in this area; and so Drake continued on his southerly course—carefully mapping the shoreline as they sailed on by. At 38° N, the lookouts finally spotted a promising break in the sandstone cliffs. They carefully threaded their way through the eye-of-the-needle that eventually came to be known as "the Golden Gate." This was Quivira Bay—a pristine, fog-enshrouded estuary that already appeared on Marco's Map.

Drake's crew found a delightful beach north of Angel Island where they spent the next few weeks completely emptying the *Hind* of all her cargo. Half of the crew attended to the chore of scraping her hull and applying a new coating of tar. The remainder of the crew hunted deer and fowl while keeping a lookout for Spanish warships along the coast. Meanwhile, the local tribe of Miwok Indians became so enchanted with their English visitors that they brought gifts of food and tobacco.

When the time came to leave, Drake left behind a brass plate bearing an inscription in honor of Queen Elizabeth and her likeness stamped on a silver coin. From this sanctuary that for many years was known as "Sir Francis Drake's Bay," they headed west across the Pacific Ocean. Many adventures were still ahead, including an incident where the *Hind* got stuck on a reef; and there was an episode where the crew gathered a crop of lemons at Sierra Leone on the African Coast. It took nearly a year before the vessel finally turned up riding at anchor in Plymouth Harbor. Then, all the tabloids went wild with rumors about the mysterious voyage.

What do Historians Think?

The reign of Queen Elizabeth is saturated with clues regarding the early English voyages to the New World. From the very outset, her Cosmographer John Dee told her stories about the legendary King Arthur who had sent a large expedition of colonists to the Western Isles of Estotiland and Norumbega in the 6th century. The locations of these English colonies were noted on a map that John Dee prepared for the Queen in 1580. The purpose of this document, which is sometimes referred to as "the Queen's Map," was to demonstrate for the benefit of the Queen and her subjects that England was not the usurper of Spanish territory in the New World as Catholic malcontents had claimed. Instead, England was presented as the rightful heir to New World territories—by virtue of the earlier Arthurian Colonies.

John Dee enlisted the services of an Oxford historian, Richard Hakluyt, who assembled quite a body of evidence attesting to ancient English voyages to the New World. Among his other sources was Gerhard Mercator—the perennial heretic and foil to the interests of Church propaganda. It was the Dutch cartographer who told John Dee about Marco Polo's maps of the New World territories. Mercator also revealed the contents of a travelogue by a Dutch journalist named Jacob Cnoyen. According to Cnoyen, he met with the descendants of King Arthur's New World colony when they were on a pilgrimage to Norway in about the year 1364. Their home of "Dusky Norway" was subsequently identified as Nova Scotia. The fact that English descendants from Arthur's colony were still practicing the Christian Faith after almost eight centuries was absolute proof that the English had established viable colonies in the New World.

The historical investigations that were undertaken by John Dee and Richard Hakluyt were intended to counter the propaganda that Spanish authorities were promulgating in an effort to deceive the Queen's Catholic subjects. The motive for this propaganda was to gain popular support for the plan to undermine the authority of the Queen. Already, she had been excommunicated; and the pope informed faithful Catholics that they would not sin if they assisted in her assassination. Meanwhile, Spanish agents hoped to foment rebellions that would weaken the English Government during the planned invasion by Spanish troops.

The very year that Elizabeth was crowned, in 1558, the Venetian writer Gian Baptist Ramusio published his book, *Viaggi*, which told the story of the New World Voyages of the Zeno Brothers. Among the places that the Zeno Brothers visited in the 1380s were such places as Estotiland and Frisland in the Western Isles. Modern historians claimed that the so-called Zeno Map showing these isles was a "fraud." And they branded the Zeno letters that served as the basis of Ramusio's publication as "a hoax." Presumably, it was all part of an ill-conceived Venetian plot to steal the glory of discovery from the Genoese hero, Columbus.

However, the cartographer Abraham Ortelius, Mercator, Richard Hakluyt, and John Dee all regarded "Friesland" as a place that was already known to English mariners before Columbus arrived upon the scene. Here's what Ortelius had to say about the western isle:

> America was not first discovered by Christopher Columbus as all the writers of our time ascribe. ... For the north part, called Estotiland, which most of all extended toward our Europe, and islands of the same, namely Groneland, Iceland, and Frisland, ... they were first discovered by fishermen of Frisland. ... Before Columbus, our European pilots sailed those seas by the help of the lodestone.[1]

During the 14th century "Frisland" was a title that was originally used to represent the Frisian Islands north of Holland. Alas, Frisian merchants and explorers used this name of their homeland to identify a region of Newfoundland that they colonized in the 5th or 6th century. Arthurian colonists followed them to Nova Scotia by the 6th century.

John Dee, much to the dissatisfaction of Columbus supporters, concluded that King Edward III had sent the Oxford Franciscans to the New World in the region of "Dusky Norway," Newfoundland, or Nova Scotia in an effort to identify the old English colonies in the region. Thus, the English claimed steady contact with colonies in the Northeast American Coast ever since the 6th century.

John and Sebastian Cabot had extended English claims as far as Hudson Bay and Florida. Francis Drake's job was to complete the English exploration of the New World by adding the West Coast. Thus, the term "New Albion" that may have been used as early as the 6th century was intended to refer to the entire Continent of North America.

American historians have grown so accustomed to regarding Francis Drake as a buccaneer that they often overlook the important geographical discoveries that were made during his circumnavigation of the world. The most important of these is the accurate portrayal of North America that we see on the John Dee Map of 1580. This map shows California as a peninsula; it accurately reflects the shape of the West Coast; it has the southern coast of Alaska bending towards the northwest—which is precisely true; and it confirms English knowledge that North America was about 3,000 miles across at the widest point. By contrast, the most popular map of the 16th century, Mercator's standard World Map of 1569/1587 exaggerates the expanse of the Northern Continent by about 2,000 extra miles. As you can imagine, knowing the distance across North America would be of great importance to colonial real estate speculators and military planners.

Francis Drake's statement regarding the shape of South America along the Chilean Coast—that there was no western bulge—indicates that he had a reasonably accurate mechanical clock on board. Indeed,

---

[1] Donald Johnson, Phantom Islands of the Atlantic, New York: Walker Press, 1994, 46-47. One reason why orthodox historians have trouble with Ortelius is his mention of the lodestone being used in early Dutch navigation prior to the 12th century.

Mercator's map of the region indicated that there was such a bulge. Drake's observation that no such bulge was present along the West Coast would have been impossible without a mechanical clock. By having such a clock—as well as a sundial to gauge local time, he was constantly aware of his actual longitude (relative to the prime meridian of London). If there was land shown on his maps where no such land actually existed, then he was able to identify the problem immediately.

By this point in time, John Dee had written a book on practical navigation which aided the training of sea captains. It was also rumored that he was equipping his captains with "very precise instruments" for determining longitude.[2]

Spring-driven mechanical clocks were available by the mid-15th century. So the idea that Drake might have carried such a device is not at all speculative. A clock the size of a small suitcase was displayed in the Brussels City Hall in 1450. A Flemish artist recorded the display in a painting that was designed to advertise the accomplishments of local clockmakers.[3] William Barents carried a mechanical clock on his 1596 expedition north of Russia—so we know that such devices were available for use in navigation even though they were seldom mentioned in ship's logs or chronicles. It was not until Norse seal hunters found the clock with the remains of Barents' winter fort at Ice Haven on the White Sea in 1871 that modern historians had any idea the ancient mariners had used such devices on their exploratory voyages.

From this point forward, historians must consider the very real possibility that any unusually accurate map we happen to examine from the 15th century onward could have been produced with the aid of a mechanical clock. Such clocks were not very reliable over long periods of time. Drake's clock apparently had gained about 40 minutes (or 10° of longitude) by the time he reached the West Coast of North America. If we examine his navigational chart from the 1577-1580 voyage, we notice that his coastline is about 10° too far west. By moving Drake's coastline by that amount to the east on a hypothetical map of North America, we find a very close correspondence of coastlines. This degree of similarity could only have been achieved if Drake had used a mechanical clock.

Captain Drake was certainly aware of the tremendous importance of his geographical discoveries; and he applied on numerous occasions to the Queen for permission to publish his journals and charts. However, he was always refused. Thus, we can be certain that the Queen and her most trusted advisors in the Star Chamber regarded Drake's discoveries as being of such vital importance to the interests of national security—and perhaps their own financial investments, as well—that the information was never made public. More than two decades after his death, the heavily censored biography by Francis Fletcher was finally published. Called

---

[2] Samuel Bawlf, The Secret Voyage of Sir Francis Drake, New York: Penguin, 2003, 202.
[3] Francis & Joseph Geis, Cathedral, Forge and Waterwheel—Technology and Invention in the Middle Ages, New York: Harper-Collins, 1994, 213.

World Encompassed, it recounted the many adventures that occurred on the voyage; but it failed to mention the most secret geographical discoveries.

Historians don't argue with the fact that Francis Drake sailed along the West Coast and subsequently circumnavigated the earth. There's simply too much documentation of that achievement to cast any doubt whatsoever. What is arguable is precisely where he landed on the West Coast of North America. In particular, historians have waged quite volatile debates concerning claims that he careened his ship in San Francisco Bay.

A promising brass plate with Drake's inscription was found in the San Francisco Bay area in 1936. It was subsequently condemned as a "fraud" supposedly due to the language used in the inscription and the type of brass used for the plate. Some writers claimed that the English didn't have rolling mills in the 16th century; and rolling mills were necessary to make this kind of plate or sheet brass. However, the Germans did have the right kind of mills; and they traded with English merchants—so the claim that "no mills in England equals fraud" does not apply in this case. In 1974, an archeologist found an Elizabethan silver coin (dated 1577) bearing the image of Queen Elizabeth at a Miwok village site near San Francisco. And this could be a relic of Drake's visit to the Bay—but it doesn't precisely indicate where he repaired his ship. A similar coin has been found in the dunes of southern Oregon.

Even more illuminating are the maps that English and Spanish cartographers prepared in the 17th century. All the early names for the Bay call it either "Sir Francis Drake's Bay" or "Sir Francis Drake's Harbor." It appears as though the English Captain George Vancouver was sent on a secret mission in 1792 to meet with the Spanish Captain Bodega Y Quadra. The official purpose of this meeting was to iron out the problems that English merchants were having with Spanish intervention in the seas around Nootka (or Vancouver) Island. Apparently, Vancouver was authorized to trade so-called "rights" to San Francisco for a guarantee that the Spanish would abandon their forts in the Pacific Northwest. It seems unlikely that the British would have been in a position to broker the deal unless they had in their possession Drake's navigational chart of San Francisco Bay. Since Drake had administered the customary rite of declaring the Queen's sovereignty in the bay and accepting the Miwok Indians as "Her Majesty's subjects," the English had obvious priority in the region.

Consequences for New World Exploration: Era of Funny Maps

In the long-haul perspective, geographical information was vital to the planning of England's colonial enterprise for the next two centuries. In the short-run, the loot that Captain Drake confiscated from the Spaniards was more than the English Crown could have expected to gain from all the taxes in the realm for the next two decades. This windfall profit enabled

England to recover economically from the long depression. There was money available for rebuilding the Navy and for establishing some of the colonial enterprises that were part of the Queen's vision for a British Empire. A lot of funding went into promoting the Elizabethan Theatre as a means of educating the public in the English language, entertaining the public, and building English pride.

The English made no public accounting of the loot that was hauled from Plymouth to London. Even the Spanish didn't know how much was lost. Chests containing minted coins were usually registered; but Drake made off with piles of gold and silver ingots. In many cases, these ingots had not yet been inventoried, or else the colonial governors didn't want to admit how much they had actually lost to the English pirate.

Following Drake's return from the Pacific Theater, Elizabeth and her councilors pressed ahead with their plans to build a "British Empire." Their goal was to establish viable farming communities in the New World that would serve as marshaling points for valuable commodities such as cured fish, furs, copper, and tar. In 1585, on the heels of exploratory voyages by Martin Frobisher and Humphrey Gilbert, Sir Walter Raleigh was dispatched with England's first colonial expedition to the Carolinas. Raleigh "planted" his band of enthusiastic volunteers on a lovely little island that seemed ideal for establishing a new farming community. The weather was pleasant; there was plenty of fresh water; and there was abundant firewood. The volunteers built a small fort and some little log houses—which they called the Roanoke Colony. It was a good start.

However, nobody who was involved in planning of this disastrous colonial experiment had bothered to really check out the area in advance. It turned out that the Carolina Coast was particularly vulnerable to hurricanes and storm surges; winters were unbelievably harsh; and the sandy soil was unsuitable for growing anything but tobacco. As the situation steadily deteriorated, and the volunteers grew desperate, they all wondered: could Drake save them?

Drake's voyage round the world from 1577 to 1580 accomplished all of its intended objectives; and it achieved a few more that proved to be frosting on the cake. He succeeded in booting King Philip II in the colonial "Rear End." Even by this early date, it was no secret that the Catholic King intended to invade England in order to remove the Protestant Queen from her throne. Indeed, Philip was so obsessed with his presumed role as God's "housecleaner," that he had ordered the construction of an Armada of huge galleons to invade the "cesspool" of Protestant heresy—that is, to invade England. So, the war that was coming between England and Spain had been on the drawing boards in the Privy Councils of both countries for a considerable time. And Walsingham's spies were watching every move of the Spanish military planners.

Drake's sudden appearance along the Pacific shores of New Spain, and his tremendous success in terrorizing the colonial governments was not just a "singing of Philip's beard," as it has been called, but a tactical triumph. King Philip was forced to stretch his Navy beyond the breaking point. His requirement that the Spanish Navy escort treasure galleons in both the Pacific and the Atlantic Oceans, defend the Spanish Main along the Gulf Coast from pirates, protect the harbors of Spain and Portugal from attack, and build up an invasion force—all at the same time—was far beyond the capability of the naval commanders. The biggest problem wasn't the size of the fleets. Spain had sufficient gold reserves, laborers, and cheap supplies from the colonies to build all the ships that were needed. The essential problem was in manning those vessels with experienced officers and crews. Many veteran captains were sent off to duties in New Spain—that is, to the New World colonies—and the leadership of the Armada was virtually left in the "Hands of God."

King Philip's governors were again caught off guard when Drake's fleet arrived outside the harbors of Cadiz and Sagres in 1586. The Armada was almost ready to sail against England; but Drake's raiders managed to burn, sink, or scuttle 130 Spanish warships. The invasion had to be postponed. On the way home from this stunning triumph, Captain Drake decided to visit the Queen's colony on Roanoke Island.

When he arrived, he found the colony in desperate straits. They had been lashed by hurricanes and winter gales. Their food supply was exhausted; they had to spend considerable efforts just to dig up edible roots. In short, they were miserable and wanted to go home. Captain Drake loaded up the survivors and sailed back to England.

The following year, in 1558, the Duke of Medina Sidonia arrived in the English Channel with the Spanish Armada. King Philip called this enormous fleet "God's Hammer of Revenge."

Admiral Howard and Francis Drake were waiting with England's "Citizen Fleet" consisting mostly of converted merchant vessels. This confrontation of elegant Spanish ladies, decked out in their finest silk banners, and motley English whores with their rag-tag sails would prove to be the Battle of the Century. But from the outset, the first impression was that the tiny English warships didn't sand a chance against the towering Spanish galleons with their skirts of bronze cannon, their legions of smartly-dressed marines, and their enormous firepower.

The small, fast English galleons didn't manage to sink a single Spanish warship. However, the pummeling that they endured from the English long-range cannon, and the terror that melted their confidence when they were set upon by fire ships in the middle of the night was sufficient to cause panic. They fled before a gale that drove them into the North Sea. Many of the beautiful behemoths were dashed against the cliffs of the Irish coast. Those that didn't sink were heavily damaged.

Spain's humiliating military defeat opened the way for English and French competition in North American real estate ventures. In retrospect, we can imagine the cunning minds at work in Elizabeth's Star Chamber by examining the maps that were published during the fifty years that followed Drake's return to England. Even though he made a very accurate map of America's West Coast, nobody in England outside the Star Chamber ever got to see what it looked like. A close copy of that map found its way to France in 1587. The map was part of deal that the Ambassador, Richard Hakluyt, brokered with King Louis to keep France out of the conflict with Spain. As was the case in England, French authorities decided to keep the contents of this map secret from their own people. That was because the best incentive for new settlers to immigrate to the colonies was the false belief that Marco Polo's Northwest Passage would lead them to the wealth of Cathay. And Drake's map was convincing evidence that the so-called "Passage" was too far north to be of any practical value to navigation.

Throughout the 17th century, French and English pioneers sailed to America; then they continued on a westward trek searching for Marco Polo's Northwest Passage and the shortcut to China. The gullibility of the colonists seems incredible to us; but they persisted because the governments of England and France deliberately published inaccurate maps in order to deceive the prospective colonists.

John Lok's Map of 1582 completely erased from existence the entire Northwest Coast Region of America. It was as though some diabolical magician had waved his wand, and "poof"—there was no Alaska, no Oregon or Washington, and no Yukon Territory that might block the passage between Newfoundland and Marco Polo's Cathay.

Another deceptive map by John Briggs in 1620 portrayed California as an Island. It was a geographical monstrosity that would endure on European maps for the next century. John Farrer, who was a scandalous real estate broker, published a very deceptive map in 1651 that made it appear as though the Colony of Virginia was only 300 miles across. According to Farrer's map, the western border of Virginia was situated right along the "South Seas" near China. As an incentive for prospective colonists to trust in his vision, Farrer pasted a portrait of Sir Francis Drake right in the middle of the ocean. "Trust in Drake"—was the deceptive message of this cunning advertisement for a new life in the New World.

The Queen's vision of a British Empire grew steadily upon the framework of courage, freedom, and geographical deception that originated in her Star Chamber. The first successful colony was named "Virginia" in honor of Elizabeth—the "Virgin Queen."

ΙΕΡΟ
ΓΛΥ
ΑΝΙ
ΦΙΚΟ
ΚΟΝ
Ο

Doctor John Dee—the "Q" of 16ᵗʰ century Espionage

Spyglasses, mechanical clocks, and codes were standard issue at Doctor Dee's School of Navigational Science. Historians tend to characterize the Queen's favorite geographer as a "charlatan astrologer." He actually had a keen insight, a firm understanding of the world's real geography, and he worked behind the scenes to prepare English sea captains. He researched mechanical clocks, cannons, explosives, geography, and marine science. His books on navigation and equipment made it possible for English mariners to map and explore the New World.

Secret Navigational Clock
Windup Steel Mainspring
London, c. 1575
Concept Ills. by author

Mechanical clock, c. 1450
Clock mechanism with steel mainspring
From painting "the Clock of Wisdom"
Royal Library, Brussels, Ms. IV, III, f. 13v.

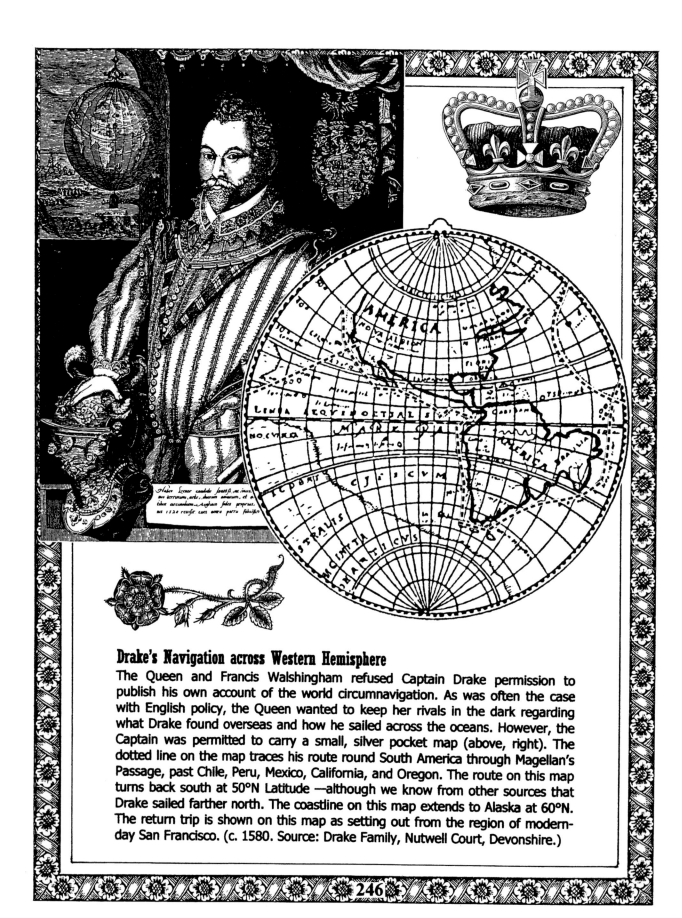

Drake's Navigation across Western Hemisphere

The Queen and Francis Walshingham refused Captain Drake permission to publish his own account of the world circumnavigation. As was often the case with English policy, the Queen wanted to keep her rivals in the dark regarding what Drake found overseas and how he sailed across the oceans. However, the Captain was permitted to carry a small, silver pocket map (above, right). The dotted line on the map traces his route round South America through Magellan's Passage, past Chile, Peru, Mexico, California, and Oregon. The route on this map turns back south at 50°N Latitude —although we know from other sources that Drake sailed farther north. The coastline on this map extends to Alaska at 60°N. The return trip is shown on this map as setting out from the region of modern-day San Francisco. (c. 1580. Source: Drake Family, Nutwell Court, Devonshire.)

**Queen's Map
1580**

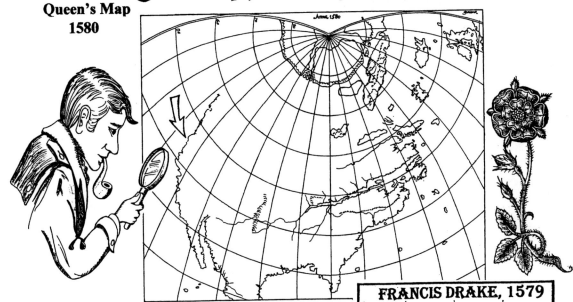

Time Detectives solve the Mystery of the "Lost Queen's Map"

Long ago, historians gave up looking for cartographic evidence of Francis Drake's route in the Pacific. They presumed that the only copy of Drake's navigation had been lost in a fire at the Queen's Palace. The map was referred to as "the lost Queen's Map." However, the author found the lost map in the British Archives—misfiled under the heading of "Dee's 1580 Map of the Northern Hemisphere". The author noticed the incredibly accurate shape of the North American Continent. By comparison, contemporary maps by Mercator showed the West Coast some 1,500 miles too far into the Pacific Ocean. In order to solve the puzzle, the author first recalibrated the oval projection to a standard Mercator Projection. It was apparent from this level of accuracy that Drake must have made his map using a shipboard clock to determine longitude. If we assume that Drake's clock had gained 40 minutes and was therefore off by 10° of longitude, and if we adjust the map accordingly, we can see from the map at right just how close Drake's navigational chart from the 1577-1580 voyage was to the actual coast. This map was kept secret and never released to the public. In modern times, portions of the map were included in a book by William Babcock and an article by E.R. Taylor.

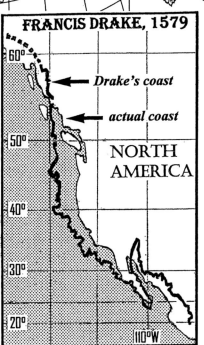

FRANCIS DRAKE, 1579

60°
Drake's coast
actual coast
50°
NORTH AMERICA
40°
30°
20°
110°W

Longitude West of Greenwich

Mechanical Clock available to Drake 1577-1580

Mercator's 1569/1587 Standard Map

This map of the Western Hemisphere from Rumold Mercator's remake of his father's standard world map shows the enormous projection of the West Coast into the Pacific Ocean. Indeed, the West Coast is between 1,500 and 2,000 miles too far west. Such an enormous distortion made it difficult for explorers to accurately determine their positions. Thus, Francis Drake's map in 1580 represented an incredible improvement over the other maps that were available. However, the Queen and her closest advisors had their own motives for keeping Drake's accurate geography of the New World a secret.

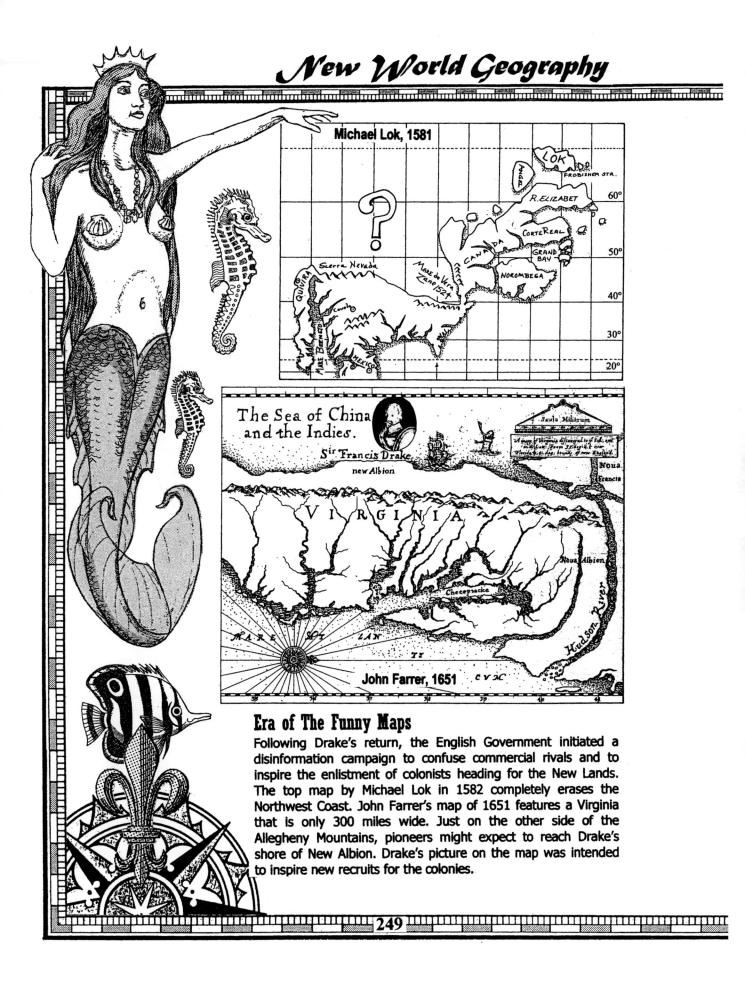

Michael Lok, 1581

LOK
Angel
FROBISHER STR.
R. ELIZABET
60°
CORTE REAL
CANADA
GRAND BAY
50°
NOROMBEGA
Sierra Nevada
MARE de Vera Zano 1527
40°
QUIVIRA
MARE BERMEIO
Cevola
30°
MEXICO
20°

The Sea of China and the Indies.
Sir Francis Drake.
new Albion
Scala Militum
Noua Francia
V I R G I N I A
Noua Albion
Checepracke
MARE SOT LAN
Hudson River
John Farrer, 1651

Era of The Funny Maps

Following Drake's return, the English Government initiated a disinformation campaign to confuse commercial rivals and to inspire the enlistment of colonists heading for the New Lands. The top map by Michael Lok in 1582 completely erases the Northwest Coast. John Farrer's map of 1651 features a Virginia that is only 300 miles wide. Just on the other side of the Allegheny Mountains, pioneers might expect to reach Drake's shore of New Albion. Drake's picture on the map was intended to inspire new recruits for the colonies.

Under the Midnight Sun

WE BEGAN OUR JOURNEY into the realm of secret voyages with the daring quest of an Egyptian Queen. She wanted desperately to understand the nature of the universe. Her legacy tempted King Solomon to sail across the seas to a New Land; and he, in turn, left a heritage of legendary voyages that inspired the Venetians, Columbus, and many other Renaissance explorers. Some found the treasures that they were seeking. However, the Golden Isles of Solomon and Marco Polo were actually a side-show to the real march of history. By finding a New World, the peoples of the Old World began to forge a New Destiny.

Relearning History

The exciting premise of the Renaissance was that the world was liberated at last from the Church dogma of Doomsday. Time-after-time during the Middle Ages, the prophets had predicted the "certain" End of the World; but it never happened. Theologians insisted to dwindling congregations that the sun orbited the earth; and they condemned the scientists who experimented with magnetism, optics, and gunpowder. But it was hard to compete with the roar of cannon; and it was impossible to police the mariners who kept a handy compass hidden in the binnacle.

The gig was up the moment that European geographers threw out their antiquated, Jerusalem-centered wheel maps. They joyously embraced Mercator's 1587 Atlas that proved to be a practical guide to their overseas expeditions and investments. Indeed, these expeditions sailed off to very real continents that the Church theologians had once claimed couldn't possibly exist.

Amerigo Vespucci's revelation of the existence of a "New World" sounded the death knell to the notion of an "Earthly Paradise." The American Continents were certainly very much like the Paradise of Elesian Fields that the Greek seafarers had described across the ocean. But Vespucci had proved that anybody could go to the New World Paradise whenever they pleased. Thus, the loyal theologians of the Mother Church had to abandon the novel idea that the Earthly Paradise was a preserve only for Christians. And they had to invent a new place for the eternal lives that were promised to loyal believers. Over time, the notion of where Heaven or Paradise might be located in a physical sense had to evolve with the progress of astronomy and the expanding universe.

Where is it now? Perhaps, it's been here all along.

The Chinese innovation in timekeeping—that is, the mechanical clock—put an end to the reliance of Europeans on the Church for keeping track of time. Before long, the need to turn the hourglass faded from memory. People began thinking of time as the perpetual turning of wheels in some enormous machine that stood in the Gild Hall clock tower. Thus, the old notion that time would ever "run out," like the sands in an hourglass, no longer made any sense. It is true that some people still use the antiquated expression—often without being able to explain the ancient origins of the concept. However, with the invention of Grandfather Clocks and pocket watches, people noticed the "ticking" sound; and then they started talking about when the "clock stops ticking." But this notion of a clock stopping only referred to the life expectancy of an individual whose heart (the "ticker") would eventually stop. Only the most ignorant fundamentalist believers still entertain notions of the entire universe suddenly coming to a complete stop. Isaac Newton ended that medieval fantasy for everyone who bothered to read about the principles of physics.

The stunning defeat of the Spanish Armada was another blow to the antiquated way of medieval thinking that for so long had held back the progress of science and technology. King Philip II, and lots of "Doomsday" thinkers, hoped that the Armada would end the cultural and religious revolutions of the Renaissance. His supporters were led to believe that the pending battle of the English Fleet with the Spaniards was the ultimate confrontation between Good and Evil. Philip and many of his followers even considered that this might prove to be the biblical Armageddon leading up to the End of the World.

"God's Hammer" made a splash in the English Channel; then it promptly sank to the bottom—with a little help of Irish banshees and Mother Nature. The effective removal of the Spanish Navy from blocking access to the New World opened up the unrestrained commercial opportunities of colonial expansion for England, France, and Holland. The flow of wealth into these countries and the enormous demand that was placed upon the shipbuilding and navigational industries caused an incredible rush in technological and scientific development. Binoculars, marine chronometers, sextants, the azimuth compass, and the inclinometer all resulted from the demand for more accurate maps of the distant isles across the seas.

Competition between the maritime powers resulted in exploratory fleets being sent to every so-called "corner" of the globe. These expeditions carried journalists, artists, and scientists whose job it was to chronicle the adventures and to inventory the valuable resources of distant islands that might be exploited for commercial purposes. By this point in time, during an Age is called "The Enlightenment," scientific societies demanded access to the journals and maps of the explorers. It was the advent of the Free Press in Europe that effectively ended the practicality and usefulness of secret voyages to the New World.

The English Geographical Society and the Admiralty sponsored Captain James Cook's three expeditions into the Pacific Ocean from 1768 to 1779. Cook is wrongly credited with "disproving" the existence of a Southern Continent. Actually, he helped to define the coast of Australia—which was but one of the southern continents that along with South America had formed the ancient Greek concept of the Antipodes. Although the English Admiralty released most of the journals from these expeditions for publication, there was still one lingering secret that haunted his expedition. Indeed, the Admiralty had ordered Cook to look for the western approach to the Northwest Passage.

He was not the last English officer to be sent on such a "fool's errand." His lieutenant, George Vancouver was given the same order in 1792. So, it seems that the British Admiralty still hoped to take advantage of a ruse that had been in operation ever since the dark days of Elizabeth's Privy Council. The English government even tried to reinforce the illusion of a shortcut to Cathay by offering a £20,000 reward for the expedition that finally located the Northwest Passage. However, George Vancouver had already figured out that the game was a "wild goose-chase." As his vessel cruised down the Thames River south of London, the veteran Captain observed the irony that his ship was sailing "on April Fool's Day."

Sequel to the Rose

On a dark and blustery night along the quays of Oslo Fjord, a desperate crew of Norwegian sailors aboard the herring smack *Gjoa* cast off their moorings and slipped out to sea. It was one more "secret voyage" that was heading towards Marco Polo's Northwest Passage to Cathay. But this time, the motive for secrecy wasn't international competition or piracy. This time, the owner of the ship, Roald Amundsen, was attempting to escape creditors who had threatened to have him arrested. It was June 16, 1903.

As far as the Norwegian authorities were concerned, Amundsen, his ship, and a crew of seven volunteers simply "disappeared" into the night. That was as good an ending as you could expect for a police report in Oslo. Indeed, the local gendarmes had little interest in putting the young adventurer in jail—especially not on such a miserably cold night. This was a time for a warm fire, ludefisk, and vodka.

It would be three years before anybody in a civilized nation ever learned the whereabouts of the fugitives or what they were doing. There were no coastguard cutters to trace their voyage to the Arctic Seas near

Baffin Island. Nor were there any Mounties in this region of the Arctic to report that they had comfortably settled into Aleut igloos to spend the winter. These Nordic desperados resided illegally in the Canadian Arctic for three years while they learned the survival skills of the Eskimos; and they gradually sailed towards the west—tracing the route of the Northwest Passage. They recorded scientific information about the Magnetic North Pole; they hunted Arctic seals and bears; and they recorded their adventures in journals and with a camera. When they emerged at the other end of the Passage in 1905, they were instant celebrities; and Roald was finally able to pay off his debts with income from books and lectures.

Historians declared that Amundsen was "the first mariner" to sail the Northwest Passage. Actually, he simply proved that the Passage did exist. It wasn't a figment of Marco Polo's imagination.

In recent times, it seems as though the Northwest Passage is beginning to reemerge from the cold, icy wasteland of the Arctic. As global warming melts the Arctic Ice Cap, the width of the Passage continues to grow longer every summer. The climate is growing warmer— thus making it possible to sail along the open Passage for longer periods of time. Certainly the Native Peoples are enjoying the warming trend because it makes for longer hunting seasons.

These days, you can ask any Aleut Native kayaking along the seas near Baffin Island about the secret voyagers; and they will nod in affirmation of their instinctive wisdom. They will point out towards the waters and say, the secret voyagers are still out there—sailing beneath the Midnight Sun. Indeed, they are. They are not the ghosts of voyagers past, but the silvery phantoms of the deep—the rorquals. In modern times, the secret voyagers of the New World are submarines from the Navies of Russia, China, England, and the United States.

On occasion, they will surface to the surprise of the native kayakers. Crews will disembark, and beneath the Aurora Borealis they will play a match of cricket or baseball. Why not? The Cold War is over—even though it's still mighty cold where the navies play.

Bibliography

Acosta, Joseph de. *The Natural and Moral History of The Indies.* (c. 1560) Edward Grimston, Trans., 1604. Clements R. Markham, Ed. London: Hakluyt Society, 1880.

Aero, Rita. *Things Chinese.* New York: Doubleday, 1980.

Aldred, Cyril. *Egyptian Art—in the Days of the Pharaohs.* London: Thames & Hudson, 1980.

Andrist, Ralph K. *Heroes of Polar Exploration.* New York: Meredith, 1962.

Andro, Anatole. *The 1421 Heresy—An Investigation into the Ming Chinese Maritime Survey of the World.* Pasadena: Author, 2005.

Ashe, Geoffre. *Land to the West—St. Brendan's Voyage to America.* London: Collins, 1962 (New York: Viking, 1962).

Babcock, William H. *Legendary Islands of The Atlantic.* Research Series No. 8. New York: American Geographical Society, 1922.

Babcock, William. H. *Legendary Islands of the Atlantic—A Study in Medieval Geography.* New York: American Geographical Society, 1922.

Bawlf, Samuel. *The Secret Voyage of Sir Francis Drake.* NY: Penguin, 2002.

Bagrow, Leo. Maps from the Home Archives of the Descendants of a friend of Marco Polo, *Imago Mundi* (V), 1948, 1-13.

Beasley, C. Raymond. Marco Polo in Dawn of Modern Geography, *1911 Encyclopedia*; www. 1911encyclopedia.org, 2003, 1-14.

Bliss, Robert Woods. *Pre-Columbian Art.* New York: Phaidon, 1957.

Boorstin, Daniel J. *The Discoverers.* New York: Random House, 1983.

Bradley, Irene. *America's Horses and Ponies.* Boston: Houghton Mifflin, 1969.

Brown, Lloyd. *The Story of Maps.* New York: Bonanza Books, 1959.

Burenhult, Göran, General Editor. *New World and Pacific Civilizations: Cultures of America, Asia, and the Pacific.* New York: HarperCollins, 1994.

Clark, Robert. *River of the West.* New York: Harper Collins, 1995.

Conlan, Roberta. *The American Indians: the Indians of California.* New York: Time-Life Books, 1994.

Cooke, Jean, Ann Kramer, and Theodore Rowland-Entwistle. *History's Timeline.* New York: Crescent, 1981.

Covey, Cyclone. Comment on the Sioux and the Atsina, *Midwest Epigraphic Journal*, Vol. 14, 2000, 90.

Crane, Nicholas. *Mercator: The Man who Mapped the Planet.* New York: Henry Holt, 2002.

Cuevas, Mariano. *Historia de la Nacion Mexicana.* Mexico City: 1940.

Davies, Nigel. *Voyagers to the New World.* Albuquerque: U. New Mex. Press, 1979.

Debenham, Frank. *Discovery and Exploration: an Atlas History of Man's Wanderings.* Garden City: Doubleday, 1960.

Delgado, James. *Across the Top of the World.* New York: Checkmark Books, 1999.

Dor-Ner, Zvi. *Columbus and the Age of Discovery.* New York: Morrow, 1991.

Edwards, Elwyn Hartley. *The Encyclopedia of the Horse.* New York: Dorling Kindersley, 1994.

Evans, Elwood, Ed. *History of the Pacific Northwest, Oregon, and Washington.* Portland: North Pacific History Company, 1889.

Everett, Felicity, and Struan Reid. *Explorers.* New York: Usborne, 1991.

Flaum, Eric. *Discovery—Exploration.* New York: Gallery, 1990.

Fox, Luke, and Thomas James. *The Voyages of Captain Luke Foxe and Captain Thomas James.* London: Hakluyt Society, 1893.

Fremantle, Anne. *The Age of Faith.* Alexandria, VA: Time-Life Boks, 1965.

Fuson, Robert H., Trans. *The Log of Christopher Columbus.* Camden MD: International Marine Publishing Co., 1987.

Galvano, Antonio. Summary Deduction of the Discoveries of the World from their first Original to the year 1555. Richard Hakluyt, Trans., Chapter I, in Kerr, Robert, and F.A.S. Edin. *A General History and Collection of Voyages and Travels.* Edinburge: Ramsay, 1811.

Gardner, Joseph L., Ed. *Mysteries of The Ancient Americas.* Pleasantville: Reader's Digest, 1986.

Gies, Frances & Joseph Gies. *Cathedral, Forge and Waterwheel: Technology and Invention in the Middle Ages.* New York: Harper Collins, 1994.

Goetzman, William H., and Glyndwr Williams. *Atlas of World Exploration.* New York: Prentice Hall, 1992

Goetzmann, William H.—*New Lands, New Men: America and The Second Great Age of Discovery.* New York: Viking, 1986.

Grove, Kindrie. *Field Guide to Horses.* Edmonton, AB: Lone Pine, 1998.

Hadingham, Evan. Ancient Chinese Explorers, in *Sultan's Lost Treasure*, NOVA Online, www. pbs.org/wgbh, 2003.

Hale, John R. *The Renaissance.* Alexandria, VA: Time-Life Books, 1965.

—*Age of Exploration.* Alexandria, VA: Time-Life Books, 1966, 1974.

Hampton, Bruce. *Children of Grace.* New York: Henry Holt, 1994.

Harley, J. B. *Maps and The Columbus Encounter.* Milwaukee: Golda Meir Library, 1990.

Harris, Hendon. *The Asiatic Fathers of America.* Taiwan: Wen Ho Co, 1975.

Harrisse, Henry. *Discovery of North America.* Amsterdam: N. Israel, 1961.

Hayes, Derek. *Historical Atlas of the Pacific NW.* Seattle: Sasquatch, 1999.

Heyerdahl, Thor. *Early Man and The Ocean.* London: George Allen, 1978.

—*Kon Tiki.* Chicago: Rand McNally, 1950.

—*American Indians in the Pacific.* London: George Allen, 1952.

Holland, Hjalmar R. *Norse Discoveries & Explorations In America 982-1362.* New York: Dover Publications, 1940 (1968).

Humble, Richard. *Marco Polo.* New York: G.P. Putnam's Sons, 1973.

Ibarra-Grasso, Dick. "Cuatro Viajes Transpacificos Precolombinos en la Historia y el Folklore," in *Revista Argentina*, 1, June 1991.

James, Peter, and Nick Thorpe. *Ancient Mysteries.* New York: Ballentine, 1999.

Johnson, Donald S. *Phantom Islands of The Atlantic: The Legends of Seven Lands that Never Were.* New York: Avon Books/Walker & Co., 1994.

Joseph, Frank. *Atlantis in Wisconsin.* Colfax: Ancient American Books.

Josephy, Alvin M., Jr. *The American Heritage Book of Indians.* New York: Simon & Schuster, 1961.

Kerr, Robert F, and F. Eden. *A General History and Collection of Voyages and Travels.* Vol. II. Edinburgh: William Blackwood, 1811.

Knkobl, Kuno. *Tai Ki.* Boston: Little Brown & Co., 1975.

Komroff, Manuel, Ed. *The Travels of Marco Polo the Venetian*. Revised from Marsden's Translation. Garden City: Modern Library, 2001.

Landström, Björn. *The Ship*. New York: Doubleday, 1961.

Larner, John. *Marco Polo and the Discovery of the World*. New Haven: Yale U. Press, 1999.

Latham, Ronald, Trans. *Marco Polo: The Travels*. New York: Penguin, 1958.

Lawrance, Scott. Buddhist Columbia, in Howard White, *Raincoast Chronicles— First Five, Collector's Edition*, Madiera Park, BC: Harbour Publishing, 1976.

Lelewel, Joachim. Atlas: *Géographie du Moyen Age* (1845). Amsterdam: Meridian Publishing (Reprint), 1967.

Levathes, Louise. *When China Ruled the Seas: The Treasure Fleet of the Dragon Throne 1405-1433*. New York: Simon & Schuster, 1994.

Lothrop, S.K., W.F. Foshag, and Joy Mahler. *Robert Woods Bliss Collection: Pre-Columbian Art*. New York: Garden City Books, 1957.

Mallery, Arlington, & Mary Roberts Harrison. *The Rediscovery of Lost America*. New York: E.P. Dutton, 1951 (1979).

Markham, Clements R. *Christopher Columbus, John Cabot, and Gaspar Corte Real*. London: Hakluyt Society, 1893.

Marsden, William. *The Travels of Marco Polo the Venetian*. New York: Doubleday, 1948.

Marshall, Robert. *Storm from the East: From Genghis Khan to Kublai Khan*. Berkeley: University of California Press, 1993.

Marx, Robert F., and Jennifer G. Marx. *In Quest of The Great White Gods*. New York: Crown, 1992.

McCurdy, James G. *By Juan de Fuca's Strait*. Portland: Binfords & Mort, 1937.

Menzies, Gavin. *1421—The Year China Discovered America*. New York: William Marrow, 2003.

Mertz, Henrietta. "The Pre-Columbian Horse," *Anthropological Journal of Canada*, 10 (2), 1972.

—*Pale Ink: Two Ancient Records of Chinese Exploration in America*. Chicago: Swallow Press, 1953 (1972).

Mitchell, James, Ed. *Random House Encyclopedia*. New York, Random H, 1990.

Morgan, Murray. *The Northwest Corner*. New York: Viking, 1962.

Morison, Samuel E. *The Great Explorers: The European Discovery of America*. New York: Oxford University Press, 1978.

—*The European Discovery of Americs*. New York: Oxford Press, 1971.

—*Admiral of The Ocean Sea*. Boston: Little Brown, 1942.

Moseley, Michael E. *The Incas and their Ancestors: the Archeology of Peru*. New York: Thames & Hudson, 1992, 2001.

Nanson, Fridtjof. *In Northern Mists*, Vols. I & II. New York: AMS Press, 1911 (AMS Reprints, 1961).

Needham, Joseph. *Science and Civilization in China*. Cambridge: U. Press, 1954.

Newton, Arthur Perceval. *The Great Age of Discovery*. Freeport: Books for Libraries Press, 1932.

Norwich, John J. *A History of Venice*. New York: Knopff, 1982.

Parry, J.H. *The Discovery of South America*. New York, Taplinger, 1979.

Purchas, Samuel. *Purchas His Pilgrimes, in Five Books, 3rd Part Voyages and Discoveries of the North Parts of the World*. London: Author, 1625, 1626.

Ramsey, Raymond H. *No Longer on the Map.*. New York: Viking, 1972.

Ratchnevsky, Paul. *Genghis Khan*. Malden, NJ: Blackwell Pub., 1991.

Ravenstein, E.G. *Martin Behaim*. London: George Philip & Son, 1908.

Riley, Carrol, J. Kelley, C. Penniglan, & R. Rands, Eds. *Man Across The Sea.* Austin: U. Texas Press, 1971.

Roe, Frank Gilbert. *The Indian and the Horse.* Norman, OK: U. Press, 1955.

Rogers, F.M. *The Travels of the Infante Don Pedro.* Harvard: Cambridge Press, 1961.

Ronay, Gabriel. *The Tartar Khan's Englishman.* London: Phoenix Press, 1978.

Rossabi, Morris. *Kublai Khan: His Life and Times.* Berkeley: UC Press, 1988.

Rydholm, Fred C. Michigan Copper—the Untold Story. Marquette: Winter Cabin Books, 2006.

Schwartz, Seymour I., and Ralph E. Ehrenberg. *The Mapping of America.* Edison: Wellfleet, 1980 (2001).

Shafer, Edward H. *Ancient China.* New York: Time-Life Books, 1967.

Sharp, William s. *Colonial History of New Jersey.* Trenton: State Press, 1890.

Sinclair, Andrew. *The Sword and the Grail.* New York: Crown, 1992.

Skelton, Raleigh A., Thomas Marston, and George Painter. *The Vinland Map and the Tartar Relation.* New Haven: Yale University Press, 1965.

Sobel, Dava. *Longitude.* New York: Walker, 1995.

Speck, Gordon. *Northwest Explorations.* Portland: Binfords & Mort, 1954.

Spence, Johnathan D. *The Chan's Great Continent.* New York: Norton, 1998.

Stefoff, Rebecca. *Marco Polo and the Medieval Explorers.* New York, Chelsea House, 1992.

Stewart, Ethel. *The Dene and NaDene Indian Migration, 1233 AD.* Columbus, GA: ISAC Press, 1991.

Stromsted, Astri A. *Ancient Pioneers.* New York: Erik Friis, 1974.

Taylor, E.R.G. John Dee and the map of North-East Asia, *Imago Mundi*, 10, 1953, 103-6.

Thomas, Hugh. *Conquest.* New York: Simon & Schuster, 1993.

Thompson, Gunnar. *Vanguard of Discovery: How Roman, English, and Portuguese Explorers set the stage for Columbus.* Seattle: Misty Isles, 2001.

—The Cantino Bridge from Antillia to America, *Information Bulletin*, 31 (1), Western association of Map Libraries, November 1999, 8-22.

—Oldest Map of America—1414 AD, *Information Bulletin*, 27 (2), Western Association of Map Libraries, March 1996, 65-77.

—*The Friar's Map of 1360.* Seattle: Argonauts & New World Discovery Institute Press, 1996.

—*American Discovery: Our Multicultural Heritage.* Seattle: Argonauts, 1994.

—*Nu Sun: Asian-American Voyages 500 BC.* Fresno: Pioneer Press, 1989.

Tronoe, J.K.R. *Columbus in The Arctic.* Oslo: Broggers Boktrykkeri, 1965.

Vignaud, Henry. *The Letter and Chart of Toscanelli.* London: Sands, 1902.

Wagner, Henry R. Marco Polo's Text becomes Propaganda to inspire Colón. *Imago Mundi*, 6, 1949, 3-13

Walker, Barbara. *Women's Encyclopedia of Myths & Secrets.* San Francisco: Harper, 1983.

Wells, H.G. *The Outline of History.* Chicago: University Press, 1960 (1920).

Wilson, Ian. *The Columbus Myth: Did Men of Bristol Reach America Before Columbus?* New York: Simon & Schuster, 1991.

Wood, Frances. *Did Marco Polo go to China?* New York: Westview Press, 1995.

Woodcock, George. *Peoples of the Coast*, Purdue: Indiana U. Press, 1977.

Worcester, G. *Junks and Sampans of the Yangtze.* Annapolis: Naval Press, 1971.

Yule, Henry, and Henri Cordier, Eds. *The Travels of Marco Polo.* London: Dover, 1905.

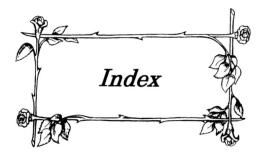

Index

photo by Karri Simmons

Author's Sketch

Gunnar Thompson is a distinguished Time Detective, actor, playwright, educator, and inventor. A Seattle resident for the past ten years, he has achieved local acclaim for his success in raising millions of dollars in funding for nonprofit organizations. He is a *Magna Cum Laude* graduate of the University of Illinois—where he also achieved High Distinction in Anthropology.

The son of Seattle natives, he was born in the Emerald City in 1946. His mother, Florence, was a gallant Public Health Nurse and nurse educator who helped to organize the Illinois Nursing Association. His father, Roy, was a talented mechanical engineer who served during World War II as the designer of equipment for landing craft and tanks. After Roy got transferred to Chicago in 1952, the family spent summers traveling across country to visit childhood friends and relatives in Seattle. During these trips, the Thompsons visited such exciting attractions as Mount Rushmore, Cahokia Mounds, Mesa Verde, the La Brea Tar Pits, Petrified Forest, and Glass Mountain, Oregon. They visited Native Reservations; and they walked in the footsteps of Sitting Bull, Chief Joseph, Lewis & Clark, and Abraham Lincoln. As a result of these inspirational encounters with America's Past, the author acquired a passion for learning the secrets of the Universe.

Gunnar has been a lifelong critic of the way that Traditional History has been taught in schools. In the Third Grade, he was asked on a test: "Who discovered America?" His response was that "the Indians discovered America." That was quite a daring answer back in the 1950s. Of course, the teacher informed him that he was "Wrong!" A few years later, when he was a Ph.D. candidate in the Anthropology program at the University of Wisconsin, he was again asked: "Who discovered America?" This time, he added "the Egyptians, the Greeks, the Romans, and the Chinese." Outraged professors told him that he was being terminated from his career as an anthropologist. Ten years later, he finally earned his Doctorate in Rehabilitation Counseling. He has served as a counselor educator at UW—Madison, Drake University, CSU—Fresno, and at the University of Hawaii. All the while, he has continued to delve into the mysteries of the past—because he enjoys solving puzzles.

Acknowledgments, continued

Seattle explorer John Jones undertook an important mission for the New World Discovery Institute in 1995. He photographed Hindu temple carvings in central India dating to the 12th century. Goddess statues in these temples hold examples of Hindu maize that was chiseled into stone. These carvings are important because they prove transoceanic diffusion of domesticated plants in ancient times. Dr. Jones also met with Jaweed Ashraf of New Delhi University who has been researching ancient maize in India for several decades in association with Carl Johannessen—a former University of Oregon geographer.

Following his discovery of the 1418 Ming Map, Beijing attorney Liu Gang brought this incredibly important document to the attention of Gavin Menzies. With the assistance of Hong Kong scholar and celebrity Frank Lee, they organized a Press Conference for March of 2006. They also invited the author to attend as an expert on ancient cartography of the New World before Columbus. The author is very grateful for the kindnesses and generosity that was given during this enjoyable outing to the People's Republic. Leon Yu, an interpreter for the Xiamen Municipal Government, assisted Frank Lee with translating the speakers' presentations. Professor Zheng Ming, Rear Admiral—retired, and the Beijing branch of the Zheng He Society was a generous host at the author's seminar. It was also a joy to meet Zhiguo Sun, Professor Zheng Xihuang, Zhang Baoyin, Xu Miaomiao, Lin Jing, Bruce Kui, Zhou Zhou, Michael Wester, Raymond Li, and Caroline Puel. Frank Lee, Liu Gang, Steve Hill, Minnie Hu Yang, and tour guide Tony Chen offered some welcome after-hours activities during the conference. Several events took place at Alex Peterson's "Bookworm Club" in beautiful Beijing.

Fred Jueneman has helped to edit and refine the author's Marco Polo manuscript along with the able assistance of Judy Davis.

Several remarkable friends and associates have accompanied the author on overseas treks to archeological sites and museums. My colleagues on these adventures have included Lyn Tebrugge, Bob Ness, Dave Berger, Susan Matland, Michaelangelo Greco, Marcia Schenkel, Tracey Baldwin, David Dutton, Laura Ovette, and Christy Freelove. They have all donned khakis, hoisted backpacks and cameras or trudged alongside the author seeking clues to the origins of New World Civilizations. Talk show host Laura Lee of the Laura Lee Show has been a frequent source of inspiration while spreading the word of innovative research to audiences throughout America; Paul Roberts of Radio Bookstore was instrumental in marketing the author's early books.

Several archivists and collectors have shared their collections with the author. Jeff Pendergraft opened up his collection of priceless Marco Polo documents that his grandfather, Marcian Rossi, had loaned to the Library of Congress back in the 1940s. Joël Sartorius at the Philadelphia Free Library showed the author a manuscript map by the English geographer John Dee, or one of his close associates, that dates to the 16th century. David Woodward at the UW—Map History Project, Mary

Galneder of the Arthur H. Robinson Map Library, and Carol Urness at the University of Minnesota have helped to track down clues.

The American Geographical Society, the Society for The History of Discoveries, the Western Association of Map Librarians, the Laura Lee Show, Donald Cyr's *Stonehenge Viewpoint*, the Wooden Boat Foundation in Port Townsend, the Hawaiian Maritime Society, and *Ancient American Magazine* provided forums for seminars and scientific papers regarding Marco Polo's Maps and Early Voyages to the New World. In July of 2006, the author gave a presentation at the "Paths Across the Pacific Conference" which Nancy Yaw Davis organized in Sitka, Alaska. It was great fun! It offered an opportunity to discuss clues with Stephen Jett, Betty Meggers, Allison Stengar, and Ben Finney.*

Among the museums and archives that have contributed substantially to the present work are the following: the British Library & Museum, the San Francisco Asian Art Museum, the Seattle Asian Art Museum, the Wisconsin State Historical Society Museum & Library, the University of Hawaii Library, the University of Washington Library, the Smithsonian Institution, the Sakler Gallery, the Boston Metropolitan Museum, the American Museum of Natural History, the Museum of Anthropology and Archeology in Mexico City, the Berlin Museum of Ethnology, and the New York City Metropolitan Library.*

Colleagues in the Society for the History of Discoveries, the Washington Map Society, Harvard University, the Western Association of Map Librarians (WAML), the Internet forum "MapHist," the "1421 Team," and the Smithsonian Institution have been very helpful with ideas and critiques of the author's presentations. Notable contributors include Dick Edgar Ibarra-Grasso, Jaweed Ashraf, Donald Cyr, Glenn Kimball, Fazi Khoury, Wesley Brown, Tom Sander, Ian Hudson, Matthew Edney, Robin Lind, Stan Hess, Rosanne Hawarden, Ian Wilson, Dick Nielsen, Betty Meggers, James Enterline, Sanford Bederman, Kathryn Womble, Eric Wolf, Greg McIntosh, and Joseph Mahan. Internet Development experts at FirstRaven.com, Sandra Stowell and Michael Pruitt, provided outstanding technical and creative support. Michelle Gagnon of the *Bremerton Sun*, Scott Wilson of the *Port Townsend Leader*, and Arthur Dürst of *Cartographica Helvetica* have helped to publicize the author's work.*

The author has gained assistance, technical expertise, and inspiration from a host of contributors, supporters, and medical specialists. Heartfelt appreciation is extended to the following: Michelle Bruns, William Ellis, Kenneth Russell, Frank Magill, Marco Sobrino, Steven Scharf, Rhude & Jennie Thompson, Gary Nelson, Hether Schenkel, Sheela Word, James Rock, Jim Westall, Jo Curran, William Stanley, Gerry Max, Athena Ovett, Dave Robison, Rhonda Eklund, David Childress, Wayne May, Frank Joseph, Kathy Ryan, Gayle Pollard, Chao Chien, Robert Cribbs, Lam Yee Din, Tai-Peng Wang, Heather Schenkel, Mike Murry, Irv Tebor, Alexa Chittick, Glenda Carberry, Anwari Thallenberg, Devon Jung, Michael Fredholm, Joe & Judy Ferem, Barbara Deloria, Ross Togachi, Laurie Strong, Heidi Lee, Len & Gite Zweig, Suzanne DeMattei, Sam Alvarado, David & Bonnie Dutton, Claudia Snipes, Magne Bolstad, Anthony Hunstiger, Madalyn Purcell, David & Della Walker, Lanny & Judy Neider, Pamela Ross, Tør & Caroline Thompson,

Tom & Nancy Word, Jeff Hammarlund, Lou & Kiyo Peverada, Aiko Oda, Dan Anderson, Elizabeth Starz, Ned & Mary Quistorff, Len & Emily Mandelbaum, Richard & Geralyn Rakowski, Pat & Don Stromberg, Lynn Nadeau, Howard Pack, Jodi Lehman, John Barr, Chris Overman, John Wills, Shaine Anderson, Ned Zineddine, Sr. Claire Joy, Brandon Gates, Rick & Aud Matland, Knut Torgnes, Mike Biskup, Jim Nelson, the Jefferson County Historical Society, and the members of the RoseWind Cohousing Community.*

Special thanks are due for the exceptional staff at the Printery and Star Copy Center in Port Townsend. Pat Kenna, Megan, Abby, Julie, Tammy, Peg, and Linda have helped to escort the manuscript through the maze of tunnels in the printing industry. Mat Bridgeway has been an incredibly overbearing and heartless editor. They say he has "perfect pitch." That is, if it isn't perfect—he pitches it! Alas, very few of my opinions regarding social policy managed to sneak past his red pen.

Many thanks for your kind and generous support! God Bless You!

*Inclusion in this list is not intended to suggest endorsement.

So grab your oars, mates, and "heave ho!"
—We're all shipmates on Gaia!

Letter to the Author—

August 30, 1993

Dear Gunnar:

Thank you for the opportunity to read your book, *American Discovery*. I have just finished reading it aloud to my wife, Ruth. We both felt that it was an eye-opener. In fact, it added considerably to the long list of things that I was taught in school and had to unlearn later. Our repeated reaction, as we went through the book, was: "so that was how it really was!" Some of it was a blast of new information; a lot of it was more in the nature of confirmation of suspicions and doubts I had been harboring all along.

Incidentally, your description of the conquest of Mexico brought to mind a poem that I wrote about 60 years ago. I bring it out once in a while. Here's how it goes. . . .

> We come now, a most cultured nation,
> And bring to your people good news:
> We'll teach you true civilization,
> And sell you new hats and new shoes.
>
> You question our great, noble mission:
> "What's civilization?" you say.
> It means, by our best definition,
> Behaving exactly <u>our</u> way.
>
> We offer now ever so sweetly
> To teach you the ways that are true.
> We prove our refinement completely,
> By having more weapons than you!

Don't expect to have the historical establishment accept your—or Thor Heyerdahl's—conclusions. Or, if they eventually come around to your point of view, don't expect any credit. They'll credit one of their own with the shift in opinion. It has always been so in many disciplines, particularly in medicine, but in others as well. Discovery Magazine recently had an article on the problem. The leaders of any academic discipline have a lot invested in time and writing about one point of view; and they feel that they will lose face if they change their teachings. Their followers and sycophants hesitate to change for fear of losing jobs and preferment.

Pioneers like you are to be commended; but they face possible trouble. I am thinking of Ignatz Philipp Semmelweiss and Alfred Lothat Wegener, for instance. Dr. Semmelweiss told the medical profession that their failure to wash their hands between patients was spreading disease; and he was hounded by the other doctors to an early grave. Mr. Wegener first proposed the plate tectonic theory; and he died fully discredited.

We much appreciate the opportunity to read your book; and we wish you well in the future.

Cordially, Wallace Bartholomew

Resources for the Future—

1421—Zheng He & World Discovery
www. 1421.tv

New World Discovery Institute
http:// www. marcopolovoyages.com

Society for the History of Discoveries
www. sochistdisc.org

Ancient American Mag. & Annual Conf.
www. ancientamerican.com

New England Antiquities Research Assoc.
www. neara.org

Laura Lee Discovery Show
www. lauralee.com

World Explorers Club
www. wexclub.com

Paths Across the Pacific Conference
Annual Meeting; Sitka, Alaska

NW Maritime Ctr. & Wooden Boat Fn.
www. nwmaritime.org

Pre-Columbiana Journal
c/o ESRS, C. Heil
505 N. Park Drive, #5
Arlington, VA 22203-2317

Thanks for your support!

*Only by relearning the Past
can we change the Future.*
Bon Voyage!